VOICES AND SILENCES

This book illuminates selected narratives to understand the lived experience of our forebears. Scholarly and thoughtful, a valuable addition to the literature on Indian indentured Diaspora.

PROFESSOR BRIJ V. LAL
The Australian National University

Thoroughly researched and sensitively written account; engages with a literary corpus and a historical phenomenon fundamental to understanding the lived experience.

PROFESSOR VIJAY MISHRA
Emeritus Professor, Murdoch University, Australia

Meticulously analyzed narratives of indenture to highlight how cultural identity has been retained in the Diaspora countries.

PROFESSOR BIMAN C. PRASAD
Leader of the National Federation Party, Fiji

A unique study; extremely useful for the community of scholars and practitioners of migration and Diaspora studies.

ARUN KUMAR SAHU
High Commissioner of India, Trinidad & Tobago

Anjali Singh utilizes her linguistic skills to discover 'a language of indenture' emerging from different locations.

PROFESSOR BRINSLEY SAMAROO
Professor Emeritus, University of the West Indies, St. Augustine

Indian indentured emigration is among the most notable social phenomena of modern history, which sent over one million men and women to tropical sugar colonies in the Atlantic, Pacific and Indian oceans. Indenture began in the 1830s and lasted till 1920; a period which finds little or no mention either in history textbooks or in literature. This book takes a closer look at some of the important narratives on indenture and evaluates them in order to highlight the experience of the indentured people across the plantation colonies in Fiji and in the Caribbean. The story of indenture is the story of betrayal, of trauma and of resistance. It is also a narrative of resilience, assimilation and acculturation. This book offers an in-depth literary study to reveal that there exists a language of indenture, one that permeates all the texts written on the subject. The texts speak to, and for each other, thereby revealing the indenture experience to the reader.

Anjali Singh is an Assistant Professor in the Department of English, Mohanlal Sukhadia University, Udaipur, India. She has a PhD in English and has travelled widely, presenting research papers in Australia and Fiji.

VOICES AND SILENCES

Narratives of *Girmitiyas* and *Jahajis* from Fiji and the Caribbean

ANJALI SINGH

Routledge
Taylor & Francis Group
LONDON AND NEW YORK

MANOHAR

First published 2023
by Routledge
4 Park Square, Milton Park, Abingdon, Oxon OX14 4RN

and by Routledge
605 Third Avenue, New York, NY 10158

Routledge is an imprint of the Taylor & Francis Group, an informa business

British Library Cataloguing-in-Publication Data
A catalogue record for this book is available from the British Library

Library of Congress Cataloging-in-Publication Data
A catalog record for this book has been requested

ISBN: 978-1-032-37704-9 (hbk)
ISBN: 978-1-032-37707-0 (pbk)
ISBN: 978-1-003-34149-9 (ebk)

DOI: 10.4324/9781003341499

Typeset in Adobe Garamond 11/13
by Digital Print Hut, Delhi 110002

MANOHAR

Contents

Acknowledgements

To 'Him', without whom, nothing is possible

THIS BOOK IS based on the research I undertook at the University of Rajasthan under the guidance of Dr Tanuja Mathur. Her sustained encouragement and infinite patience led me to put in my best and I owe her my grateful thanks for everything.

My research rests under the shadow of great academic giants and my writing owes a huge debt to their scholarship. I am indebted to Prof Brij V. Lal, historian extraordinaire, his conversations and suggestions, which helped my writing and made it richer. Prof Biman Chand, 'Visionary' leader of the National Federation Party in Fiji, and Dr Rajni Chand, Director in the University in Suva, graciously hosted me in Fiji and answered all my myriad questions on indenture. Dr Satish Rai in Australia gave me directions on how to approach *girmit* in Fiji. Ms Shubha Singh, an expert on Fijian history and contemporary affairs, gave me the primary material I needed while answering all my questions with an extraordinary amount of patience. I am also extremely grateful to Dr Vagish Singh and Ms Archana Singh (the Hony. Consul of India in Queensland), who went out of their way to assist me in my research. Prof Sarva Daman Singh in Brisbane invited me to browse through his personal library and gave me valuable material to aid my writing.

H.E. High Commissioner of Trinidad and Tobago, Shri Arun Kumar Sahu was magnanimous in his support and inspired me to get this book printed. Mr Ashwini Kumar in Canada couriered me his own copy of a hard-to-find book on indenture. Dr Peggy Mohan's suggestions helped me connect the links that eventually shaped this literary mosaic.

Grateful thanks to Prof Pradeep Trikha, Dr Minakshi Jain, Dr Khushpal Garg and Mr Saurabh Meena, who helped me refine my thoughts through countless ideation sessions.

A very special thank you to Mr Ramesh Jain and the entire team at Manohar Publishers, whose vast experience and professionalism made the entire process smooth and memorable.

I also owe a huge debt of gratitude to my support system—my family—along with good friends and strong critics . . . You know who you are . . . Thank you!

Arjun, Aditi and Adhiraj, you ensured I kept my momentum. Akansha, I could not have succeeded in this endeavour without your constant support, especially through the long 'unproductive' days.

I have saved the most important acknowledgement for the end, because as T.S. Eliot writes in *Little Gidding*, 'The end is where we start from'. To my parents, Nirvikar and Asha—of all the identities I hold in this world, the one I would truly fight for, and the only one I am most proud of is the privilege of being called 'your daughter'.

And finally, to the *Girmitiyas* and the *Jahajis* . . . you are not forgotten. . .

Jaipur ANJALI SINGH
7 January 2022

Preface

INDENTURE WAS A form of contract labour initiated by the British just after slavery was abolished. It has, so far, remained either largely absent from or underwritten in the public discourse. Historically, it is placed just after the period of the Atlantic slave trade and outlines the movement of the Indian and the Chinese (to a lesser degree) populations, among others, across four continents. Although indenture was not slavery, it shared some characteristics of that system, and so was, labelled little more than 'a new system of slavery'. The nineteenth century witnessed large scale global journeys of migration. One of the significant flows in trans-national migration from India comprised the 1.3 million Indians who left as indentured labourers to the plantation colonies of the British Empire.

This book takes a closer look at some of the important narratives on indenture and evaluates them in order to highlight the experiences of the indentured people across the colonies in the Caribbean and Fiji. While indenture was a global phenomenon, the Indian indentured communities in the colonies developed different historical trajectories based on their diverse experiences. The fragmented nature of these experiences necessitates a closer look at the indenture paradigm to interpret the contexts that have given rise to a distinct social formation and sensibility in the Indian diaspora.

The Indian indenture system resulted in the transportation and displacement of men, women and children from their homes to the plantation colonies in the Indian Ocean, in Africa, in the Caribbean and Fiji. The first Indian indentured labourers were sent to Mauritius in 1834 and the Caribbean in 1838. The last was Fiji, which received the first set of indentured labourers only in 1879. While some migrants indentured willingly owing to several push factors in India, it is also true that many left their homes without complete knowledge of the length of the journey they were undertaking, or how far they would be travelling and even where they were going. Force was applied by the recruiters through coercion, misrepresentation and even kidnapping. The exploitation of the indentured subject continued right from the moment they were 'caught' in the web of indenture up till their contract period ended.

The story of indenture is the story of betrayal, trauma and resistance. It is also a narrative of resilience, assimilation and acculturation. Leading historians writing on indenture have analysed the experience on either of the two polarities: colonial and postcolonial. In doing so, they have largely ignored the voices of the indentured people and their personal histories. With the third and fourth generation descendants of the indentured labourers writing about indenture, an entire discipline of literature has opened up to situate their narratives and focus on the issues they highlight. Their works raise a challenge to the earlier narratives that have focused largely on official records and, following a colonial mindset, have stereotyped the indentured Indians as misfits both in India and in the countries where they went/were sent.

Literary pioneers of indenture diaspora include Nobel Laureate Sir V. S. Naipaul from the Caribbean and Satendra Nandan from Fiji. These stalwarts have contributed to a formidable body of work that interrogates the legacies of indenture across a wide spectrum of diverse genres. Their works have managed to place indenture on the literary map. Recent works by the younger generation of writers, who are descendants of the indentured diaspora, have become involved in a process of 'reclamation' around the word *coolie*. They are writing about indenture poetics and highlighting a distinct vocabulary that is required to be read and understood to comprehend the experience.

According to the latest UN world migration report, the Indian diaspora is the world's largest, with slightly more than 15.6 million people from India living overseas. Descendants of the indentured labourers, who were taken by the British to work in the plantation colonies, now number approximately 4.5 million and comprise 28.8 per cent of the total Indian diaspora. It is imperative to study the diaspora sensibility of the indentured diaspora to trace the development arc of the Indian diaspora. As a system of the colonial period, this diaspora is also termed the 'capital diaspora' or 'labour diaspora' to mark its distinction from the new and contemporary Indian diaspora. Indenture, as a colonial labour system, encouraged forced migration of the Indian people, resulting in exile, whereas the migration patterns of the new Indian diaspora are voluntary and are thus marked by dislocation.

Indenture literature is as old as indenture itself. During the period of indenture, literature written on the subject centred on debates, with one side supporting the system and the other side likening it to a 'new system of slavery'. The colonists took on the role of apologists and professed indenture as beneficial to the Indians, while the abolitionists used their voices to campaign against the system. During the later stages, indenture literature focused on looking at the voyage as a formative factor in constructing a diasporic identity. The colonial archive does contain extensive documentation but it also hints at racial stereotyping of the indentured people and hence, cannot be read objectively. It is only in the last two decades that there has been a revival in indenture literature with the third and fourth generation of the indentured diaspora revisiting the past and writing narratives that are based on revealing testimonies and anecdotes. The authors have also mined the rich oral tradition in indenture to project the voices of the original *girmitiyas,* who have recounted their experience in the *bidesiya* songs. These resources have enabled the writers to piece together the real history of the period. Indenture began just after slavery ended in the 1830s and lasted till it was 'abolished in all its forms' in 1920. This translates to almost a century of indenture; a period which finds little or no mention in either Indian history textbooks or literature.

The key narratives taken up for in-depth study in this book were selected based on criteria that allowed for a broader understanding of the system. Accordingly, Totaram Sanadhya's polemical text, *My Twenty-One Years in the Fiji Islands* (translated) narrated by him after returning from Fiji (after completing his indenture) has been taken up for analysis. Sanadhya was an indentured labourer whose recounting of indenture illustrates a lived experience in the protagonist's own words.

Rajendra Prasad's book *Tears in Paradise: Suffering and Struggles of Indians in Fiji, 1879-2004,* is written by the third-generation descendant of an Indian indentured labourer in Fiji. Prasad combines family history, anecdotes and archival records to deconstruct the story of indenture in Fiji. He pays special emphasis to the *bidesiya* songs in his emotional work.

The other two texts are written by women and were selected to project the gendered perspective and depict a holistic view of the colonial labour system. Peggy Mohan's *Jahajin* starts as a linguistic project about uncovering the reasons for the vanishing of the Bhojpuri language from the indentured peoples' vocabulary. Written by a fourth-generation descendant of an indentured person who was sent to Trinidad in the Caribbean, it is a framed narrative that works on four different levels. The feminine voice takes centrestage in the book and the reader is given a glimpse of indenture from the female point of view.

Coolie Woman: The Odyssey of Indenture is a genealogical search by a fourth-generation descendant's literary journey undertaken to uncover the trajectory of her great-grandmother's indenture in British Guyana. It follows a historiographic narration, with Gaiutra Bahadur uncovering many of the marginalised and silenced female voices in the history of indenture. She draws from the historical memory and personal narratives of the indentured labourers while analysing the *aporias* in the colonial documents and national archives.

The first chapter 'Cartographies of Indenture: Historical Overview' defines indenture, along with its distinct parametres, and places it in a historical context. It outlines the structure of analysis used in the book, which is based on literary and theoretical frameworks. The chapter also comprises a review of the literature of the main texts analysed in the work.

The second chapter 'The *Girmitiyas* of Fiji: A Forgotten Generation' explores the *girmit* experience in Fiji. It highlights the formation of a collective identity, that of *jahaji bhais* and *jahaji behens*, among the indentured diaspora and also takes into account the trials and tribulations faced by them on the long voyage, as well as on the plantations. The themes of trauma and nostalgia pervade the indenture experience in Fiji. The chapter questions the loss of identity of the *girmitiyas* and looks at indenture as *narak* from a racist point of view. It presents the real, lived experience in direct contrast to the hegemonic colonial discourse and brings to light the existence of other histories through memories and testimonies. The chapter also juxtaposes the themes of home, homeland, loss, exile and betrayal with the themes of resistance and accommodation.

Indenture was a heterogeneous experience. To highlight the differences in the experiences of the people in the host colonies, the third chapter 'The *Jahajis*: Indentured Indians in the Caribbean' encapsulates the indenture experience in the Caribbean, with special reference to Trinidad and British Guyana. Women in indenture have traditionally been seen as gendered beings standing on the intersection of morality and sexuality. This chapter lays greater focus on the role played by the *coolie* women and re-positions the colonial (his)tory of Indian indenture as (her)story. It also analyses the ethos of assimilation and acculturation which was a distinct feature of indenture in the Caribbean.

Chapter four 'The Aesthetics of Narrative: Poetics of Indenture' evaluates the narrative techniques employed by the authors in their texts. It discusses the literary framework, including genre, plot, setting, point of view, characterization and style, used by the authors. The epistemic frame of this chapter highlights the specific techniques used in the texts, such as magic realism, polyphony and frame narration.

The fifth chapter 'Emerging from Indenture/ship: Evolving Being and Belonging' concludes the work by summing up the research. It offers a comparative analysis while highlighting the points of convergence and divergence underlying the experience of indenture in Fiji and the Caribbean. How different or similar were these experiences and how were they projected in literature? The chapter also identifies the research gaps and limitations in the study. Finally, it looks at the way ahead by opening up the research and broadening its scope, while also delineating future trajectories for further study on the subject.

This in-depth literary study of the narratives reveals that there exists a language of the indenture, one that permeates all the texts written on the subject. The texts speak too, and for each other, thereby enhancing the indenture experience for the reader.

Jaipur
7 January 2022

ANJALI SINGH

CHAPTER 1

Cartographies of Indenture: Historical Overview

> 'Before all else, India to us Biharis,
> Is a small village in the north.'
> (Buckhory 1979: 65)

SUBMERGED WITHIN THE burgeoning texts of the Indian diaspora is a special category of literature. This includes the narratives of and about the Indian indentured diaspora, which have recently come of age as a special field of study in their own right. The last three decades have witnessed the emergence of serious research on the institutionalised system of indenture and in particular, on the old capital diaspora. Writers of indenture literature bring out the lived experience of the indentured people. They affect serious literary engagement by bringing to the fore, the lost voices of a generation that need to be recovered and heard. Historically, we have only 'heard about' these people who were sent as indentured labour to the plantation colonies. Their narratives, both first person and second person accounts, allow the readers to actually 'hear from' them and develop a better sense of their lived experience.

The nineteenth century was witness to the greatest trans-continental migrations in world history; two of the important movements were of the Europeans to the Americas, South Africa and Australasia; and of the Asians, especially the Chinese and the Indians, to the plantation colonies. Slavery and indenture, both historical movements, one preceding the other, brought about the mass migration of human resources across continents. Postcolonial theorist Bill Ashcroft (1998: 58) states, 'Diaspora, the voluntary or forcible movement of peoples from their homelands into new regions, is a central historical fact of colonization. . . the practices of slavery and indenture resulted in worldwide colonial diasporas'. Indian indentured emigration is widely regarded as the successor to the erstwhile African slave trade. Post the abolition of slavery in the British Empire, large scale recruitment of Indian indentured labourers was undertaken to compensate for the shortage of labour in the sugar plantation colonies in the Indian, Atlantic and Pacific oceans.

Etymologically, the word 'diaspora' comes from the Greek *dia* (meaning 'through') and *speirein* (meaning 'to sow' or 'scatter'). Historically, it is associated with the dispersion of the Jews. Over the years, the word has gathered complex connotations and 'is now used broadly to refer to the cultural connections maintained by a group of people who have been dispersed or who have migrated around the globe' (Encyclopedia.com). Adesh Pal (2004: xiv) quotes theorist Jasbir Jain in the 'Introduction' to *Theorizing and Critiquing Indian Diaspora* where she 'critiques and problematizes the very concepts of diaspora—homeland, history, identity and self'. Jain opines that all these categories 'are fluid and unstable with multiple layers of meanings' (ibid). According to her, 'Diaspora is not merely a scattering or a dispersion but an experience made up of collective and multiple journeys: an experience about who travels, where, how and under what circumstances' (ibid). Her view sums up the sensibility of the indentured diaspora.

India was revered as the common ancestral homeland for the approximately 1.3 million Indians who were (in most cases) forcibly taken away as indentured labour to the plantation colonies spread across the globe. Historian Brij V. Lal, in his 'Introduction' to *The Encyclopedia of the Indian Diaspora* (hereafter referred to as *EOTID*), opines that India 'retains its place in their consciousness as a marker of their distinctiveness and difference, reinforced perhaps by the sense of exclusion and marginality in their home country' (Lal 2007: 14).

He goes on to suggest that there 'is a sense of cultural, religious and historical ties with India, in various combinations of longing and nostalgia' (ibid.: 14).

When the British East India Company arrived in India in 1600, India was under Mughal rule. However, the Company brought with it a Charter signed by Queen Elizabeth I, which effectively gave them a monopoly over the British trade from Asia to Europe (ibid.: 23). With the decline of Mughal power and supremacy in the mid-eighteenth century, and more specifically after its win in the Battle of Plassey (1757) and the Battle of Buxar (1764), the East India Company transformed from a mere trading company in India to an administrative arm of the British colonial empire. The active acquisition of territories in India by the East India Company between 1757 and 1856 had allowed them to interfere in the politics of the region and entrenched them firmly in the country. The First War of Indian Independence of 1857 managed to push back the East India Company for a short period but this was not the end of British influence in India. In its place, the British government stepped into India in the role of a coloniser. Consequently, India was placed directly under the British Crown by the enactment of the Government of India Act of 1858 (ibid.: 24).

Globally, the British had been actively caught up in the transatlantic slave trade for around 200 years (from the early seventeenth to the nineteenth century) and different forms of slavery were being practised in the British colonies across the globe, particularly in the Caribbean and in North America. Based on information available online in the UK National Archives section on slavery, the British had first settled in the Caribbean in 1623. The new colonies were henceforth, rapidly converted from predominantly white European settlements with small-scale agriculture into slave colonies employing thousands of African slaves on large, white-owned plantations. Historian Richard Oluseyi Asaolu (2011: 67) marks the chronology of the abolition of the slave trade. The Abolition of the Slave Trade Act was passed by the British Parliament on 25 March 1807. Under this Act, a fine of £100 was imposed for every slave found aboard a British ship. After the 1807 Act, slaves were still held, though not sold, within the British Empire. In the 1820s, the Abolitionist Movement became active again, this time campaigning against the institution of slavery itself. On 23 August 1833, the Slavery Abolition Act outlawed slavery in all the British colonies.

Slavery was finally abolished on 1 August 1834 but only children under the age of six were freed immediately under the terms of the Emancipation Act of 1833. The others were still tied to their former owners in an apprenticeship system which was finally abolished in 1838. In the *Routledge Handbook of the South Asian Diaspora* (hereafter referred to as *RHSAD*), Brij Lal states, 'Indian indentured emigration was started in direct response to the shortage of labour in the tropical colonies caused by the abolition of slavery in the British Empire in 1833' (Chatterji 2013: 80). The planters had continued to obtain slave labour until the termination of the system of apprenticeship in 1838. Richard Oluseyi Asaolu (2011: 28) highlights, 'Full emancipation for all was legally granted on 1 August 1838, making Trinidad the first British colony with slaves to completely abolish slavery'.

According to the *Note on Emigration from the East Indies to British Guyana* written on 8 May 1847 and quoted in *RHSAD*, once slavery had been abolished:

> The greater part of the Negroes abandoned not only field labour, but service of every kind, almost as soon as they were at liberty to do so. No present kindness, or memory of past benefits, no persuasion or pecuniary inducements could prevail upon them to remain; and it is to be feared that the time is yet distant when motives of interest, or the press of necessity, will bring them back to serve as agricultural labourers. (Chatterji 2013: 80)

The apprenticeship system failed because once freed, the former slaves refused to succumb to the system (in any form) again. The pattern of resistance was the same across all the colonies where slavery had been in force.

Lal explains how the plantation owners in Trinidad attempted to procure labour from the neighbouring countries of Grenada, St Christopher and Nevis, engaging captains of small trading vessels with a bounty and a promise of returning them to their homes after the completion of their contracts. However, with no legal provisions specifying the terms and conditions of service, or making the contract enforceable, and 'being ill-contrived and injudiciously managed,' this attempt too, succumbed to failure (ibid.).

The Chinese were considered a better prospect as labour for the plantations, as they were believed to be 'further developed in civilisation'. According to the report in a Parliamentary Paper from the House of Commons cited in *RHSAD*, the British officials found that 'the Chinese tended to move out of the plantations at the earliest possible opportunity to set themselves up as market gardeners and small shopkeepers, becoming in time, rivals to the very planters whom they were supposed to serve' (ibid.).

These successive failures to find an alternative for slaves on the plantations put the focus on India as a reliable source of labour. While the pre-colonial movement of Indian peasants was limited to internal migration, the British rule in India opened up the possibility of overseas migration. Certain factors operating in India during the same period became instrumental in encouraging Indians to look for work overseas. Owing to various push and pull factors, India became the principal source of labour supply to the sugar colonies of the British Empire. 'Coolitude' (a term coined by noted poet and writer Khal Torabully to symbolize indenture) thus became the inheritor of 'Negritude'. Coolitude attempts to disclose the 'Coolie's story which has been shipwrecked ('erased') in the ocean of a Western-made historical discourse as well as a world of publication and criticism' (Torabully 2002: 15).

The northern parts of India in the nineteenth century had witnessed a surge in the labour market. With the coming of Oudh and Rohilkhand Railways, whole villages of *Kahars* (an occupation-based caste) whose livelihood depended on bearing *Palkis* (a mode of transport) had become unemployed. The end of the Kabul War in 1842 had also created a large section of unemployed youth in Punjab. Critic Kapil Kumar writes in his article, 'Colonial Expansion, Resistance and Forced Migrations', 'There was tremendous pressure on land as a result of the colonial practices of disbanding the armies of local rulers, the weavers and the artisans being thrown out of their professions as one after another, the local kingdoms fell prey to British expansion' (Kumar 2014: 26). The only livelihood left for the retrenched soldiers, and out-of-work weavers, spinners and craftsmen was agriculture.

The changes in land revenue in India at the time, however, were not conducive to shifting to agriculture as a source of livelihood. Kapil Kumar's book *Peasants in Revolt: Tenants, Landlords, Congress and the Raj in Oudh, 1886-1922* informs about one of the most drastic and exploitative changes that were put into force by the British after the First War of Indian Independence of 1857. The new legislation catered to the granting of permanent hereditary rights to the *talukdars* (land revenue collectors during the Mughal period). This act turned them into landlords while the peasants were converted to 'tenants-at-will' who could be evicted any time by their new landlords (Kumar 1994: 10-16). The rise in the rentals became arbitrary and the tenant's indebtedness was on the increase. With money lenders forming the third angle of the nexus, along with the British officials and the Indian landlords, the peasants were the ones who suffered the most. Once evicted from the land, the peasants had no other means of sustenance except to become indentured. The push factor was thus twofold. Before 1857, it was the destruction carried out by the East India Company which gave rise to famines, misery and abject poverty. After 1857, the alliance between British colonial officials and the Indian feudal aristocracy ensured that people would be forced into indenture as they were left with no other alternative.

Emigration offered under indenture was one of the few outlets available for unemployed peasants and labourers. Researcher Anand Yang has noted in his paper 'Peasant on the Move: A Study of Internal Migration in India' that historically, in the Saran district of Bihar, thousands of labourers used to migrate to Bengal for work and then return for the agricultural season in their villages (Yang 1919: 41). Historian G.A. Grierson has been quoted by Shahid Amin in *A Concise Encyclopedia of North Indian Peasant Life* mentioning the former's tenure as the Collector of Gaya. Grierson found that people from Bihar used to move to Nepal in search of work (Amin 2005: 30). With the advent of the indenture, it became easy to recruit such people to travel to the plantation colonies as labour. Having once left their home in search of work, if they failed to do so, the Indians found it feasible to enter into indenture rather than return home empty handed and without any employment.

It is pertinent to note here, however, that it was not just the people of the 'low castes' who chose to get indentured to save themselves from the caste exploitation that existed in India. According to British historian Hugh Tinker, who cites the *Protector of Emigrants Annual Report 1872-3,* in his book *A New System of Slavery*, '2521 high castes, 4974 agricultural castes, 1537 artisans, 5309 low castes and 2910 Muslims were indentured during the period' (Tinker 1993: 55). These figures question the theory propagated by the supporters of the indenture, who claimed that it was only the low caste Indians who chose to get indentured to escape the ill-treatment meted out to them under the garb of the social order in India. Owing to various push factors, Indians from a cross-section of the society were indentured into the system. Brij Lal's extensive research conducted to classify the indentured people in Fiji based on social stratification has also trounced the commonly held belief which claimed that only the low-class Indians emigrated as indentured labour.

Academicians Marina Carter and Crispin Bates in their paper 'Empire and Locality' have written about the suppression that followed the First War of Indian Independence of 1857, which brought about a drastic change in almost all fields of life in India. The out of work and ostracised people who had fought against the British found that the only work open to them was agriculture. However, with the already escalating pressure on land, owing to the new land regulations, taxes and other natural calamities, even this option was not a sustainable one. It was suggested by the British that these people, along with their whole family, should be indentured. It was also proposed that 'if the transportees, averse to plantation labour, should commit suicide', their bodies should be handed over 'headless, bound in chains, the head planted in a conspicuous quarter, near the habitation of the living' (Carter 2010: 56).

According to Benjamin Elisha Sawe (2019), 'mass migration of contract labour from India was sent first to the island of Mauritius in 1834 and then to British Guyana in 1838'. The last of the colonies to receive indentured labour from India was Fiji in the year 1879. Based on the statistical analysis and extensive research conducted by Brij Lal, which he later published in his book *Girmitiyas: the Origins of the Fiji Indians* (hereafter referred to as *Girmitiyas*), it was found that 'between the years 1838 and 1916, a total number of 238,909

Indians were indentured and sent to British Guiana. Trinidad received 143,939 indentured emigrants between 1845 and 1916. Fiji was home to 60,965 *girmitiyas* between 1879 and 1916' (Lal 2004: 13).

As a prime capitalist model, the system of indenture allowed the British to bring cheap labour from India that would, in return, offer them the highest form of productivity. It is for this reason that the indenture diaspora is also termed the 'old capital diaspora'. The question that arises here is what makes the indentured diaspora (also classed as the labour capital diaspora or plantation diaspora) different from other Indian diaspora categories. The answer to this is not simple. Rather, the complexity involved in answering this question is supported by the quantum of research that has been conducted on this topic. The indenture diaspora was taken forcibly from India and in a majority of the cases, had not migrated willingly. This sets the context of their migration apart from the later diaspora which had migrated voluntarily and willingly to other lands. The departure from India was final for the indentured people, although they did not know it at the time of their departure. The temporal and spatial distance from the homeland, which they witnessed during their period of indenture, heightens a sense of nostalgia that finds effective communication only in their literature.

In *Fiji's Indian Migrants,* historian Ken Gillion highlights that more voices supported rather than opposed or denounced indenture. He states that indenture was viewed by the British as being 'universally beneficial' (Gillion 1973: 20). Some supporters in the British establishment even considered indenture a humanitarian venture which sought the welfare of the labouring class of India who had become 'melancholy' owing to the periodic famines in India. The expression of 'melancholy' was given by Lord Salisbury, the Secretary of State for India, in the House of Lords in 1877. Thus, where indenture was concerned, the British adopted a paternalistic view towards India and sought to encourage the system as beneficial to the labourers.

However, even while it was being commended by its supporters, the indenture system was strongly protested against by humanitarians, both in India and in England. They saw it as a revival of the abolished slave trade. Their protests bore fruit and for some time, indenture was stopped owing to the public pressure against it. However, the need of the colonial planters soon made the colonists reconsider their stance and the ban against indenture was lifted. 'By 1840, indenture had been extended to other colonies in the West Indies, and subsequently to Natal' (ibid.).

Historian Ahmed Ali informs in his book *Girmit: Indian Indenture Experience in Fiji* (hereafter referred to as *Girmit*), 'The *girmit* contract stipulated that an individual had to work nine hours on five consecutive days of every week, plus five hours on Saturday, and for each full day's work he would receive one shilling' (Ali 2004: 7). 'Girmit' was the vernacular term given by the indentured people to the contract (agreement) they had put their thumbprint on. The English term was not easily pronounced by the illiterate indentured people and over time, the simple mispronunciation of the term became a synonym of indenture. While Ali's work pertains largely to indenture in Fiji, the terms of the agreement were more or less similar in the other colonies. Sociologist Morton Klass notes in *East Indians in Trinidad: A Study of Cultural Persistence*, that work hours were very long and arduous (stretching between twelve and sixteen hours a day) with minimal wages of about ten cents per day. Further, there was a reduction in the wages, from which about one third was taken for the rations that were supplied to the labourers (Klass 1988: 14-15).

The literature pertaining to the period of Indian indenture comprises the narratives of indentured labourers, who were lured away by the false promises of the recruiters. A majority of these narratives indicate that indenture was not a passive event with the poor and low castes walking willingly into it. Almost all accounts talk about the different methods of force adopted by the recruiters, i.e. *akratis* (also referred to as *akratis*) to lure unsuspecting men and women. They made fake promises and gave assurances of a better life in the plantations. Where their talk failed to move the people to indenture themselves, the *akratis* resorted to using force and kid-napping them. The indentured people were even deceived about the actual distance to the plantation colonies. Almost all indenture voices agree that they were not told about the living conditions they would be offered in the plantations. Nor were they given a fair summation of the money they would earn. Among the list of deceptions practised by the recruiters, the recurrent complaint was about the lack of information on the return to the homeland. It was only when they reached the plantations that the indentured people learnt they would have to pay for their food from their salary, that the food given to them for a week would not be enough for even five days. They soon learnt that they would be punished for the smallest of 'offences', which would entail their money being deducted by the overseer. They would also have to face extreme humiliation at the hands of the overseers, and be treated like animals, violently thrashed and beaten, while their women would be sexually assaulted. They would have no recourse to legal measures and the natives and indigenous people would continue to remain hostile to them. This was the fate that greeted the indentured labourers on their arrival in the plantation colonies.

Some female migrants did look upon indentured migration as a means of moving out from patriarchal oppression. In *Coolies of the Empire,* Ashutosh Kumar quotes G.A. Grierson's (who was then a British revenue officer in India) report, 'Enquiry into Emigration, Revenue and Agriculture', which lists the four categories of women who enlisted to emigrate as indentured labourers:

> The first category was that of the wives of emigrants, the second category was widows without friends or kin, who were starving, the third category comprised married women who had been socially ostracised for absconding from their husband's house (with or without a lover) and had been shunned by him, and finally, women who were regarded as prostitutes and had no other means of support. (Kumar 2017: 41)

There were comparatively more push factors for women to migrate than for men. Historian P.C. Emmer (1986: 247) views indenture as a means that allowed women to 'emancipate themselves from an illiberal, inhibiting and very hierarchical social system in India'. It offered them an escape route. In some cases, widows and socially oppressed women themselves searched for recruiters and chose to get indentured. On the other hand, there were various pull factors at work, which facilitated the Indian women to become emigrants. The colonial government was keen on their recruitment into the system in order to offset the acute familial separation that would result during the long term of indenture. The Indian Emigration Act of 1864 made it compulsory for women to comprise 32 per cent of the passengers on each ship that was sailing to the colonies. This translated to a ratio of 40 women for every 100 men indentured into the system. The British also had another motive for ensuring the presence of women in the colonies. They were 'keen to weaken and displace the indigenous population or previously resident group by forming a new permanent community that could be utilized to meet colonial labour needs' (Kumar 2017: 48).

The Indian indenture system was state-regulated and was based on a written and 'supposedly' voluntarily 'agreement' which the emigrants would sign before leaving India for the plantation colonies. The term 'indenture' thus, broadly refers to a written contract entered into by a person to work for another person for a given period. In *Voices from Indenture,* Mariana Carter (1997: 101) informs that 'an indentured migrant was an individual who had not paid his or her passage but had entered into an agreement to receive transported assistance to a colony in return for a fixed period of labour'. While the exact terms of engagement for indenture were varied across the plantations, the general agreement was for an indentured person to work for an employer for five years. The indenture contract regulated the terms of employment of labourers and defined the general standard of living since it specified wage rate, working hours and the type of work, rations, housing and medical attendance. According to the agreement, once the indenture period of five years was complete, the labourer was free to 'either re-indenture in the same plantation or work elsewhere in the colony; and after ten years, depending on the terms of the contract, he or she was entitled to a free or partly paid return passage to India or to receive a piece of crown land on the colony in lieu of the fare' (ibid.: 108).

By 1834, Calcutta and Madras in India had become official depots for the indentured emigrants. Ajay Kumar Sahoo and Laxmi Narayan Kadekar recount in *Global Indian Diaspora: History, Culture and Identity,* 'when slavery was abolished in the French colonies in 1846 and the Dutch colonies in 1873, the French and Dutch planters came to an agreement with the British colonial authorities in India to obtain labour for their colonies under the indenture system' (Sahoo 2012: 31). This raised the demand for the supply of indentured labourers from the Indian hinterland.

The question about whether indenture was *The New Slavery* (Joseph Beaumont) or not has been debated since Hugh Tinker's seminal book *A New System of Slavery* was published in 1974. Tinker termed the indentured labourers 'imperial auxiliaries'. Enlarging on this debate, writer Kowlasar Misir in his article 'Indentureship was a Clever Euphemism for Slavery', states:

> The idea of indentureship as a form of slavery is not new. It occupies a central place in indentureship research. Tinker's position reinforced the abolitionists' views that deception, kidnapping and coercion were the hallmarks of indentureship; the exploitation and oppression to which the servants were subjected made them victims of a new form of slavery. Indeed, indentureship was the new avatar of slavery. (Misir 2009)

Tinker also notes that 'indentureship incorporated many of the repressive features of the slave system and induced in Indians, many of the responses of the African brothers in bondage' (Tinker 1993: 19). Frank Birbalsingh (1998: 8) argues that the 'conditions under which indentured Indian immigrants existed suggested that they were slaves in every other respect other than name'. Further, he notes that the 'Indentured labourers on arrival in the colonies were housed in the same living space vacated by the freed slaves and performed their exact tasks' (ibid.). Misir adds, 'For all intents and purposes, indentureship was a clever euphemism for slavery since labour became a commodity to be bought and sold' (Misir 2009). Following the emancipation of the African slaves, a large number of Indians were either tricked and kidnapped, or forced and pushed into immigrating as indentured labourers to the plantation colonies of the empire. Most of them were illiterate and could not understand the agreement they were putting their thumb impression on. They did not realise that the act of putting their thumb impression was symbolic of signing off their freedom. Research has revealed that a majority of the indentured people were not even aware of their final destination. Further, a large number of suicides by the labourers attests to the fact that they were forced into indenture. The pre-existing slave trade in British India made it relatively easy for the indentureship system to develop.

Colin G. Clarke (2010: 9) gives out the statistics in *South Asians Overseas: Migration and Ethnicity*. 'About 1.3 million indentured

Indian workers migrated to the following colonies/countries: Mauritius, British Guyana, Natal (South Africa), Trinidad, Fiji, Guadeloupe, Kenya, Uganda, Jamaica, Dutch Guiana/Suriname, Martinique, Seychelles, St. Lucia, Grenada and St. Vincent'. While some south Indians were indentured, their number was very small. It was the region of north India that became the largest supplier of indentured labour to the British colonies. Brij Lal highlights that a large number of the indentured labourers came from the present-day states of Uttar Pradesh and Bihar. The first lot were sent to Mauritius in 1834 and then to British Guiana in 1838. Trinidad received the first batch of indentured people from India in 1845 while Fiji received the first *girmitiyas* much later in 1879 (Lal 2004: 12).

According to information available online in the 'Discovery' Section of The National Archives in the United Kingdom, 'The Dutch West India Company had been occupying Demerara, Berbice and Essequibo from 1621. These territories were captured by Britain in 1796, restored to the Dutch in 1802, recaptured in 1803 and formally ceded to Britain in 1814. All three were united as British Guiana in 1831' (nationalarchives.gov.uk). Trinidad had been a Spanish colony until 1797 when it was taken over by Britain and formally ceded to the British in 1802. 'Fiji was ceded to Britain on 10 October 1874' (*The National Archives*, 30 May 2018).

Owing to reports of ill-treatment of the labourers in Mauritius and under pressure from the anti-slavery forum, the Government of India decided to incorporate the Act of 1837. Brij Lal enumerates the salient features of the Act:

> The emigration of contract labourers was to be subject to orders from authorities from India; that the emigrants should be required to appear before an official appointed by the provincial government; that the contract, in English and the mother tongue of the emigrant, must specify wages and the nature of employment in the colonies; that contracts for over five years, which did not include the provision for a return passage, were not to be approved; and that recruiters who obtained labourers through fraudulent means were to be fined or imprisoned. (Chatterji 2013: 81)

During the early years of indenture, the agreement was not very concrete. The terms and conditions kept changing and there was confusion over the exact wordings. Later, a more uniform document was put in place. It fixed the terms of indenture across the colonies, including, the remuneration to be paid, living arrangements in the plantations and medical facilities. It also fixed a 'free' return passage to India after ten years from the date of arrival on the colonies. This proves that indenture was meant to be only temporary in nature and that the labourers would return to their homeland. In pursuance to this, Lal's research of the archival records confirms that 'up to 1870, 21 per cent of the emigrants had returned, and in the decade after 1910, one emigrant returned for every two who had embarked for the colonies' (ibid.: 82). However, for a majority of the contracted people, who had expected only a temporary stay overseas to earn money, indenture became a permanent displacement.

Lal also elaborates on the features of the Government of India Act of 1842, which 'provided for the appointment, on a fixed salary, of an Emigration Agent at the ports of embarkation in India.' The Emigration Agent 'was required personally to examine each emigrant and to ascertain that he or she fully understood the contract they were signing.' The Act also prescribed for the emigrant ships to be 'fully licensed by the government' and to 'conform to certain prescribed standards'. It also set down the dietary and medical supplies for the emigrants, as well as their accommodation on board the ship. Looking at the drawbacks of the Act, Lal reveals that it 'was a good start, but it had no provision for the enforcement of the regulations. Nonetheless, this piece of legislation formed the basis for further reforms and amendments in the latter half of the nineteenth century' (ibid.).

Most of the Indian indentured labourers came from North India. 'Among the largest recruitment districts in Bihar in the 1850s and 1860s were Arrah (Shahabad), Sahebganj (Gaya), Hazaribagh, Patna, Purulia, Ranchi and Chapra (Saran)' (ibid.: 85). Indentured recruitment was also done from the United Provinces of Agra and Oudh. These provinces remained the principal suppliers of labour for the remaining period of indentured emigration. Within the United Provinces, the emigrants came from the eastern districts of Basti, Gonda, Faizabad, Sultanpur, Azamgarh, Gorakhpur, Allahabad and Ghazipur. Ayodhya, Aarah, Baliya and Chappra also witnessed high levels of recruitment. There were varied factors that were responsible for recruitment in these districts. 'A depressed economy, dwindling property rights, fragmentation of landholdings, subdivision of property, heavy population density, the effects of periodic droughts, floods and famine and, finally, an established pattern of migration' (ibid.).

It was not just individuals, single men and women, who migrated. In some cases, entire families migrated to the plantation colonies. In the case of Fiji, '70 per cent of women migrated as individuals while the remaining 30 per cent migrated as members of families' (ibid.: 87). Not all potential emigrants who were taken (forcibly or otherwise) to the district depot were sent to the colonies, '18 per cent-19 per cent would be rejected for various reasons, mostly because they were found to be unfit' (ibid.: 88). Later, at the port of embarkation, a similar percentage would become either deserter or simply refuse to embark on the journey.

The journey undertaken by the indentured people became the greatest leveller of social hierarchy in the system. The long voyages aboard the ships, which could take up to three months on sailing ships, brought new relationships into play. The new association of *jahaji bhais* and *jahaji behens* (ship brothers and ship sisters) became the much needed emotional anchor during the journey and translated into becoming the most enduring of all relationships during indenture. The *jahaji* brotherhood was the only tie that sustained the indentured people in the new and alien (sometimes hostile) landscape. These relationships were considered most sacred and they endured and persisted long after indenture was over.

Once they arrived in the colonies, the indentured labourers were sent to different plantations based on the planters' requirements. On the whole, families were kept together on the same plantation but it was for the benefit of the planters to break up groups of people, such as those who belonged to the same district in India, to prevent protests and strikes. Almost all narratives on indenture lament the long days of work. The indentured people had to wake up around 5 a.m. (women had to wake up earlier to prepare food), go to the fields and work late till about 4 to 6 p.m. Included in the narratives of indenture were the constant beatings and punishments, as well as the brutal violence, not to mention the virulent diseases that plagued the labourers. Added to this trauma was a life of complete and absolute isolation from the homeland.

New research on indenture depicts the system as being 'simultaneously an enslaving as well as a liberating experience for many (ibid.: 90). The stringent diktats of social stratification in India had confined many, right from their birth, to the lower stratum of Indian society. Caste was an identity marker and there was no escape from it in India. To such people then, indenture represented an alternative and gave rise to the possibility of being able to rise above their low status which had been decided based on their birth. To them, indenture was a 'god-sent opportunity' to set aside caste, class and birth distinctions. Instead, a new social order, without the traditional notions and taboos held sacred in India, seemed possible. Anthropologist Chandra Jayawardena (1971: 90) extrapolates, 'Caste as a social institution became anachronistic, its protocols of approved behaviour unenforceable'. At the plantations, everyone had to do the same work, eat the same food and live in the same dwelling units. The indentured labourers were also paid based on the task performed and not based on their caste order. This further diluted the strong bindings of the Indian caste system.

It would be misleading to assume that women had absolutely no agency in the indenture system. While it is true that they were subjected to the worst forms of sexual violence in the colonies, it is also correct to say that they enjoyed a fair measure of independence that would have been unimaginable for them in India. In *Lakshmi's Legacy*, Marina Carter (1994: 142) states emphatically that women 'played a critical role in facilitating the transmission and practice of folk religion and tradition-based sanctions'.

Indenture diaspora comprises a specific group of subjects who have been driven out of their country of origin owing to economic or other needs or pressures. They were sent as contracted labour to other colonies under the British system of indenture. Theorist Lily Cho, in her paper, 'Diasporic Citizenship: Contradictions and Possibilities for Canadian Literature', suggests that these are people whose 'agonized relationship to home engenders a perpetual sense of not quite having left and not quite having arrived' (Cho 2007: 99).

Theorist Vijay Mishra offers a relevant definition that connects the word 'diaspora' 'with the complex history of twentieth-century capitalism':

1. Relatively homogeneous, displaced communities brought to serve the Empire (slave, contract, indentured, etc.) co-existing with the indigenous/other races with a markedly ambivalent and contradictory relationship with the Motherland(s). Hence, the Indian diasporas of South Africa, Fiji, Mauritius, Guyana, Trinidad, Surinam, Malaysia; the Chinese diasporas of Malaysia, Indonesia. Linked to high (classical) Capitalism.
2. Emerging new diasporas based on free migration and linked to late capitalism: post-war Asian, Chinese, Arab, Korean communities in Britain, Europe, America, Canada, Australia.
3. Any group of migrants that sees itself on the periphery of power, or excluded from sharing power. (Mishra 1993: 1-2)

Home and belonging, as well as the notions of identity and citizenship, are quintessential concepts in the diaspora. While the common concept of a diaspora is understood to include the people living outside their homeland, the definition is not as literal or simple. There are fundamental differences between all diasporas that resist the clubbing together of the term as homogeneous. In *Cartographies of Diaspora: Contesting Identities*, theorist Avtar Brah (2003: 190) delineates the term diaspora as one based on the idea of 'multiple journeys', of 'settling down, about putting roots "elsewhere"'.

Diaspora literature highlights the themes of nostalgia, identity and belonging, as well as of adaptation, assimilation and acculturation. Since identity is a fluid concept, particularly in the case of the indenture diaspora, it spills over and navigates all three elements of construction, deconstruction and reconstruction in the new land. Several writings by diaspora writers and theorists incorporate these themes to offer a critical perspective to the readers. In 'The Turn to Diaspora', Lily Cho cautions, 'Diaspora must be understood as a *condition of subjectivity* and not as an object of analysis' (Stierstorfer 2018: 109). She argues that diaspora is 'not divorced from the histories of colonialism and imperialism' and that '. . . these histories and practices form a crucial part of the condition of diaspora's emergence'.

Cho contends that diaspora emerges from the '. . . deeply subjective processes of racial memory, of grieving for losses which cannot always be articulated and longings which hang at the edge of possibility' (ibid.). Post-colonial theorist, Homi Bhabha's seminal work, *The Location of Culture* explores the 'unhomeliness of migrancy' and maps the loss of home with '. . . the feeling of dislocation and dispossession' with respect to understanding diaspora (Bhabha 1997: 18).

Yoon Sun Lee examines the structures of works written by and about the displaced population and suggests that in these works, '. . . identity emerges as something radically contingent on performance, on performing certain types of acts, gestures or styles' (Stierstorfer 2018: 198). Author Salman Rushdie too, suggests in his famous essay 'Imaginary Homelands' that diasporic writers are 'haunted by some sense of loss, some urge to reclaim, to look back, even at the risk of being mutated into pillars of salt' (ibid.: 227). To him, the resultant work that articulates such a loss is a '. . . novel of memory and about memory'. He opines that a 'writer who is out-of-country and even out-of-language may experience this loss in an intensified form' (ibid.: 228).

Theorist Dibyesh Anand in 'Diasporic Subjectivity as an Ethical Position' grounds an understanding of diaspora as one that '. . . entails excavating marginalised, silenced and dissenting voices as well as dominant ones' (ibid.: 114). Diaspora narratives discuss the nature of the exile, the role of nostalgia, the importance of memory, the feeling of alienation, 'the state of inbetweenness' and the resultant identity crisis. The diaspora sensibility, thus is, in a sense, a search for the self, for roots, for identity and belonging. It attempts to decode the 'I' and is essentially a quest for identification.

In his essay 'Cartographies of Diaspora', Avtar Brah opines that the word diaspora 'invokes the imagery of traumas of separation and dislocation. . . but diasporas are also potentially the sites of hope and new beginnings' (Stierstorfer 2018: 237). This also holds true for indenture narratives, which can be associated with the subaltern entering the colonial space of the English language and using it as a mode of resistance to the hegemonic discourse. In *The Literature of the Indian Diaspora: Theorizing the Diasporic Imaginary* (hereafter referred to as *Literature of the Indian Diaspora)* Vijay Mishra extrapolates that narratives on indenture have taken into greater account the experience of the indentured men. However, he highlights, '. . . equally miserable and much more abject were the bodies of women, the silent rarely written underside of indenture experience' (Mishra 2014: 84). One of the underlying themes of these narratives is the belief that the indentured people were tricked into the system. Their shared sense of betrayal and trauma originates from this belief. These narratives also talk about the unifying experiences of the voyage that gave birth to a new poetics and return to the ideas of 'roots' and 'routes'. Vijay Mishra believes that the indentured diaspora '. . . lives out its trauma through a constant return to an original moment' that can be '. . . glimpsed only through its re-inscription in a narrative of departure and loss' (ibid.: 107). If, as Mishra suggests, 'the force of trauma lies in its repetition', then indenture narratives offer a cathartic return to the trauma to secure a cathartic release (ibid.: 118). Thus, the entire experience of *girmit* pervades the psyche of the indentured diaspora and their writings work on the ethos of memory that situates, in the words of Vijay Mishra, an 'impossible mourning' (ibid.: 108).

The texts selected to encapsulate the sensibility of the indentured diaspora in this book are chosen with special care to include the different perspectives of the writers towards projecting the lived experience of indenture. The authors are divided equally between Fiji and the Caribbean. One of the writers was an indentured worker in Fiji while the other three writers are the third and fourth generation descendants of the indenture diaspora. Keeping in mind that a holistic understanding of indenture is imperative for a balanced point of view, the gendered perspective has been carefully scrutinised in the choice of texts selected. Thus, an equal number of authors are women and offer a subaltern outlook to the system of indenture.

Totaram Sanadhya's autobiography, *My Twenty-One Years in the Fiji Islands*, is a unique account of the lives of the indentured labourers in Fiji. It was written during the time of indenture and is a first-hand account of the experience of an Indian *girmitiya*. Initially written in Hindi as *Fijidwip mein Mere Ikkis Varsh*, Totaram Sanadhya dictated the account of his life in Fiji to Benarsidas Chaturvedi, who penned the book on his behalf. It was then translated into English by anthropologists John Dunham Kelly and Uttra Kumari Singh in 1991. Sanadhya claimed that he had been deceitfully recruited in 1893 and had spent his first five years in Fiji working as an indentured labourer. After he had completed his tenure of the indenture, he established himself as a farmer, and then as a Hindu priest, dedicating himself to removing the plight of other Indian labourers indentured and sent to Fiji. He took the help of Indian freedom fighters and missionaries and encouraged the migration of Indian teachers and lawyers to Fiji to help improve the working conditions of the indentured Indians living on the islands. Sanadhya returned to India in 1914 after spending twenty one years in Fiji and narrated his experiences in a book. So powerful was his account that this book was used as campaign material in the movement that started to end the indenture system. According to Brij Lal (2012: 262), Sanadhya's narrative shows 'a perception, idealism, wit, tolerance, balance and shrewd practicality seldom matched by any of his European or Indian contemporaries'. John O'Carroll (2012) in 'Totaram's Ghost' believes that while the text 'generated a huge impact and produced a change in its time, it still lingers not as a literary masterpiece (though the style of the text and its story-telling does bear considerable scrutiny), but as part of a wider scene, perhaps as a synecdoche of a dimension of that scene'. Vijay Mishra states that Sanadhya's account, 'the clearest contemporary account of the early fragment as it comes into being, traces a number of key developments surrounding indenture that will resonate in the early histories of Indian indentured communities elsewhere as well' (Mishra 2014: 98).

Tears in Paradise: Suffering and Struggles of Indians in Fiji 1879-2004 written by Rajendra Prasad is an explosive book that captivates the reader and narrates the story of the indentured labour taken to Fiji from British occupied India in the years 1879-1916. Prasad highlights the brutal exploitation of the Indian immigrants on the British and Australian run sugar cane plantations. Published in 2004, the book weaves a riveting account of the suffering, sacrifices and struggles of the Indians during the *girmit* (indenture period of 1879-1919) in Fiji. In this book, Prasad has painted a very vivid picture of the indentured Indo-Fijians. Dev Nadkarni (2011) describes it as '. . . an amazing work of research, compiled historical facts, personal stories, anecdotes, even stories within stories . . . the book is a genuine eye opener that makes us aware of such pain, inequities, their indentured lives'. Nadkarni highlights how in the narrative, 'Prasad alternates between being a personal diarist and a dispassionate chronicler, writing equally with the heart and the head' (ibid.). The book describes plantation life and the new culture in vivid detail and narrates the onerous circumstances of the powerless *girmitiyas*. If they failed, whether through sickness or pregnancy, to perform their back breaking, 12-hours-per day, 6-days-per-week tasks, they were fined from their paltry wages and prosecuted. Gideon Polya (2015) notes, 'In 1886, 6566 *girmitiyas* were registered in Fiji and 8835 charges were laid against them'.

Peggy Mohan's debut novel *Jahajin* illustrates the extraordinary experience of the journey undertaken by the indentured Indians from Calcutta to Trinidad, crossing two oceans to reach their new 'home' on the other side of the world. The novel encapsulates the memory of the train ride taken by the 110-year-old Deeda (the protagonist of the novel) from Faizabad to Calcutta (now Kolkata). She vividly describes the subsequent passage down the *Hooghly* in a ship, as well as the three-month-long voyage around the stormy Cape and up the Atlantic Ocean to Trinidad. Here, the '. . . weary migrants settled into life as indentured labourers on the sugar plantations of *Chinidad*'. Raka Banerjee (2013) reviews *Jahajin* on wordpress.com and finds that the author is interested in how the indentured women helped preserve and propagate Bhojpuri in the sugar estates, who would have otherwise spoken the *Khari Bholi* dialect which is the present standard dialect in UP, or would have altogether abandoned their mother tongues for English or Creole. Banerjee describes it as '. . . a remarkable tale, celebrating the triumph of the human spirit and imagination. *Jahajin* is, for all the stories it brings together, the story of a diaspora—a culture and community that has strayed away from its roots and struggles to both discard as well as preserve, some of the legacy (and cruelty) of a culture inherited . . .' (Banerjee 2013). Peggy Mohan's story of a lost homeland captivates readers and the novel comes alive with compelling characters, gathering different voices in various narratives of relocation and transformation across a century. Rukmini Bhaya Nair in her article 'Ladies Coop' describes it as '. . .

an "autoethnography", a hybrid genre where the author's fictionalised biography ultimately mirrors the story of her community and is a compelling mix of truth . . .' (Nair 2008: 68).

Shortlisted for the 2014 Orwell Prize for Political Writing, and winner of the 2014 Gordon K and Sybil Lewis Prize, Gaiutra Bahadur's seminal book, *Coolie Woman: The Odyssey of Indenture* (2013), explores complex issues of migration and the post-slavery exploitative system of indentured labour. According to Sara Wajid, 'It is a genealogical page-turner interwoven with a compelling radical history of the colonial period from the perspective of the indentured women'. She finds that 'The collective voice of the *jahaji behen* (ship sisters) has been barely audible across the centuries, until now. . . ' (Wajid 2013). Reviewing the book for *The Indian Express*, Pratik Kanjilal writes, 'One of the book's strength is that, it goes beyond a solely Indian or Indo-Caribbean perspective, to consider our intertwined relationships to different parts of the world, as well as to each other (i.e. Indo-diasporic and Indian, Indo and Afro, or Indo and European)' (Kanjilal 2014: 9). The book is a record of the women who made their way to the Caribbean, whose stories remain elusive, partly because they wanted it to be that way. Shrabani Basu (2013: 9) believes that it is also '. . . a tale of extreme violence that the women faced from their partners on the plantations. The machete—to be used in the sugar cane fields—was often the weapon used against them'. *Coolie Woman* straddles a memoir in the literary non-fiction genre exploring the origin and legacy of the life of Gaiutra Bahadur's great grandmother who was brought to British Guiana around 1903 to work in a sugarcane plantation. It explores a subaltern woman's point of view.

This book explores the migration experience of the indentured diaspora, along with issues of exile, rootlessness, alienation, language and culture dislocation, marginalisation, and racial and gender discrimination. It makes a comprehensive study on how cultural identity is retained in the host country, as well as discusses issues of adaptation and assimilation and the birth of a cultural hybridity. The objective of this book is to analyse and research socio-cultural issues like place of origin, destination, resultant identity, cultural continuity and change, as well as cultural identity and integration. It also aims to discover how indenture literature acts as a 'cathartic release' of long-held trauma, and grievances against the system. Further, it seeks to explore the impact of the indentured system on the social, historical, economic, psychological, anthropological and sociological changes that were brought about in the lives of the indentured people. It does this by projecting their lost stories and their lost selves as well as highlighting their sense of longing to belong to the homeland. Finally, the book highlights the experience of displacement and homelessness that has been a source of unrelieved sadness and trauma, consequently giving rise to the distinct social group of indenture diaspora.

This work undertakes a close textual analysis of various narratives including those of Totaram Sanadhya, Rajendra Prasad, Gaiutra Bahadur and Peggy Mohan to explore the lives and experiences of the indentured labourers. It explores their writings with relevance to the issues of migrancy and also generates aesthetic evaluation while negotiating, interrogating and navigating the cultural and theoretical constructs involved in aiding the emergence of a new hybrid identity. The book also takes into account the historical contextualisation of the primary source material through archival research, i.e. with the help of secondary source material.

Indenture was a product of the colonial period and while interpreting the works under study, critical perspectives and theoretical frameworks have been applied to bring out the issues of isolation and alienation, as well as the sense of home and homeland from a postcolonial point of view. This book studies the key facets in the retention of the Indian ethos in the indentured diaspora, while also analysing the notions of socio-cultural transformation, identity reconstruction and acculturation. The indenture perspective highlights the 'collective consciousness' of the social group and evaluates the role of memory in their viewing of India as an 'imagined homeland'. The outlook of the indentured diaspora plays a big role in their 'longing to belong' to the land of their ancestors. Theoretical concepts about diaspora have been taken into account while analysing the affective dimensions of the forced migration. The book also analyses the ways through which literature of the Indian indenture diaspora develops a poetics different from the one embodied in other diaspora writings.

Drawing from historical records and documented resources, as well as from the personal narratives of the indentured labourers and their descendants, this work charts the changing processes of labour migration and the subsequent emerging forms of identity in the indenture diaspora communities, specifically in Fiji and the Caribbean. It takes individual narratives into account while tracing the history of Indian indenture. The study also attempts to correct the History, with a capital H, which was written by the British Empire to further its own interest. Instead, it endeavours to replace the colonial discourse by incorporating private histories. This process of (re)visioning indenture history takes place at the level of the individual narratives, tying them with the larger community of the indentured diaspora spread across the world.

In his essay 'Mauritius: The Overcrowded Barracoon', Nobel laureate Sir V.S. Naipaul answers the quintessential question asked in India—'Where do you come from?' This roughly translates to mean 'To which place do you belong?' Naipaul says that it is '. . . the Indian question of people who think in terms of the village, the district, the province, the community, the caste' (Naipaul 1972: 43). The answer to this seemingly innocuous question opens up a Pandora's Box as far as indenture is concerned. This book looks at ways through which indenture literature, through negotiating the concept of identity in its diaspora, can deliver the answer to this question.

WORKS CITED

Ali, Ahmed, *Girmit: Indian Indenture Experience in Fiji*, Suva, Fiji: Fiji Museum, 2004.

Amin, Shahid, William Crooke, J.R. Reid and George Abraham Grierson, eds., *A Concise Encyclopedia of North Indian Peasant Life: Being a Compilation from the Writings of William Crooke, J.R. Reid, G.A. Grierson*, New Delhi: Manohar, 2005.

Anand, Dibyesh, 'Diasporic Subjectivity as an Ethical Position', *The Routledge Diaspora Studies Reader*, ed. Klaus Stierstorfer and Janet Wilson, Oxon: Routledge, 2018, pp. 114-18.

Asaolu, Richard Oluseyi, *Slavery: Abolition*, New York: Pedia Press, 2011.

Ashcroft, Bill, Gareth Griffiths and Helen Tiffin, *Key Concepts in Post Colonial Studies*, London: Routledge, 1998.

Bahadur, Gaiutra, *Coolie Woman: The Odyssey of Indenture*, London: Hachette, 2013.

Banerjee, Raka, 'Jahajin: Fable and Facts', *Wordpress*, 17 October 2013, Web. 22 April 2017, www.southasainwomenwriters.wordpress.com/reviews-home/2013-reviews/

Basu, Shrabani, 'The Women Who Came from the Sea', *Telegraph*, 1 December 2013, p. 9.

Beaumont, Joseph, *The New Slavery: An Account of the Indian and Chinese Immigrants in British Guiana,* University of Warwick, Guyana: The Caribbean Press, 2011.

Bhabha, Homi, *The Location of Culture,* London: Routledge, 1997.

Birbalsingh, Frank, *Jahaji Bhai: An Anthology of Indo-Caribbean Literature,* Toronto, Ont: TSAR, 1988.

Brah, Avtar, *Cartographies of Diaspora: Contesting Identities,* New York: Routledge, 2003.

———, 'Cartographies of Diaspora', *The Routledge Diaspora Studies Reader,* Ed. Klaus Stierstorfer and Janet Wilson, Oxon: Routledge, 2018, pp. 235-8.

Buckhory, Somduth, *The Call of the Ganges*, New Delhi: Vikas, 1979.

Campbell, Gwyn, *The Structure of Slavery in Indian Ocean Africa and Asia,* London: Frank Cass, 2006.

Carter, Marina, and Crispin Bates, 'Empire and Locality: a Global Dimension to the 1857 Indian Uprising', *Journal of Global History* 5.1, 2010, pp. 51-73. Web. 21 November 2018.

Carter, Marina, *Lakshmi's Legacy: the Testimonies of Indian Women in the 19th Century Mauritius,* Mauritius: Editions de l'Océan Indien, 1994.

———, *Voices from Indenture: Experiences of Indian Migrants in the British Empire*, Leuven: Leuven University Press, 1997.

Chatterji, Joya and David Washbrook, eds., *Routledge Handbook of the South Asian Diaspora,* Oxon: Routledge, 2013.

Cho, Lily, 'Diasporic Citizenship: Contradictions and Possibilities for Canadian Literature', *Resituating the Study of Canadian Literature*, ed. Smaro Kamboureli and Roy Miki, Waterloo, ON: Wilfred Laurier University Press, 2007, pp. 93-109.

———, 'The Turn to Diaspora', *The Routledge Diaspora Studies Reader*, ed. Klaus Stierstorfer and Janet Wilson, Oxon: Routledge, 2018, pp. 109-13.

Clarke, Colin G., Ceri Peach, and Steven Vertovec, *South Asians Overseas: Migration and Ethnicity*, Cambridge: Cambridge University Press, 2010.

Clifford, James, 'Diasporas', *The Routledge Diaspora Studies Reader,* ed. Klaus Stierstorfer and Janet Wilson, Oxford: Routledge, 2018, pp. 10-16.

'Discovery' *The National Archives*, n.p., n.d. Web. 30 May 2018. <https://discovery.nationalarchives.gov.uk/discovery/>

Emmer, P. C. and E. Van Den Boogaart, *Colonialism and Migration: Indentured Labour before and after Slavery*, Dordrecht: M. Nijhoff, 1986.

Gillion, Kenneth L., *Fiji's Indian Migrants: a History to the End of Indenture in 1920,* Melbourne: Oxford University Press, 1973.

Jayawardena, Chandra, *The Disintegration of Caste in Fiji Indian Rural Society,* Sydney: Angus and Robertson, 1971.

Kanjilal, Pratik, 'The Books of Exodus', *Indian Express*, 2 March 2014, p. 9.

Klass, Morton, *East Indians in Trinidad: A Study of Cultural Persistence*, Prospect Heights, IL: Waveland Press, 1988.

Kumar, Ashutosh, *Coolies of the Empire Indentured Indians in the Sugar Colonies, 1830-1920*, Cambridge: Cambridge University Press, 2017.

Kumar, Kapil, *Peasants in Revolt: Tenants, Landlords, Congress and the Raj in Oudh, 1861-1922*, New Delhi: Manohar, 1994.

———, 'Colonial Expansion, Resistance and Forced Migrations', *Resistance and Indian Indenture Experience: Comparative Perspectives*, ed. Maurits S. Hassankhan, Brij V. Lal and Doug Munro, New Delhi: Manohar, 2014, pp. 19-49.

Lal, Brij V. and Clem Seecharan, *Girmitiyas: the Origins of the Fiji Indians*, Lautoka, Fiji: Fiji Institute of Applied Studies, 2004.

Lal, Brij V., Peter Reeves and Rajesh Rai, eds., *The Encyclopedia of the Indian Diaspora*, New Delhi: Oxford University Press, 2007.

Lal, Brij V., *Chalo Jahaji: On a Journey through Indenture in Fiji*, Canberra: ANU Press, 2012.

Lee, Sun Yoon, 'The Postcolonial Novel and Diaspora', *The Routledge Diaspora Studies Reader*, ed. Klaus Stierstorfer and Janet Wilson, Oxford: Routledge, 2018, pp. 196-200.

Mishra, Vijay, 'Introduction', *SPAN Journal of South Pacific Association for Commonwealth Literature and Language Studies*, 34. 35, 1993, pp. 1-17.

———, *Literature of the Indian Diaspora: Theorizing the Diasporic Imaginary*, London: Routledge, 2014.

Misir, Kowlasar, 'Indentureship was a Clever Euphemism for Slavery', *Kaieteur News*, n.p., 19 May 2009. Web. 21 Jan 2019. <https://kaieteurnewsonline.com/>

Mohan, Peggy, *Jahajan*, New Delhi: HarperCollins, 2007.

Nadkarni, Dev, 'Tears In Paradise. Suffering and Struggle of Indians in Fiji 1879-2004', *Blogspot*, 27 August 2011. Web. 09 August 2017. www.rajendraprasadsite. blogspot.in

Naipaul, V.S., 'Mauritius: The Overcrowded Barracoon', London: Allied Newspapers, 1972.

Nair, Rukmini Bhaya, 'Ladies Coop', *Outlook*, Outlook Publishing (India) Private Limited, 31 March 2008. Web. 31 May 2018. <https://www.outlookindia.com/ magazine/story/ladies-coop/237061>

O'Carroll, John, 'Totaram's Ghost', *Australian Humanities Review* 52.6 (2012): n. pag. Web. 22 May 2017. < http://australianhumanitiesreview.org/2012/05/01/ totarams-ghost/ >

Pal, Adesh and Tapas Chakraborty, *Theorizing and Critiquing Indian Diaspora*, New Delhi: Creative Books, 2004.

Polya, Gideon, '"Tears In Paradise. Suffering and Struggle of Indians in Fiji 1879-2004" by Rajendra Prasad – Britain's Indentured Indian "5 Year Slaves"', *Countercurrents*. 4 March 2015. Web. 9 August 2017.< www. countercurrents. org/polya040315.html>

Prasad, Rajendra, *Tears in Paradise: Suffering and Struggles of Indians in Fiji, 1879-2004,* Auckland, N.Z.: Pindar, 2010.

Rushdie, Salman, 'Imaginary Homelands', *The Routledge Diaspora Studies Reader,* ed. Klaus Stierstorfer and Janet Wilson, Oxford: Routledge, 2018, pp. 227-9.

Sahoo, Ajay Kumar, and Laxmi Narayan Kadekar, *Global India Diaspora: History, Culture and Identity*, Jaipur: Rawat Publications, 2012.

Sanadhya, Totaram, *My Twenty-one Years in the Fiji Islands*, tr. John Dunham Kelly and Uttra Kumari Singh, Suva, Fiji: Fiji Museum, 1991.

Sawe, Elisha Benjamin, 'Aapravasi Ghat Of Port Louis, Mauritius', *WorldAtlas*, n.p., n.d. Web. 30 May 2019. <https://www.worldatlas.com/articles/aapravasi-ghat-of-port-louis-mauritius.html>

'Slavery', *The National Archives,* n.p., n.d. Web. 27 May 2018. <http://www.nationalarchives.gov.uk/slavery/about/>

Tinker, Hugh, *A New System of Slavery: The Export of Indian Labour Overseas 1830-1920,* London: Hansib, 1993.

Torabully, Khal and Marina Carter, *Coolitude: an Anthology of the Indian Labour Diaspora,* London: Anthem Press, 2002.

Wajid, Sara, 'Journey of the Coolie Woman in the History of the British Empire', *The Guardian*, 19 November 2013, Web. 1 May 2016. < https://www.theguardian.com/lifeandstyle/womens-blog/2013/nov/19/journey-coolie-women-history-british-empire-indentured-labourers>

Yang, Anand, 'Peasant on the Move: A Study of Internal Migration in India', *Journal of Interdisciplinary History* 10.1, 1979, pp. 37-58.

CHAPTER 2

The *Girmitiyas* of Fiji: A Forgotten Generation

> '*Girmitiya*, my maker
> Your journey
> Has broken my heart'.
> (Mishra 1992: 13)

WHILE THE BINARY of *desh* (own country) and *videsh* (abroad) attempts to put a clear divide between the homeland and the rest of the world, and posit one against the other as diametrically defined opposites, it is able to do so successfully only in terms of the geographical space. Identity is a fluid concept and while, on the one hand, leaving the *desh* seems to put a 'dash', a hyphen, in the identity of a diaspora, on the other, it opens up a site to explore the narrative of the displaced. In *The Literature of the Indian Diaspora,* Vijay Mishra (2014: 185) suggests that it is through the hyphen that the diaspora can retain the 'problematic situating of the self as simultaneously belonging "here" and "there"'. However, he purports that 'the politics of the hyphen itself is hyphenated because, in the name of empowering people, the classification indeed disempowers them; it makes them use a hyphenated term, "empoweringly-disempowered"' (ibid.: 184).

Indenture literature attempts to give a concrete shape to the real and imagined worlds, but, as Salman Rushdie points out in *Imaginary Homelands,* it '. . . is obliged to deal in broken mirrors, some of whose fragments have been lost . . .' (Rushdie 1991: 10). Such literature then, exemplifies the epistemology of the hyphenated diaspora, of the rootless subject who has been lost along the route, the one who now belongs to no particular landscape and who has arrived, but not to his 'home'. The narratives of indenture juxtapose the themes of home, loss, trauma, exile, nostalgia, memory and betrayal with the themes of resistance, accommodation, acculturation and assimilation. Narratives by the descendants of indenture are drawn on a different scale and the ambivalence that is still present—within their being, which is fragmented between 'Indianness' and their homeland, and between their identity and their 'home'—works in very different ways.

While the colonial master narrative suggests that most of the indentured people belonging to the lower castes were using indenture to flee poverty, starvation and other forms of depravity, the factors contributing towards the migration of Indians belonging to the upper castes into indenture were diverse. They had either been tricked into indenture or abducted by the *akratis* (vernacular Hindi term used for a recruiter, middleman or agent; also spelt *akrati* by some authors). The account of Totaram Sanadhya, narrated by Sanadhya to Benarsidas Chaturvedi, who published the same as *Fijidweep mein Mere Ikkis Vars* in 1973, is one such instance. This account was translated into English as *My Twenty-One Years in the Fiji Islands* (thereafter *My Twenty-One Years*) in 1984 by John Dunham Kelly and Uttra Kumari Singh and is one of the rare accounts narrated by an indentured person while undergoing the period of indenture. It is a first-hand experience of the life led by the indentured labourers in the Fiji Islands and offers a point of view that questions the colonial discourse. This polemic book became in its own right, an anti-indenture campaign, and contributed to the abolishment of the indenture system in Fiji in 1920. Data provided by Kelly and Singh shows that '. . . between 1879 and 1916, approximately 60,537 Indians came to Fiji under contract as part of the British system of indenture to work in the sugarcane plantations for a period of five years' (Sanadhya 1991: 1). In 'Voices from the Diaspora', Vijay Mishra explains the origin of the word *girmit.* The recruited labourers had to sign an indenture 'agreement'—vernacularised in Hindi as *girmit*—and they were thereafter known as *girmitiyas* (Lal 2007: 122).

Totaram Sanadhya was a Brahmin, a high caste under the Hindu system of caste hierarchy. As a 17-year-old, he was brought to Fiji to work on the plantations on 28 May in the year 1893. He lived in Fiji for 21 long years before returning to India in 1914, where he devoted his life to fighting for the end of indenture. Sanadhya had been tricked by an *akrati* in India who, unknown to Sanadhya posited him as a 'Thakur' on his indenture pass. The loss of identity for him began even before he had left the shores of his motherland. Sanadhya lists the sum of the *girmitiya* experience as being one of trauma that included the loss of caste as well as the social and moral degeneration faced in the lines on the plantation. In *The Literature of the Indian Diaspora*, Vijay Mishra (2014: 197) argues that since the British do not have a theory of their own postcoloniality, they '. . . see themselves not as a racial entity but as a people who have transcended race, leaving race and ethnicity for everyone else'. Sanadhya specifically details the brutalities committed by the white overseers on the *girmitiyas*, as well as the hardships and issues faced by the indentured people in general. As a first-person account, his book offers a rare insight into the indenture system. Not only does it report facts, but it also reflects the truth from the *girmitiya* perspective. Kelly and Singh suggest that '. . . it is our bridge into the participant's point of view in a particular historical episode, the cultural beliefs of a particular time and place' (Sanadhya 1991: 11). After spending 21 years in Fiji, first as an indentured labourer, then as a farmer, as well as a Hindu priest, Sanadhya returned to India in 1914. His experience in Fiji testifies what being a *coolie* meant—it covers the life of an indentured Indian labourer, starting with his betrayal by an *akrati,* the sufferings faced at the depot in India, his journey aboard the ship carrying him to the islands and finally, a critique of the life of subjugation lived on the lines in the plantations. He also lists the initiatives taken by people like him in Fiji to put pressure on the British government to end the system of indenture.

Historian and Christian Methodist Missionary J.W. Burton based in Fiji during the period of indenture has summed up the *girmitiya* perception and equated the life of an indentured worker living in the lines to that of a life in *Narak* (Hell). Historian K.L. Gillion (1973: 129), in his book, *Fiji's Indian Migrants* too alludes to the Indians calling 'their life on the plantations in Fiji *narak* which means "hell"'. In his testimony, Sanadhya marks a departure from this train of thought. He stresses instead on *kasht*, i.e. the hardships, distress and troubles faced by the indentured Indians (Sanadhya 1991: 14). He marks this distinction by saying that in Christian theology, hell is a place for sinners. The hapless Indians who had the misfortune of being indentured were not sinners. Sanadhya states that the mainstay of the Hindu belief system is *karma.* He defines it as '. . . a realm of activity in which no other agent is a factor, and one's fate is entirely in one's own hands as the quest for deliverance' (ibid.: 15). The question which then arises is whether indenture was woven into their *karma* or was it the fate of these people? Not all *girmitiya* voices agree on this but Sanadhya lays great emphasis on *kasht,* along with *dukh.* He defines *dukh* as mental stress and *kasht* as a definitive of difficult material situations (ibid.: 16). He also discusses the connotations of *atyachar* which comprised physical violence and injustice meted out to the indentured people by the authority figures in the British, as well as by the indigenous population in Fiji. 'Overseers beat them, lawyers steal their money, merchants pay them less for what they sell and charge them more for what they buy, and government officers consistently fail to do their duty and provide the Indians protection' (ibid.: 17).

Author and descendent of a *girmitiya* in Fiji, Rajendra Prasad, in his book *Tears in Paradise: Suffering and Struggles of Indians in Fiji 1879-2004* (hereafter referred to as *Tears in Paradise*) contests Sanadhya's voice on *girmit* not being a state of hell for the *girmitiyas.* He argues, 'The *girmitiyas,* with low wages, hard tasks, scant food and appalling conditions, called their term of indenture "narak" (hell)' (Prasad 2010: 60). Prasad also quotes Rev. Burton who said of the CSR Company (the Australia-based sugar company hiring the indentured Indians in Fiji) that 'it has no soul, its prime motive being the exploitation of labour to increase its profits' (ibid.). This essentially means that indenture was *narak* with this rider: sinners and sufferers formed a fractured-hyphenated unit, with sinners being some others and sufferers living in 'hell-like' conditions. *Karma* belongs to the first half of the unit and its consequences were faced by the other half.

The indenture diaspora has been termed the old capital diaspora because, in its very essence, it was established to make profits for the plantation industry. Where the ends justified the means, the barbaric and dehumanising abasement of the *girmitiyas* was nurtured by the unholy nexus of the *sardaars* (overseers), the CSR officials and the British judicial system in Fiji. Prasad quotes British historian Hugh Tinker in *A New System of Slavery*, who also blamed the system for the violence on the fields. 'An industry which provided almost nothing for the workers by way of incentives succeeded in keeping them hard at work by a system of penalties and punishments. The role of the taskmasters was grim and their capacity to exploit the coolies included the sexual exploitation of women' (ibid.: 61).

In his book, Prasad terms indenture '. . . a system of manipulation, domination, intimidation and exploitation of human labour, and mental and physical violence were mercilessly used to increase productivity and raise the profitability of the white planters' (ibid.: 9). He also laments that the psychological impact of the system on the lives of the successive generations is an 'inherited stigma of shame' (ibid.: 11). From a period of physical hardship, *girmit* turned into a period of mental anguish and finally a psychological trauma for the indentured. The stigma of shame carried so much weight that the people undergoing indenture refused to recount the extent of the harsh brutalities they faced in the hands of the *sardaars* (mostly overseers of Indian origin) and the *columbers* (the colonials). The word *columber* is a linguistic breaking down and rendering of the English words 'call number' and was used as a form of address by the emigrants to refer to the white plantation heads who called out the numbers assigned to the indentured labourers to mark their attendance. The indenture period has thus been acknowledged by most historians and critics as a period of collective trauma with the word *narak* coming up repeatedly in most narratives.

The geographical position of the plantation also played an important role in the conflicting and contradicting testimonies about indenture. Eminent historian, Brij V. Lal, talking about his grandfather's *girmit* in Labasa, Fiji, in his book *Chalo Jahaji* says, 'Indenture was generally a hard, brutalising, disorienting experience, but Indenture in Labasa was pure *narak*, hell. The *girmitiyas* were more vulnerable because they were cut off and stationed on another island, remote, isolated: out of sight, out of official mind' (Lal 2012: 30). In *Bittersweet: The Indo-Fijian Experience,* Lal (2004: 4) maintains, 'People recalled *girmit*—when they recalled the past at all—as a period of brutality and violence and debauchery, of poverty and degradation, of moral disintegration and cultural and social chaos, altogether a dark period best left unexplored to the obscure pages of a fading history'.

In *The Literature of the Indian Diaspora*, Vijay Mishra traces the *girmit* ideology based on the varied accounts of indenture:

> The story of indenture begins with the work of recruiters who never explained the full conditions of the indenture, nor the distances to be travelled. Labourers were just loaded into ships like animals; mocked and caned by the officers. Upon arrival, the coolies were randomly sent to different estates. Removed from the new bonds of friendship created on the ships, a few committed suicide. The purchasing power of the Rupee was low in Fiji and few were able to save enough for themselves. The rape of women by young officers from Australia and New Zealand was not uncommon. It was not unusual to hear about the murder of these women by their husbands, although they were not at fault (Mishra 2014: 35).

Mishra talks about 'the girmit ideology as a structure (of feeling) that grew out of the experience of the plantation diaspora' (ibid.: 39). He also includes the concepts of home, trauma and return in his writing. Mishra's view on one of the key components of indenture is that of a sense of betrayal. In Sanadhya's and Prasad's accounts, betrayal forms the very core of the narrative. Starting from the betrayal by the *akratis*, the betrayal at the depots where his caste is changed on the emigration pass, the betrayal on the ship where he is forced to eat and dwell with others belonging to lower castes, the betrayal on reaching the plantations where he is 'bought' for a sum of Rs. 210, the betrayal of the overseer in assigning him to work more than his capability, the betrayal of . . . , the list is endless for Sanadhya. The final betrayal comes in the form of his own people shunning him as an outcaste, a *tapuwalla* when he returns to his home after 21 long years in Fiji. An 'Indian' when he left 21 years ago, Sanadhya is 'welcomed' back as an outcaste. His identity had undergone a shift several times over in the process. He is addressed as a *girmitiya* when he signs the agreement, a *coolie* when he boards the ship and also during his period under the indenture, and finally, a *tapuwalla* when he returns to India. The home he left belongs to a past that cannot be retrieved and is in a country that is now lost to the indentured, maybe forever.

Mishra goes on to suggest that 'the diasporic imaginary is a condition of impossible mourning that transforms mourning into melancholia'. He explains that '. . . traumatic moments heighten the sense of mourning occasioned by a prior "death" of the homeland which in a sense is part of the entity, the dasein, of the subject' (ibid.: 9). Explaining further, he states, 'there is no immediate cure for the condition because the loss remains abstract; it is not compensated for by the happiness in the new nation-state and is, therefore, internalised' (ibid.: 10). Poet and critic Sudesh Mishra (2006: 14) in his book *Diaspora Criticism* defines indenture as an 'atemporal ontology of suffering, hardship and deceit'. In his paper 'Time and *Girmit*', he explains the derivation of the word *girmit* as a vernacularised form of the word 'agreement' (Mishra 2005: 16). Scholar Maebh Long in her paper 'Girmit, Postmemory, and Subramani' recognises 'the term as naming a visceral response to the emptiness of the arrangement made' (Long 2016: 165). Sudesh Mishra surmises that the indentured people were misled when they boarded 'the wrong ship, to undertake the wrong voyage, to disembark at the wrong destination' (Mishra 2006: 22).

The force of trauma lies in its repetition. In both, Sanadhya's and Prasad's accounts, the traumatic experience is recollected and enacted in the narrative. Vijay Mishra (2014: 118) suggests that in one sense 'writing' may be seen as a cure for trauma. Writing the experience offers a cathartic release to the author. According to one of the lectures delivered to reformist groups after his return to India, Sanadhya traced the specifics of the indenture system or *coolie-pratha* as he termed it. History, for him, was not an abstract, remote discipline, but a lived reality. He believed that he lived not above or beyond his history, but within it as an active, engaged observer. Prasad too recollects the indenture of his grandfather from his memory. While Sanadhya's book is a first-person account, Prasad's work is based on (re)memory of an actual life lived in the past. Marianne Hirsch's work on postmemory can offer an insight into the diasporic experience. Her book *Family Frames: Photograph, Narrative, and Postmemory* look at a condition in which the 'home' is inaccessible or impossible since it is located in a different time and a different country. While her work is based on the Holocaust survivors, the trauma transcends the situation and can relate to the experience of the children of the indentured diaspora. In her paper 'Past Lives: Postmemories in Exile', Hirsch (1996: 662) says that '. . . although they have not themselves lived through the trauma of banishment and the destruction of home' the children of the exiled, '. . . remain always marginal of exiled, always in the diaspora'. Maheb Long (2018: 167) broadens Hirsch's concept of post-memory as a '. . . a relationship that subsequent generations have to trauma suffered by the predecessors, a trauma passed down in stories and accounts, but with such an impact as to become a memory, something as if personally experienced by the listener'. Hirsch (2012: 34) explains that in the case of postmemory, 'Loss of family, home, of a sense of belonging and safety in the world "bleed" from one generation to the next'. In her paper, Hirsch (1996: 664) projects mourning as '. . . a loss that cannot be repaired. And, because even the act of mourning is secondary, the lost object can never be incorporated and mourning can never be overcome'. The history of the previous generation is thus entangled in the present of the next generation. Prasad's narrative also shows how the trauma and grief of *girmit* have been internalized. 'This pang of separation was the most painful I have ever experienced. . . . This union and separation were so deeply etched that time has failed to diminish the grief that I experienced. . . . Because of this event, I have lost my emotional symmetry: tears speak in place of words in moments of reflection' (Prasad 2010: 40).

As an indentured person and part of the plantation machinery, Sanadhya remained on the periphery and was never fully integrated into it. From his ambivalent position (both outside and inside), he questions the very notion of home. His narrative captures precisely the nature and effects of indenture on the individual and, more importantly, the effects that the notion of home has on our own beliefs. It questions the certainty of our identity and our convictions about our own and others' cultures. From a Brahmin born in India, his identity was changed in the depot even before embarking on the voyage that would take him to Fiji. His travel pass lists him as a *thakur*. The change in identity is further brought out by the way he is addressed. Sanadhya's identity (like that of others indentured with him) is changed from that of an Indian to that of a *girmitiya* and finally, to a *coolie* on the lines.

Critics of the indenture, Khal Torabully and Marina Carter, in their seminal work, *Coolitude*, discuss the voyage as an essential component in indenture poetics. 'It is to be understood as a place of destruction and creation of identity, which is preliminary to the "enracinement" in the host country, itself comprehended as a dynamic space of the diversity of perceptions and cultures' (Torabully 2002: 15).

French social theorist, Michel Foucault's work on deconstructing and decolonising texts deals with the exploration of power as set up by binaries. A reading of his lectures leads to the discovery of the colonial discourse as an act of power, with narrations becoming hegemonic over time, and becoming History with a capital 'H' (Foucault 1997: 110). The colonial master narrative promoted indenture as the option for the unemployed labourers, as well as for the widows and single women in India as a means to escape poverty and oppression in India. On the other hand, the literature of the indentured diaspora presents the real lived experience in direct contrast to the hegemonic colonial discourse. It brings to light the existence of other histories through memories and testimonies. An instance of this is externalised in *My Twenty-One Years* when Sanadhya (1991: 17) recounts, 'The *girmitiyas* are treated like prisoners and dogs. On the ship, they get dog biscuits to eat, and prisoners' clothes. . . They have been made into a new kind of people, forced into a new social place. They are now "coolies"'. Sanadhya's outlook is not a conventional re-telling of life (it is more than just an autobiography) but is narrated through the echoes of his memory from his present location after returning home. The difference between history and memory is that while history supports a bias towards a particular point of view and is promoted as fact, memory refers to a lived experience and is a more personal narration.

While the colonial narrative showcases the labourers belonging to the lowest rungs of society in India, the counter-narratives, in the form of testimonies of those who had laboured under the system, present indenture as an inhumane and debilitating experience into which a cross-strata of Indian society had been tricked. Indian indentured emigrants came from all parts of India but a majority came from the United Provinces (present states of Uttar Pradesh and Bihar) in north India. Brij Lal elaborates that in the nineteenth century, all strata of rural north Indian society were affected by the changes resulting from British colonization. These included the introduction of new forms of land tenure, heavy land revenue and taxes, increased commercialization of crops, and the ultimate subordination of the economic interests of India to those of Britain (Lal 2004: 74). The strata of Indian society, the high castes, low castes, landlords and landless labourers were affected by the changes in the land and revenue system put in place under the British governance. Everyone was suffering, though not equally. Some of them tried to ride the change and stayed on in their villages, clinging to their ancestral homes. It was not just the men who migrated. Women and along with them, the whole family also went through migration. They were looking to migrate domestically to either Calcutta or the tea gardens of Assam. It was during their search for an alternative place of livelihood that the *akratis* were able to dupe the illiterate and naïve people by painting a rosy picture of indenture outside India.

Indenture history would be incomplete if it ignores the deportation of thousands of Indian sepoys, who fought in the First War of Independence, in India, to the plantation colonies. Rebels against British rule also faced the same fate. These migrations come under the category of 'forced migrations' as they were not induced by poverty. Instead, these were punishments meted out to the rebels. Martina Carter and Crispin Bates in 'Empire and Locality' express the psyche of the British which forced the wholesale transportation of every mutineer. 'Their families should be forced to travel with them, and if the transportees, averse to plantation labour, should commit suicide, hang their bodies, headless, in chains and plant the head in a conspicuous quarter, near the habitation of the living—the fashion will soon cease' (Carter 2010: 51).

Ahmed Ali, in his introduction to the Indian indenture experience in Fiji, highlights that 'between 1879 and 1916, some 60,553 Indians arrived in Fiji as indentured labourers. Of these, approximately 755 boarded their ship in Calcutta and the rest in Madras' (Ali 2004: 1). Of these, 85.3 per cent were Hindus, 14.6 per cent Muslims and 0.1 per cent Christians (Gillion 1973: 209). The narratives of indenture also highlight how the colonial powers institutionalized the exploitation of the labourers.

Sanadhya's journey begins from his home in Firozabad, where he lived till he lost his father at the age of 11. His eldest brother had to travel to Calcutta (now Kolkata) to look for work in order to support the family. Unable to see his mother's suffering, Sanadhya too left his home in 1893 to look for work in Prayag, where he was accosted by an *akrati* who promised to find him a very good job that would make him happy. At the *akrati's* house, he met 100 men and 60 women who were already housed there. They were forbidden to speak to each other while the *akrati* kept telling them that the place where they would be sent to work '. . . would be without any sorrows and that they would be able to eat a lot of bananas and sugarcane. . .' (Sanadhya 1991: 34). This group of people was taken in front of a magistrate where they were asked to respond with 'yes' to all of the questions else they would be charged and put in jail. Within a matter of 20 minutes, the magistrate had registered the 165 illiterate and unemployed people into going to Fiji. He asked each one, 'Tell me. Have you agreed to go to Fiji? The magistrate did not tell each person where Fiji was, what work they would have to do, or what punishment they would be given on not doing the work' (ibid.).

Soon afterwards, this group of registered passengers was put on a special train to *Havra*, from where they were taken in closed vehicles to the Depot where they met the immigration officer. They were informed that they were bound for Fiji, where they would earn 12 *annas* a day and would have to perform plantation labour for five years. If they chose to return to India after five years, they would have to pay their return fare but if they decided to return after 10 years, the government would pay their fare (ibid.). Sanadhya protested at this arrangement and asked to be allowed to leave but instead was locked in a room without food and water until he agreed to travel. Two days before boarding the ship, the group was examined medically. They were given prisoners' clothes to wear along with a tin jar and a plate to partake water and food. Caste was obliterated with Chamars,

Kolis, Brahmins, etc., all wearing the same clothes and eating from the same communal pot. In his book, Ahmed Ali projects, 'Those recruited had ceased to be individuals, they were all labourers together, that was the only recognized common denominator; caste, religion and status by birth were of little or no consequence' (Ali 2004: 3).

Other accounts of indenture carry the same description about the role of the *akratis*. Ahmed Ali (2004) and Rajendra Prasad (2010) also emphasise the duplicity of the *akratis* in getting the labourers to board the indenture ships to Fiji, while the labourers have been portrayed as ignorant of the spatial and temporal dislocation from India and the realities of the harshness of the plantation environment. Ahmed Ali claims, 'All who have written about the indenture system have been consistent in emphasizing the role of the *akrati* or the recruiter's agent in enticing Indian peasants away from village life in the quest of wealth' (ibid.: 2). One of the *girmitiya* voices in his book narrates, 'I was lured away by someone painting a glorious picture of my being able to obtain work. I was young and attracted by the recruiter's story. I came quite willingly, simply because I was drawn by the offer of money' (ibid.: 41). Another voice reports, 'I met some men who asked me if I were interested in work. They promised me to work in Jamaica. I had no idea where Jamaica was. When we went as far as Singapore we were told we would be going to Fiji' (ibid.: 69). Yet another *girmitya* voice narrates 'There were four of us at the depot that I was taken to and offered a job. I was unwilling. I was told that Fiji was near Calcutta and all I needed to do was to go there for six months' (ibid.: 71). These accounts question the colonial master narrative that portrays indenture as a consensual and humane activity owing to the bad living conditions in India, which included family problems, unemployment and caste discrimination.

The literal meaning of an agreement stipulates that both parties willingly and knowingly enter into an understanding after agreeing upon the said conditions. It is pertinent to question the veracity of the indenture agreement since it did not spell out all the terms and conditions. How could illiterate Indians be a fair party to any such agreement they were coerced into signing or putting their thumb impression? They were not made aware of the social, cultural, religious and legal conditions to which they would have to adhere to in the plantations. Did the indentured Indians know what fate awaited them? Were they aware that the Hindus would not be allowed to cremate their dead or that neither Hindu nor Muslim marriages would be recognised? Further, children born to them would be termed illegitimate (inherently denoting an insult to the mother of the child and calling to question her moral character). Did they know, for instance, that they would be penalised for all manner of supposed wrongs committed by them or that the dead would be thrown from the ships into the sea? Their families would be separated and if they wanted their children to be educated they would have to convert to Christianity (8).

Prasad's book *Tears in Paradise* recounts the story of his grandfather, an *Ahir* by caste, who was tricked into setting sail for Fiji as an indentured labourer along with his cousin. He mentions the fact that migration was common in India, with whole families migrating owing, either to the vagaries of nature or to the burden of debts that had led them to lose their farms to the moneylenders (Prasad 2010: 32). People often left homes for better opportunities and employment in other parts of India. This was common practice and was a decision born out of poverty, struggle and frustration. Twenty years after their disappearance, Prasad's families in their ancestral village in India received a letter informing them that the two cousins and their wives were working in Fiji in the sugarcane fields. They even enclosed 10 pounds 'requesting that it be used for digging the communal well for the family' (ibid.: 34). It is pertinent in this context to refer to Caribbean author Lomarsh Roopnarine's paper 'A Critique of East Indian Historiography in the Caribbean' which draws attention to the millions of pounds that were saved and sent back to India by the indentured people but never reached the country. Instead, the money benefitted the Bank of England owing to a complex system where the bills of exchange could only be negotiated in India when the first, second and third bills were presented together (Roopnaraine 2014: 392).

Aboard the ship that was to take them to Fiji, the *girmitiyas* found their identities further wiped out. Sanadhya (1991: 36) says that they were housed in 'a space one and a half feet wide and six feet long'. Further, they were given four 'dog biscuits' and one-sixteenth of a pound of sugar. The biscuits were such that 'they were broken by fists, and soaked in water, then eaten' (ibid.). His ship set sail in the evening and when they were woken at dawn the next day, they 'saw nothing but the blue sky'. He narrates, 'At that time many emotions were born in our hearts. In just the way a free bird is imprisoned in a cage, we were all locked in' (ibid.: 37). It is interesting to note here that the ship does not signify freedom. Instead, the metaphor carries a sinister tone in that it is likened to a collective prison. 'Coolitude explores the concept of the ocean as a nodal moment of migration, a space for destruction of identity, yet also one of regeneration, when an aesthetics of migration was created' (Torabully 2002: 17). Spaces can thus be both, a place for contestations, as well as convergences.

In this respect, theorist Homi Bhabha's concept of the liminal space is expounded further by author Penney Peirce in her book, Transparency: Seeing Through to Our Expanded Human Capacity where she quotes American author Richard Rohr, who describes it as the 'crossing over' space—a space where you have left something behind, yet you are not yet fully in something else. Rohr refers to it as:

> An anthropological term, the in-between, often in rituals or rites of passage, the place of disorientation where an individual sheds their former status or identity but has not yet become what they will be. . . . It is when you have left the tried and true, but have not yet been able to replace it with anything else. It is when you are between your old comfort zone and any possible new answer (Pierce 2017: 182).

Peirce suggests that in such a space 'Continuity of tradition may become uncertain, and future outcomes once taken for granted may be thrown into doubt. Your sense of belonging, purpose and identity can be compromised' (ibid.).

In his 1967 lecture, *Of Other Spaces,* French philosopher Michel Foucault (1997: 48-9) outlined the concept and principle of heterotopias. He argued that places are defined and given meaning and substance based on their relationship to other places. A ship is a place that has a relationship to other places in that it contests and challenges the relationships according to which other spaces are constituted. Foucault described the ship as the best example of a heterotopia. It is also a liminal space, in that it is a space between boundaries and it operates as a threshold. Ships, as heterotopias, hold the space between one time and another, one place and another, a kind of suspension between feeling a part of one culture or context and then feeling a part of another. Sarah McLean (2016) suggests in her article 'Places Where Reality Feels Altered', 'Liminal spaces, such as waiting rooms, parking lots, stairwells and rest stops, make you feel weird if you spend too much time in them because these spaces exist for the things that come before or after them. Their "existence" is not about themselves. Thus, they mark differences in time and space.'

The *girmit* experience on the ship was unlike any the newly indentured labourers had faced. These ships had earlier been used to transport slaves and carried a strong connection to a dark past. In *Tears in Paradise,* Prasad narrates that even the clothes given to the *girmitiyas* were the same as those worn by the prisoners in British India. The ships, whether sailboats or steamers, were specially fitted for the transport of indentured labourers and were designed looking at the expediency for travel. They definitely did not think about the comfort of the immigrants. In *Chalo Jahaji,* Brij Lal gives an evocative account of the emotions of the people on board the ship.

> They seemed to be shipwrecked by fate in a place they did not, perhaps could not, fully embrace, and they could not return to the place they so dearly loved. They were a people caught in between the tensions of culture and history, resisting assimilation into the ways of their adopted homeland by re-enacting archaic customs from a remembered past. (Lal 2012: 26)

He further elaborates on the sentiments of the indentured people undergoing the voyage, ' "Floating caravan of barbarian tourists" someone called these ships, while some *girmitiyas* remembered them as floating funeral processions: *chalta firta, jeeta jagata janaza*' (ibid.: 29). Sanadhya also narrates his experience aboard the ship on similar lines,

> We each got bottles of water to drink twice each day. We didn't get more even if we were dying from thirst. The same was true about eating. Fish was cooked and rice was cooked. Many people suffered from sea sickness. Some unfortunate vomited and vomited and then left this world forever. Those people were thrown into the ocean! (Sanadhya 1991: 37)

Sanadhya also believes that it is on account of their black colour that the indentured people had to endure so many hardships on the steamers. 'I was made to sit where pigs and other animals are kept' (ibid.: 46). There is a strange dichotomy that comes to the surface here. While caste has been negated, race (in the form of colour) comes to the fore. Caste is a distinctly Indian (Hindu) concept while race carries European (Christian) undertones. It would be pertinent to point out here that for the indentured Muslims on the ships (Muslims believe in a casteless society), this would have been a new experience of 'othering'.

It took three months by sail ship and one month by steamship to reach Fiji and it was during this time that a unique bonding was established among the new recruits travelling to the islands. Brij V. Lal (2012: 13) has extrapolated the indenture experience as a 'very important, formative and defining period in the history of overseas Indian communities, particularly in the Caribbean, Mauritius, South Africa and Fiji, because that is the site of the initial social transformation'. He suggests that it is at the point of the intermingling of the old and new world that change happens. A different social order takes the place of the old, which has lost its relevance. In the case of the indenture, the caste system, with its rigid social structure, collapsed. Everyone was a 'coolie' in the cramped quarters of the lines on the plantation. Lal further views 'the indenture process as the death of one world and the beginning of another. The details vary from colony to colony, but the process is the same everywhere' (ibid.: 13).

Some of the indentured people equated leaving the homeland with the exile of Lord Ram in the *Ramayan* by quoting lines from the epic, *Chaudah Baras Ram ban Basi*. (Lord Ram was exiled for fourteen years). 'What was five years in front of fourteen?' (ibid.: 29). While the men compared their departure to Lord Ram's banishment, women sang the *birha* (song of separation) to describe the pain of being exiled and separated from their home. The *birha* was even sung on the ships to depict the painful separation from the beloved. These folk songs were composed from the emotional lament of the soul and did not need any musical instruments to accompany them.

From the east came the rail, from the west came the ship,
And took my beloved away. (ibid.: 113)

'Inevitably, the ship became the site of massive social disruption. The voyage was a great leveller of hierarchy and status: the immigrants were all coolies in the eyes of the sahibs' (ibid.: 29). The dreaded voyage across the *kalapani* (black water) was a traumatic experience for the indentured Indians with the forced interaction hastening the breaking down of social and cultural mores. The first to break down was the social hierarchy-based caste system. After that, it was nothing less than a vertical descent into 'Hell'.

The cramped living quarters below the decks initiated the breaking down of customs and traditions. The quarters below the deck were divided into three sections—single women were placed under the toilets, married couples were placed in the middle section, along with their children, and single men were put up under the galleys. Thus, great care was taken to house the men and women separately. 'Everyone, irrespective of social status, took turns cleaning decks, pumping water and cooking' (ibid.: 142). Most of the migrants who had come from the land-locked hinterland of India had never seen a ship before. Onboard they had to contend with the crowded living quarters, seasickness and other diseases, such as typhoid, dysentery and cholera. The loss of caste and the seasickness were not the only qualms that the indentured people faced on the ships. 'Fire and wrecking on treacherous reefs or in heavy storms stalked the emigrant ships' (Torabully 2002: 40). One of the worst maritime tragedies of the period occurred on 11 May 1884, when the Indian immigrant ship *Syria* was wrecked on a reef off the coast of Fiji. It resulted in the death of 56 indentured immigrants and three Indian *lascars* (seamen). 'Between 1879 when indentured Indian immigration to Fiji started, and 1916 when it finally ended, immigrant ships made 87 voyages to Fiji carrying over sixty thousand indentured adults and children to the islands' (Lal 2012: 154). The *Syria* was carrying four hundred and 97 indentured immigrants along with a crew numbering 43 (including the three Indian *lascars*). Very few knew how to swim and were at the mercy of the rescuers.

Apart from maritime disasters, shipboard mortality owing to disease and ill nutrition was another cause for concern, both for the immigrants as well as for the British. Diseases contracted at sea soon became epidemics and were dreaded killers. In 1859, eighty-two immigrants died of cholera en route to Guyana, and 124 died of fever in 1863 on the same route. The dead on the ship could not be given the kind of cremation that would appease the religious sensibilities of the migrants. The bodies were thrown overboard into the ocean. This practice was a grave cause of concern and further undermined the psyche of the survivors. Since the Surgeon-General on the ship was 'paid a commission for every recruit safely delivered to the ultimate destination', better sanitary reforms were introduced by the British to enable healthier living conditions for the labourers on the high seas (Prasad 2010: 54). The British doctors on board the ships lacked the knowledge to treat indigenous Indian diseases. The stark change in the diet of the *girmitiyas* also led to the under-nourishment of the immigrants on the sea voyage. As this oversight on the part of the colonial powers led to greater mortality, they put certain dietary regulations in place, which also included the accommodation of religious beliefs in meat provisions. Authorities took sheep and goats instead of cows and pigs on the ships in order to appease both the Hindus and Muslims. Further, Muslim butchers were also taken on board to ensure the slaughter was done in the *halal* (cut made in the throat of the animal) manner of killing.

In *Coolies of the Empire*, Ashutosh Kumar (2017: 116) informs, 'On one hand, the ship was like the temple of Jagannath for many villagers, and on the other it was the coming of Kaliyug, where Brahmins and other high caste became alienated from their religion'. Poet Sudesh Mishra in his book *Diaspora and the Difficult Art of Dying* puts it thus, '. . . many things were lost during that nautical passage, family, caste and religion, and yet many things were also found, chamars found Brahmins, Muslims found Hindus, biharis found marathis, so that by the end of the voyage we were a nation of jahaji bhais . . . all for one and one for all. . .' (Mishra 2002: 12).

The voyage had allowed new relationships to be forged in the form of *jahaji bhais* (ship-brothers) and *jahaji behens* (ship-sisters) which were based on 'a shared sense of servitude' and became even more enduring than intimate familial relationships left behind in India. When they were not working on cleaning, the immigrants used to spend time singing songs and playing drums to keep depression at bay. In *The Location of Culture*, theorist Homi Bhabha (1997: 2) states, 'It is in the emergence of the interstices—the overlap and displacement of domains of difference—that the intersubjective and collective experiences of *nationness*, community interest, or cultural value are negotiated'. In the foregoing discussion on the new found relationships aboard the ship, Totaram Sanadhya and Rajendra Prasad's accounts further the description of Bhabha's concept of interstices and elucidate how it ties in with their description of life on board the ships.

Despite the use of steamers, instead of the sailboats that had been used earlier, it still took a long time to reach the Islands (sailboats took about three months while the steamers covered the distance in a month). Depression became a cause for great worry during these long voyages. In *Fiji's Indian Migrants*, K.L. Gillion cites from Dr Lang's Handbook for Surgeons Superintendent of the Coolie Emigration Service:

> I know that many people died from nostalgia pure and simple . . . and can it be wondered at with all their caste prejudices, their leaving their native land, perhaps never, to see it again, and being thrown among people of strange habits, language, and even colour? The excitement of the newness of everything keeps them up for a time, but soon dies away, and is followed by depression when they realise what they have done (Gillion 1973: 62).

Prasad (2010: 56) highlights the journey to Fiji which took 'seventy-three days for a sailing ship, and thirty days by steamship'. The wreck of the ship *Syria*, carrying 497 passengers was the only maritime disaster among the eighty seven ships that had carried the labourers to Fiji. It resulted in the deaths of fifty-six indentured labourers and three *lascars* (Indian sailors) (ibid.). Coming from the landlocked hinterland, most of these people had never gone aboard a ship before and, coupled with the rough seas and harsh winters of the Pacific Ocean, they found themselves in a very weak state both, mentally and physically. The first few days were extremely traumatic for the voyagers. Seasickness and the resulting depression owing to loss of homeland, identity, melancholy, nostalgia, as well as the much feared crossing of the *kalapani* were strong fears on board the vessel.

In order to combat these ills, the Surgeon-General on the ship encouraged participation in singing, dancing, playing musical instruments and indulging in various forms of games and entertainment to keep the depression at bay. Surgeon-General Liang's diary entry comprises a careful note of his solution to keep depression on the ship at bay. '. . . I would urge their being employed as much as possible while on board and encouraged in every available means of entertainment' (Gillion 1973: 62).

On board the ship, punishments were meted out for non-compliance in broad view of everyone in order to act as a deterrent to the others. Prasad (2010: 55) narrates, 'Bizarre methods of punishment were used. People caught stealing, or committing other offences, were sometimes frogmarched with faces painted black, accompanied by people of low caste yelling and ridiculing them as others laughed'. In the Indian cultural context, painting someone's face black was tantamount to one of the most demeaning ways to ridicule that person. These punishments also led to a number of suicides. Unable to bear the ignominy of shame, and already reeling under the pressures of the voyage, the migrants could not cope and chose to drown themselves by jumping overboard.

The journey marked a shift from the homeland to the adopted land. In a sense, it was the point from where all moorings would be removed and a new beginning would be made. Author Amitav Ghosh, in his historical fiction, *Sea of Poppies,* has looked at the experience of indenture and forced migration by chronicling and giving a voice to the *girmitiyas.* In his novel, the ship *Ibis* carrying indentured labourers and *lascars* to Mauritius is cast as '. . . an adoptive ancestor and parent of dynasties yet to come. . .' (Ghosh 2015: 328). The coming together of the motley group of people from a cross-section and strata of society on the *Ibis* is reminiscent of the bonding which grew between the *jahaji bhais* and *behens* aboard the ships carrying the indentured people overseas to the plantations. These bonds would survive the test of time and the generations to follow would realise their sense of belonging in a distant land from these new moorings.

Mariam Pirbhai (2009: 55) in *Mythologies of Migration: Vocabularies of Indenture: Novels of the South* talks about the liminal space of the ship becoming a metaphor for displacement, and eventually collective 'transplantation'. She projects the ship as 'a unifying symbol for indentured peoples just as it did for those who endured the middle passage'. Pirbhai compares the labourers' journey to the search for El Dorado (the mythical city of gold) while the ship serves as a metaphor for the process of transculturation. It attempts to show the chaotic nature of an identity in flux and steady continuum of deeply rooted beliefs that are carried across in the process of migration. The ship thus, carries both—continuity and change. The symbolic importance of the ship, the water, and the sea serve as sites not only of flux but also of a counter discourse of cultural and political reconfiguration.

Thus, while the individual's sense of identity is destabilised, both in the process of transplantation and the moment of contact, there is a counter impulse toward a transcendent spiritual fraternity. The ship and, by extension the sea, nonetheless serve as the primary arena for the reconfiguration of identity (ibid.: 57). Both, Sanadhya and Prasad's accounts of the voyage support this hypothesis.

Prasad narrates that as the journey progressed, most of the labourers began to accept their fate and mix and mingle with the others on board. He suggests that the environment on the ship was conducive to the forming of new relationships which 'took root, strengthened and endured. People of different castes, cultures and languages found common ground in their new identity' (Prasad 2010: 57). They took to calling themselves *jahaji bhais* (ship-brothers) and *jahaji behens* (ship-sisters). Pirbhai (2009: 60) opines that 'jahaaji-hood' transformed 'the dehumanisation of the subaltern migrant as a homogeneous labour force (or 'unit of labour') into a spiritually united group'. This new identity of calling each other *jahaji bhais* and *behens* can be seen as a subtle wresting of control by the indentured people to enforce their own identity. With the loss of caste at the depot and the subsequent change in identity, this act of community naming can be viewed as the first instance of resistance by the indentured people.

However, this little sense of home and belonging that they had found in the close physical proximity with each other on the ship proved to be short lived since another separation was eminent as soon as they would reach the Islands. Here they would be herded over by the plantation owners to different plantations. 'During this separation, none had the opportunity to break the muster to bid farewell to others. . . . The mustering was so rigid and so heartless that it was not uncommon for husbands and wives to be separated from each other, never to meet again' (Prasad 2010: 57).

Referring to the geographical position of Fiji, Sanadhya (1991: 38) narrates that it comprised 254 islands in the South Pacific Ocean. The physical landscape was as far removed from the Indian hinterland as was possible. Here, for the first time, they saw on the shores of the ocean, coconut trees, yams, sweet potatoes and oranges. The mental landscape carried images of India that were hard to reconcile with the new images of their physical reality in Fiji. The landscape of the sugarcane plantations '. . . was lush and green compared to the dusty plains from which the Indians had come, and the life on the plantation was also very different from that they had known in India' (Gillion 1973: 103). By the time Sanadhya arrived in Fiji on the *Jumna*, there were 12,000 indentured labourers already there in Fiji. Some even had Fiji-born children (Mishra 2014: 27). Sanadhya's narrative further informs that on disembarking from the ship, they were termed *coolies* and immediately surrounded by the police so that they could not escape. He explains that his *jahaji bhais* and *behens* were separated and assigned to five different plantations, thus obliterating the temporary sense of belonging that had come into play and acted as solace during the long voyage.

In a telling statement, Sanadhya (1991: 39) compares the indenture system to that of slavery and asks, 'People say that slavery has been ended in all civilized countries. Do you understand less of this coolie system than of slavery systems?'. When he highlights that the planters paid 210 rupees for each person to the Immigration Department, he again raises the question that is central to indenture. Was indenture not a new form of slavery if the *coolies* were bought for a price paid in currency? He says that the agent informed them:

> 'For five years from today you are a servant of this particular sahib.'
>
> I said, 'I am not a servant! I am not sold! My father and brothers have not received anything from anyone!' (ibid.)

Narratives of slavery carry references to the immigrants being addressed as animals and being treated in a similar manner. Narratives of indenture carry the same tone and sense of being likened to animals and treated at par with them. In Fiji especially, the word *coolie* in the local Fijian language means 'dog' and thus carries an added insult. The word *coolie* in the Indian context has its root in the Tamil language and means 'to hire'. Sanadhya externalises how the *girmitiyas* were perceived as beasts of burden by their employers. Prasad reconfirms Sanadhya's perception, 'The white planters treat us as if we were donkeys or dogs'. He also refers to CSR company officials referring to them as 'hordes of coolies, swarms of locusts, yellow fangs' and of 'out-animalising the horde of near-human apes' (ibid.: 89).

Sanadhya was housed by the Colonial Sugar Refining (CSR) Company plantation at Nausori along with 140 other indentured labourers. The living quarters assigned to the indentured people in the plantations were very small with each room being 12 ft long and 8 feet wide. 'If a man is together with his wife then they are given this room, and otherwise, three men or three women stay in one room . . . And it is usually arranged this way, that Brahmans have to live with Chamars' (ibid.: 40).

In his testimonio, Sanadhya narrates that for the first six months after their arrival, the estate was responsible for providing the food staples and provisions for which an amount of two shillings and four pence was deducted from each week's pay. Needless to say, the provisions barely covered the needs of the labourers who were putting in 10 hours a day of hard manual labour. A week's provision barely lasted four days and the remaining three days were spent on a forced fast.

Sanadhya attributes his survival to his reading of the *Pandava Gita*, a book written by his elder brother. He also narrates an incident in which he had no food for six days, became sick and delirious with fever and yet was made to work in the fields. On the third day, he attempted suicide by hanging one end of a jute rope to the rafter in his living quarters but was stopped from doing so by some Fijians, who were the earlier inhabitants of the living quarters. They had come in search of food and forcibly searched his home for food to eat, where they were able to find a little leftover rice which Sanadhya had forgotten. In order to repay his hospitality, the Fijians brought back 'four sacks of sweet potato and yams' for him (Sanadhya 2003: 12). Sanadhya believed that it was his prayers that had saved him.

Prasad too assigns the role played by religion and culture as pivotal in shaping the lives and times of the indentured labourers. In his paper 'Colonial Exploitation, Resistance and Forced Migrations', historian Kapil Kumar (2014: 42) cites psychologist Sandili Ramdial-Maharaj's paper presented at a conference in Suriname in June 2013. She mentions that when the *girmitiyas* were looking at possible conversions, they imbibed an important psychological stance that had to do with '. . . retaining the culture/religion as a means of retaining the sense of the familiar in an unfamiliar environment. This paradoxically meant that the more their culture/religion was threatened, the more they adhered to it, perhaps even more than they had ever cared to in India itself'.

Couplets from the *Ramayan* were quoted often and parallels were drawn between the exile faced by Lord Ram in the epic and the hapless *girmitiyas* on the plantation. Both, religion and culture played an important role as coping mechanisms adopted by the indentured people in Fiji. They had carried with them religious texts from India which were recited at gatherings. This was possible owing to the emergence of the common language called Fiji *Bhat* (Fiji Hindi), which is a vernacular form of the dialects spoken in Hindi, Bhojpuri and Awadhi in the north Indian states from where the *girmitiyas* had come. They kept the language of their homeland alive in the plantations and absolutely refused to let go of it. Over the years, it became a determinant in their identity. Together with religion, culture, festivals, dress and food habits, the language of their homeland gave them a sense of belonging to each other while at the same time marked them as distinct and diverse from the indigenous population on the islands. Holding onto the Indian tradition under such traumatic conditions also goes to show that the indentured Indians had no intention of settling permanently in Fiji. They were always looking back and longing to return to India.

The Indians in Fiji celebrated all the major festivals and organised community readings of the sacred texts. Both the Hindus and Muslims held and attended alike, the festivals of Holi and Muharram. From 1902, *Ramlilas* were staged in several places across the islands and saw greater participation and attendance by Hindus, Muslims and even the Fijians. Sanadhya renders high praise for the Hindu-Muslim unity in Fiji. 'It is a pleasure that the Muslims of Fiji are mixed with the Hindus. They never sacrifice cows on Bakra Eid. . . . This much mixing among uneducated people like us is no ordinary thing' (Sanadhya 1991: 70). He is ironical, however, when he observes that the most celebrated festival was that of Christmas.

A *santani pandit* himself, Sanadhya had managed to build a fairly large following in the plantations. He narrates that during the later part of the indenture period, Fiji saw an influx of *sadhus* and *fakirs*, especially from the sects of the Kabir Panth, Ramanadi Panth, Arya Samaj and Nanak Panth among others. Gillion ascribes that the importance given to the Arya Samaj was not due to the sheer number of followers but owing to its leaders demonstrating genuine concern instead of just an outward show of religion to gain disciples (Gillion 1973: 148). The Arya Samaj, with its emphasis on improving education and its objective of ensuring the social advancement of the *girmitiyas,* opened a school in 1908 on government-leased land. It was among the first Indian schools to be successful in Fiji and offered a new sense of hope for the children of the indentured labourers.

While there existed missionary schools in Fiji, sending children there would have been tantamount to their accepting conversion to Christianity. Initially, the religious life of the *girmitiyas* was impoverished. The causes for this were 'the isolation from India and family religious practices, the lack of pundits, and . . . the pollution of *coolie* status' (Sanadhya 1991: 111). Faced with very little choice, some people did convert. Crossing the *kalapani* had cost them their caste and a return would have been impossible. Sanadhya opines that 'Having gone there [to Fiji] saying "Jay" to Sanatan Dharm, they follow the rules of the Messiah' (ibid.: 63). Still, conversion was not very successful in Fiji and there were very few Hindu Christians. The reason for this was the counter movement launched by the Hindus against conversions, as well as the numerous attempts made to resuscitate the religion. 'And if they become Christian, then we convert them [*shuddh karna*, literally, purify them]' (ibid.: 66). However, this process of cultural rejuvenation was not always easy. The *girmitiyas'* struggle to preserve their culture and religion was an act of resistance against the conversions being pressed upon them by the colonial powers. Against the numerous Christian missionaries in Fiji, there were hardly any Hindu religious teachers or books available. Totaram Sanadhya's encounter with Methodist missionary, Rev. J.W. Burton, detailed in the former's book, depicts how he refused to embrace Christianity despite his genuine affection towards Rev. Burton. When Sanadhya was informed by Burton that the employees of CSR attended church and were true Christians, he replied:

You call them true Christians? How can that be when these people treat their workers like animals and skin them alive? Their cruelty knows no bounds. They pay them a pittance. Look at the atrocities they commit against our women. And yet in a court of law they take the oath on the Bible and deny their evil deeds. Does baptism wash away all their evil deeds? (Lal 2012: 256)

It is ironical to note how it was actually the British made system of indenture that created all the *dukh* and *kasht* as well as the feeling of living in *narak* for the *girmitiyas;* yet, in order to alleviate their suffering, the only alternative offered to them was conversion to Christianity by the British missionaries.

Among the religious texts listed by Sanadhya and Prasad in their narratives, the most popular was the *Ramcharitmanas* written by Tulsidas. It details the story of Ram's exile, Sita's abduction, the war with Ravan in Lanka and the subsequent return of Ram and Sita to Ayodhya. 'The story of Ram struck a particular chord with the Fiji Indians who themselves came from the region of Ram's kingdom… His story gave them hope and consolation: one day, they, too, would escape the exile of indenture' (ibid.: 241). Sanadhya also mentions that the path of bhakti 'provided hope, negated most functions of the lost castes, and was the buttress against Christian pressure' (ibid.: 114).

Religion and culture are important markers in identifying the sense of self. In his narrative, Sanadhya talks extensively about the religious ceremonies governing the birth of children, as well as marriages and funerals. He mentions the disappearance of the practice of wearing the *janeau* (sacred thread worn by Brahmins diagonally across their chest) suggesting that most *girmitiyas* had become apathetic to the practice. Births were celebrated according to the social status of the family. Mostly, in families following the Kabir Panth, the *baba* (religious preacher) would name the child and sing *bhajans* (religious hymns) along with his disciples. With respect to marriages, Indian marriages were not considered legal or valid and to this end, the bride and groom had to go to the marriage court and register their marriage after paying a princely sum of five shillings. Such marriages were termed *marit.* If the marriage was not registered, the widow or heirs would not receive the wealth of the departed. Instead, it would be sent to the Immigration Department. Another kind of marriage was the *andhadhundh paddhti* (indiscriminate system of marriage) and was performed between Hindus and Muslims, entailing the presence of a *pandit* and a *maulvi*, who had to recite the *Satyanarayan Katha* and the *Maulud Sharif*, respectively (ibid.: 49). Concerning funeral rites, Sanadhya highlights that the Hindus in Fiji buried their dead instead of cremating them. Post the ceremony, religious books were read and *bhajans* were sung to mark the mourning period.

However, confusion reigned supreme among the descendants of the indentured people. Sanadhya quotes a court record from 1907 and reveals 'the next witness cannot be sworn as she says she does not know whether she is a Musalmani or a Hindu and does not know the meaning of religion having been born in Fiji' (ibid.: 111). Religion is a very powerful orientation in identity and determines essential aspects of thoughts and behaviour. Loss of religion then would render the person rootless in an already alien environment and create further anxiety. The 'Fiji Indian community as a whole remembered its faiths, resisted the Christian Mission, and despite the decomposition of caste relations, maintained a vital Hindu (and Muslim and Sikh) tradition' (ibid.: 112). According to Sanadhya, *bhakti* even provided a new organizational form of religion through the Ramayan Mandali Egalitarian Cooperatives that were organised to express devotion by singing the Tulsidas version of the *Ramayan* (ibid.: 114).

While Hindus made up the majority of the indentured people in Fiji, 14 per cent of the *girmitiyas* were Muslims. After the First War of Independence in 1857, the Muslims faced greater oppression under the British in India. There was also increasing discrimination against them by the Hindu nationalists who opposed cow slaughter. All in all, these factors collectively worked to favour their emigration as an escape mechanism from the religious persecution in India. It is noteworthy that Muslim women emigrated in a greater percentage (17 per cent) than their male counterparts, suggesting that the factors for emigration weighed more heavily on them than on the males. Their indenture passes showed their caste as Muslim, Musalman and Mohammedan (Ali 2004: 99). While the Hindus proclaimed their *girmit* as *narak*, the Muslims too faced a level of trauma that was heightened by the racist environment on the plantations. Ahmed Ali (2004: 105) quotes Rev. C.F. Andrews' views on the Muslims in Fiji in 1916, 'The religious decline had not been so rapid with them as amongst Hindus. They held together more … they were Musalman, and this gave them a dignity of their own'. Muslims and their faith were inseparable.

Gafur, a Muslim, who was indentured and sent to Fiji in 1905, claimed that it was their religion that saved them and gave them the incentive to survive and sustain their identity. Their learning could be transmitted orally and some *girmitiyas* who were educated could recite the Holy Quran in Arabic. Others were literate in Urdu. They held the belief that the 'survival of the Indian Muslims in a culturally recognisable form was directly linked with Urdu' and to this end, they continued the demand for Urdu to be taught in Persian script (ibid.: 112). Some Muslims, despite the rigours of *girmit* observed the 40-day Ramadan fast. Muharram was permitted to be celebrated by the colonial regime and *tazias* (tall paper edifices) were taken out in procession on the streets.

Muslim women, already marginalised in the indenture system, were further brutalised and scarred under the violence and horrors of the indenture system. They carried memories of bitterness, shame and a sense of loss of *izzat* (self-respect). To them also goes the credit of keeping their faith and belief alive while living in the plantations. They were the communicators of the culture to their children; 'they were their first teachers, the primary agents of essential socializing processes' (ibid.: 118).

Suicide was a legacy of indenture. Owing to outrages committed by the overseers on the poor labourers, suicide became the only resort for many. Sanadhya informs, 'Many of our brothers there make a noose and hang themselves' (Sanadhya 1991: 43). In his article, 'Veil of Dishonour: Sexual Jealousy and Suicide on Fiji Plantations', historian Brij Lal (1985: 215) highlights, 'Between 1884 and 1925, over 300 Indian immigrants in Fiji committed suicide'. A majority of the suicides was committed by male indentured workers with the primary cause being sexual jealousy over women. This was not entirely true. While the dispute over women may be said to have been a contributing factor, the real cause lay elsewhere. It was the complete disruption of the social and cultural order (family support system) away from the homeland that led to conditions for suicide. 'It was both a cry of despair and an act of protest directed ultimately at the principles and ethics of the indenture system itself' (Lal 2012: 18). The suicides attracted wide attention within Fiji, as well as in India. Anthropologist John D. Kelly (1991: 9) in *Fiji Indians and the Law, 1912* says, 'Our sample of cases under-represents suicides, in part, because only suicide attempts that failed ended up in court'. According to him, confessions of those who attempted suicide revealed a sense of shame and perception of hopelessness. In *The Story of the Haunted Line,* Sanadhya (2003: 106) furthers this sense of helplessness that led to him attempting suicide. He projects the suicide rate in Fiji in great detail. '… while there were 37 suicides per one million in India, there were 662 suicides per million among the coolies …'. Brij Lal also informs that the Fiji Indian suicide rate 'was the highest among all Indian labour importing colonies in Africa and the middle east and much higher than India itself' (Lal 2012: 135). A quarter of all suicides were committed within the first six months of arriving in Fiji, with the Colonial Sugar Refining (CSR) Company plantations in Ba, Lautoka and Macuata being particularly notorious for ill-treating the indentured labourers. These three areas accounted for 43.6 per cent of all Indian suicides. It appears that for many indentured labourers, the horrors of life overwhelmingly outweighed the terrors of death. This situation was sympathetically explained by one *girmitiya* who managed to overcome his suicidal urges, 'There were times when our work became so tough that we thought death would be easier than some of the things we had to endure' (ibid.: 320). Suicide is taboo for Muslims and is considered a mortal sin, but even here, Fiji had the worst record in suicides committed by Muslims. Lal informs that the 'suicide rate for Muslims was 2.9 per thousand' (ibid.: 238).

Sanadhya recounts how the overseers used to punish the workers with hard labour and put them to work in separate areas where they would be beaten up severely. 'The ones being punished are made to do hard work separate from all the others. Overseers go to where these people are alone and beat them up severely'. He highlights how it was impossible to get justice. 'If anyone does complain, then because there is no witness the case is dismissed' (Sanadhya 1991: 43). Narrating one particular incident, he says that the overseer used to harass him a lot. 'Whenever he came to see my work, a couple of blows were deposited on my face' (ibid.: 87). The day began at 4 a.m. for the indentured people. They prepared their own food and arrived on the fields by 5 a.m. Women who had children were left with no choice but to bring the children to the field. Each labourer was assigned a lane of cane which was about 1200 to 1300 ft long and 6 ft wide to weed with a hoe. This was termed as a 'full task'. Needless to say, this was too much work for one person to accomplish in a day. 'For any work left incomplete, the labourer was produced before a magistrate the very next day and fined between ten shillings and one pound. This amount meant the loss of 15 to 20 days of wages per month. On an average, the indentured labourers were able to earn only seven and one-half rupees per month' (ibid.: 42).

Prasad (2010: 60) too externalises the case of the overseers who were perpetrators of violence against the *girmitiyas*, 'The *kulambars* of the CSR Company gained notoriety for inflicting heinous acts of cruelty against the *girmitiyas*' (60). Taking up the excuse of punishment, the overseers would outrage the modesty of the female labourers. John Weir Burton (1910: 60) in *The Fiji of Today* exposes the indiscretions of the *kulambars*. 'The young and brutal overseers on the sugar estates take all sorts of liberties. . . and torture them and their husbands in cases of refusal'. Many women had migrated to Fiji. There were more than forty thousand Indians in Fiji, of which 35 per cent were women and 55 per cent were men. While some had come with families, the others had been tricked by the *akratis* into coming to the islands.

Owing to the arguments and fights with close relatives, and ill-treatment in their widowhood, many women were forced to go to the islands and become indentured in the system. Sanadhya highlights the plight of women indentured in Fiji:

In Fiji, women are forced to bear more sorrows than men. First of all, they have to get up at half-past three in the morning and cook *roti*. After that,

> for ten hours they have to do hard labour in the fields, and then have gone back to the house, make more *roti.* When women return from work, there is corpse-like shading to their faces.... Many child widows were misled and sent to Fiji. Listening to their sorrowful stories, the hardest heart could melt. (Sanadhya 1991: 61)

Women in indenture suffered the most. Coincidently, as Brij Lal (2004: 97) points out, they also 'unwittingly played a very large part in the movement to abolish the indenture system'. The Indian public had been aware of the 'sorry plight of the Indian labourers overseas, but it was the news of molestation and abuse of Indian women on the plantations that outraged them the most'.

One of the most widely documented cases of the ill-treatment of females during indenture is that of Kunti, who along with her husband, was fooled by the *akratis* in Lakhupur district of Gorakhpur. Sanadhya highlights that she was 20 years of age when she was indentured and brought to Fiji where a *sardar* and overseer made 'a great effort to destroy her virtue' and tried to rape her on 10 April 1912 (ibid.: 44). To save her virtue, Kunti ran away and jumped into the river, where she was fortunately saved from drowning by a man named Jaidev, who owned a dingy. When she informed the white plantation owner about the incident, she was turned away and when she did not report to work the next day as a form of protest, her husband was beaten up very badly. She reported her story to the newspaper *Bharat Mitra* which led to an investigation. The immigration office tried to threaten her to take back her report during the investigation process, but Kunti refused and in an exemplary show of courage stuck to her version. Her story in the newspaper prompted the Government of India to ask the Government of Fiji to enquire into the treatment of Indian indentured women (ibid.).

The case of Narayani, also documented by Sanadhya in his book, was no different. Despite the law allowing for three months leave post-delivery, she was severely beaten up by the overseer for not returning to work three days after the death of her four-day-old baby. When the case reached the Supreme Court in Fiji, where Narayani was carried on a stretcher on account of her injuries, the overseer was pronounced 'not guilty' and was freed. Narayani suffered such trauma—being severely beaten so soon after the death of her newborn—that she went mad (Sanadhya 1991: 44). Ahmed Ali has also documented Narayani's agonising experience in his book in detail, suggesting that her experience underscored the *girmitiyas'* portrayal of their *girmit.* The sexual molestation of females by *sirdars* and overseers; was prevalent throughout *girmit,* from 1879 to 1919. According to Ali (2004: 96), *Girmit* was always, from the beginning to the end, a form of slavery. Lal (2004: 98) contests the common view that 'the indentured women were mostly stray 'loose' women who had been deceived into migrating by unscrupulous recruiters'. Instead, he suggests that while some women may have certainly been duped into *girmit,* the 'others may have left of their own volition to escape the drudgery and degradation of Indian life'. Lal has also presented extensive data in support of his research on the proportion of women to men in the indentured population. He externalises the prescribed proportion which varied greatly during the entire period of Indian indenture. In the early days of *girmit,* the proportion of women to men was very low owing to colonial planters' requirement of 'able-bodied efficient workers' (ibid.). However, once indenture had become firmly established it became apparent that a sex ratio would need to be fixed.

The Colonial Office, in 1867, finally fixed the proportion at 40 females to 100 males and this rule remained in force throughout the period.

A majority of the women were tricked into indenture owing to their being susceptible to the craftiness of the *akratis.* It was difficult to fill the stipulated quota and to this end the *akratis* were paid a premium sum for women. Other push factors included the plight of the 'unwanted' women in India. These women came from a cross-section of Indian society and included young and old widows, childless women who had been deserted by their husbands, as well as women with unsympathetic in-laws demanding dowry.

Indenture was especially cruel to the women. Vijay Mishra affirms that while narratives of indenture are more about men, yet 'more abject were the bodies of the women, the silent, rarely written underside of the indenture experience' (Mishra 2014: 84). This is not to say that the women did not have agency. The imbalance between the ratio of men and women gave rise to issues of plantation infidelity and increasing and violent crimes against women by the men. The abnormal living conditions in the barracks, together with the collapse of rigid village social structures (as they existed in India) combined to give rise to the problems of sexual politics and barbaric violence against women on the plantations. While life had been difficult enough for the women in India, it became even more traumatic on the plantations. They had no real security to speak of. To make matters worse, Indian marriages came under the Heathen Marriages Act and it was only in 1856 that marriage ordinances were enacted, largely due to the efforts of Thomy Hugon (ibid.: 85).

The women who migrated to the colonies had already been gendered in different ways in India. The language in their place of origin, Bhojpuri, had brought them into the discourse. In writing the g*irmitiya* experience in his book, researcher Ashutosh Kumar looks at the terms collected by J.R. Reid (Settlement Officer of Azamgarh in 1871-2) which were used to characterise some of the women in India who were living with a man outside wedlock:

> *dolnarhi* – a woman who has been taken to the bridegroom for whom the bridegroom did not take her *barat; gharkaili* – a woman who has taken up a residence with a man without marriage; *dhenmani* – a woman living with a man to whom she is not married; *urhari* – a woman who has been enticed away; a woman, not his wife, who lives with a man. (Kumar 2017: 173)

The lopsided male-female ratio was also responsible for the crimes committed against women by Indian men. Since they were attuned to violence on the plantations, the men, when they were not fighting others, fought with themselves. The pattern of violence against the *girmitiyas* was varied but the culture of violence on the fields had permeated into their family life. The degree of brutality used in the attacks on women could hardly be conceived by any man in his right senses. Kelly (1991: 11) contends, 'This violence was what psychologists call a "displacement" of aggression and hostility towards sardars and overseers, i.e. the girmitiyas were truly motivated by a hatred of overseers and the system, but attacked women because they were weak and not overseers because they were powerful'.

Prasad (2010: 64) highlights the fact that religious marriage rituals carried no legal sanction in Fiji, and hence, the sanctity of marriage was violated with the *kulambars* taking advantage of the women. The comparatively smaller ratio of women to the men in the plantations was also a factor in the degrading social and sexual standards in Fiji. Since men now faced competition if they were to have any kind of relationship with a woman, even if she was his wife. 'The world of adultery and prostitution which existed in the interstices of Indian society, beyond the proper confines of family duty, was not difficult to reproduce in Fiji' (Burton 1910: 15). Thus, the operation of power and competition within relationships also provoked violence among men against women.

Sanadhya too laments the plight of women in Fiji and mentions that even the native Fijians were appalled at outrages meted out to the Indian women. The Christian missionaries were also aghast at the way Indian women undergoing indenture were being treated in the plantations. He reproduces a letter in his book by Australian Methodist missionary, Hannah Dudley, which was sent to the newspaper *India*:

> They arrive in this country timid, fearful women not knowing where they are to be sent. They are allotted to plantations like so many dumb animals ... they are punished by being struck or fined and are even sent to gaol. Life on the plantations alters their demeanour and even their faces...The look on those women's faces haunts me ... only about 33 women are brought out to Fiji to every one hundred men. I can not go into details concerning this system of legalized prostitution ... every few months some Indian man murders for unfaithfulness the woman he regards as his wife. (Sanadhya 1991: 71)

Dudley begs for the system to be 'utterly abolished'. Sanadhya also mentions Rev. Burton (1910: 74), who in his book *The Fiji of Today*, writes about the inhuman outrages committed by the planters and terms the Indians 'human agricultural instruments'.

Cases of torture and physical assault by the *kulambars* and the *sardars* against the *girmitiyas* continued to rise during the period of indenture. Sanadhya (1991: 43) is caustic in his remarks while alluding to the torment faced by his brethren at the hands of the CSR officials, 'This is the coolie from India—you punch him with a fist, kick him, you don't give him wages, send him to prison, and no one hears about it at all'. Prasad informs that the victims of these punishments resorted to their own sense of justice with the aid of the knife they used for cutting the cane. 'Many of the *kulambars* and *sardars* were decapitated in these circumstances and the culprits, unrepentant, marched to the gallows' (Prasad 2010: 59). It is important to note that the children of the *girmitiyas*, once they reached the age of 12 were automatically indentured into the system and were also punished in a barbaric manner. They were whipped for small mistakes and were abused and beaten up on the smallest pretext. To complain to the magistrate was foolhardy because firstly, the magistrates 'invariably sided with the perpetrators', and secondly, invited further physical assault and mental torment by the plantation officials. 'In addition, *girmitiyas* did not have the liberty to leave plantations without the consent of the *kulambars*, and this effectively prevented many from reaching the Inspector of Immigrants to lodge complaints or going to the courts to give evidence' (ibid.: 62).

To curtail any idea of resistance in its nascent stage, the colonial powers used the practice of breaking up the connections formed on the ships by separating and sending the new arrivals to different plantations. Care was also taken to ensure that the *girmitiyas* from the same region in India were not put on the same plantation. This would help curb resistance and not allow a collective voice or uprising to gather momentum against the system. In some cases, families were broken up and sent to different plantations to guard against fostering and grouping. Brij Lal (2012: 171) mentions the ordinance passed in 1886 which made it unlawful for more than five labourers to absent themselves at the same time from any plantation without authorisation of the employer. Violation of this rule would invite a fine of two pounds or imprisonment of two months.

Prasad (2010: 71) also documents the different punishments meted out to the labourers where the patterns of violence varied from pouring boiling water over a *girmitiya's* genitals to making them drink kerosene. Hugh Tinker (1993: 179) notes that 'in folk-art, the indentured Indian was always portrayed with his hands bound together, and shoulders hunched: for he was now a tied creature, a bondsman'.

This is not to say that the *girmitiyas* were a docile lot and bore all the torture meted out to them without any form of protest. There were individual and collective acts of both active and passive resistance. Just as there were different forms of punishment utilised by the *kulambars* and *sardars*, similarly, there were different forms of resistance practised by the *girmitiyas*. Their first course of action was to lodge a formal complaint or petition in the Immigration office against the plantation owners. In most cases, this did not solve their problem as the very machinery that was enabled to serve their interests, sided with the plantation officials against the *girmitiyas.* In some cases, labourers attempted to run away and desert the plantation (desertions were common and the runaways were protected by the Indians who had finished serving their *girmit*), some feigned illness and absented themselves from work while others vented out their rage on the crops of the plantation owners (Ali 2004: 11). Some of these actions were not premeditated and were an individual form of resistance. In more severe cases, some *girmitiyas* committed suicide owing to the helplessness of their situation, while 'others took matters into their own hands and killed the *kulambars* and *sardars* in an act of vengeance' (Lal 2012: 189).

One of the most courageous acts of organised resistance narrated by Rajendra Prasad (2010: 70) centres around thirty *girmitiya* women on the Rarawai plantation who attacked a *kulambar* because he had verbally abused and called one of the women *randi* (an extremely derogatory Hindi term used for a woman, addressing her as a prostitute). The women got together and pulled him down from his horse, beating him up and soaking him in their urine. In the plantation in Rewa, a few *girmitiyas* got together and started a contributory fund to pay fines and fight the court cases. In their paper 'Non-Resistance in Fiji', Brij Lal and Doug Munro mention the courage and fortitude shown by the *girmitiyas* in Rewa.

> In 1917, they burned an effigy of the indenture system. This old friend of the European planters, and the enemy of Indian national self-respect, national honour, national name and fame—a hideous monster preying on Indian womanhood and torturing its victims into a life of misery and shame, and bringing up its offsprings in sin and filth. (Lal 2014: 152)

Singing the Bhojpuri songs *bidesiya* (literally meaning 'foreigner') were also a form of resistance for a non-literate generation of *girmitiyas*. They were moving cries for help and were sung by the men and women in the plantations with tears rolling down their cheeks. The songs illuminated their feelings about *girmit.* Lamenting the betrayal by the *akratis*, one song in *Chalo Jahaji* reads thus,

I hoe all day and cannot sleep at night,
Today my whole body aches,
Damnation to you, *akratis.* (Lal 2012: 114)

Prasad also documents many songs in his book, which he claims acted as a release valve for the intense emotional pressure the indentured people were facing during *girmit.*

Resistance also took the form of writing letters to Indian National Movement leaders in India. Sanadhya narrates the event in which he reached out to Mahatma Gandhi in India for help. Initially, the call for help was not geared towards setting up an abolitionist movement for indenture. Rather, the Indians in Fiji were seeking an Indian barrister to come from India and help them in their legal troubles because the *girmitiyas* believed that the 'white lawyers were writing something and telling us something else' (Sanadhya 1991: 52). To this end, the Indians in Fiji called a meeting during the monsoon season of 1907 and the result was a unanimous decision to write a letter to Mr Gandhi with a brief account of their troubles, beseeching him to send a barrister to Fiji. Gandhi published an article about this letter in the *Indian Opinion.* It was read by Manilal Doctor, a barrister-at-law who was in those days, working in Mauritius and looking after the welfare of the indentured Indians who had gone there. He answered the call and arrived in Fiji on 27 August 1912.

Meanwhile, in India, along with the drive for a free and independent India, the cause for abolishing the system of indenture was gaining momentum. This impetus came in many forms. Gillion (1973: 172) highlights, 'From 1913 the Indian critics of the indentured labour system concentrated their attack on Fiji, which then was taking more migrants than any other colony'. Burton's *The Fiji of Today* had been published in the periodical *India* in London, along with the letter written by Hanna Dudley, at the end of 1912. Manilal Doctor's articles from Fiji were also being published in India and depicted a view of the stark reality of the indenture system in Fiji. One of these reports in the Indian newspapers was about the sexual abuse faced by the Indian women on the plantations. This led to widespread protests in India. The cases of Kunti and Narayani had already been well-documented in India with Kunti's letter being published in 1913 in *Bharat Mitra*. Gillion believes that their stories 'enlisted wider public support than any other movement in modern Indian history, more than the independence movement' (ibid.: 182). Rajendra Prasad (2010: 121) informs that Pandit Madan Mohan Malviya and Gopal Krishna Gokhale, who served on the British Imperial Council were arch critics of the system. In 1912, Gokhale moved a motion in the Indian Legislative Assembly seeking the abolition of indenture. While the motion was defeated, the cries against the system could not be ignored any longer and the British government in India was thus forced to look into the matter with a modicum of seriousness.

Owing to the campaign against indenture by the people in India, the British government in India appointed a commission of two men in 1913 to look into the system—Mr. McNeill and Mr Chimman Lal. However, this commission was not a success as the Indians on the plantations were interviewed in the presence of the planters, and facing severe punishment and oppression, did not give any evidence against them. The commission also did not take the pain to interview Kunti. 'Far from recommending the end of the indentured labour system, McNeill and Chimman Lal praised it' (ibid.: 173).

The other cry for the end of indenture came in the form of returnees to India. Australian film-maker Satish Rai's (2013: 29) book *In Exile at Home: A Fiji Indian Story* highlights that 60 per cent of these labourers, chose to settle in Fiji on completion of their indenture while the remaining returned to India. Totaram Sanadhya returned to India in May 1914 to campaign for the abolition of indenture. To achieve this goal, he made several public speeches and joined the Indian National Congress to attend its sessions and further the cause for abolition. He also published his book *Fijidwip Mein Mere Ikkis Varsh* with the help of journalist Benarsidas Chaturvedi, which served as a platform for spreading the cry for abolition among the masses.

Just as the cry for abolition was becoming louder, the world was plunged into the Great War. On 5 November 1915, Gandhi sent Rev. Charles Freer Andrews and Rev. William Pearson to Fiji, who 'were so traumatised by what they saw of *girmit*', that they immediately began to engage the planters to sensitise them to the 'high rate of suicide, murder, low wages and inhuman working and living conditions' (Prasad 2010: 122). Their report created the base for a sustained campaign against indenture.

The indenture system or *girmit pratha* as it was called, lasted 37 years in Fiji, beginning on 4 March 1879 and finally ending with its abolishment on 20 March 1916. It was the mass public mobilization, backed by Gandhi's support, which compelled the then Governor-General of India, Lord Hardinge, to announce the termination of the indenture system. During this period, 87 voyages had been made to Fiji, and 60,965 Indians had been indentured and sent to work there. A majority of the labourers worked on the Australian Colonial Sugar Refining (CSR) Company's sugar plantations while others either worked on *copra* (coconut) and rice plantations or were employed by the colonial government to build roads and railway lines.

The abolition announcement by Lord Hardinge proved to be short-lived since Lord Chelmsford took over as the Viceroy of India in 1916 and revived the indenture system, extending its term of operation by five years. Mahatma Gandhi vehemently opposed this announcement and threatened picketing of the ships if the system was not ended by 31 May 1916. For the first time in Indian history, Indian women moved out of their traditional confines and went to meet Lord Chelmsford. Finally, the recruitment to the plantation colonies was stopped on 12 April 1917. This did not mean that the *girmitiyas* serving their indenture were now free. They were still expected to complete their stipulated term.

Regarding those who had completed their indenture period before its abolition, the CSR company wanted the *khulla* (free) immigrants to re-indenture themselves as it was cheaper than getting new labourers from India. However, most of them did not want to go back to the plantations, bringing to mind, similar denials by the free Negro slaves after slavery was abolished. When this strategy did not work, the Fiji government offered leasehold land to the free immigrants to induce them to stay. Under increasing pressure from Indian nationalists, such as Mahatma Gandhi, Pandit Madan Mohan Malviya, Gopal Krishna Gokhale, Sarojini Naidu, as well as with the sustained efforts of Rev. Burton, Rev. C.F. Andrews, Totaram Sanadhya, Kunti and

Naraini, Lord Montague finally abolished indenture in all its forms on 1 January 1920.

Sanadhya and Prasad's accounts reveal the position of the returnees, both during and after indenture was abolished. While Sanadhya returned to India and was one of the voices instrumental in bringing about the end of indenture, he found that not all returnees were welcomed in India. 'Sanadhya describes the fear of losing one's caste and being penalized for crossing the sea as the reasons that kept the emigrants permanently in Fiji' (Kumar 2017: 191). They feared losing their status among family and friends in India. Sanadhya (1991: 62) also highlights the cases of many returnees who were looted by their own brethren in India. 'The selfish priests casually cause some of the wealth to be extended in ceremonies of atonement'. The homes of many returnees were also occupied by their relatives. Sanadhya laments the trauma faced by the returnees, 'The man who reaches home without any earnings empty-handed is treated by the rest like a stranger who is there for a temporary stay' (ibid.: 63). Prasad also informs that some of the *girmitiyas,* who had entered into inter-caste or interreligious marriages in Fiji refused to return as they would not be accepted by their caste-rigid families in India. Greater was the plight of the women in such marriages. There were reports of the men leaving their wives at the depot on their return to India. Since such women would never have been welcomed by their in-laws or their own families, they were left to either live away from their families or re-indenture themselves as a single traveller. They could also remarry another man at the depot who was headed to Fiji (ibid.: 39).

However, debating the myth of return related to the *girmitiyas,* critic Kapil Kumar in his paper 'Colonial Exploitation, Resistance and Forced Migrations: The Indian Scenario in the Era of Indenture Labour' argues that it is not factually correct that those who returned to their villages were not welcomed. Kumar (2014: 32) believes that 'The number of returnees would have been much more had the agreements not been tampered with and changed as per the vested interests of the planters.' In fact, at times the returnees would even be duped of their savings during their return voyage. Kumar also highlights the 'lack of communication modes which increased the gaps in the family ties but the very emergence of *birha* songs in Bihar and eastern Uttar Pradesh are sufficient indicators that the wives, families and lovers, not only remembered those who went, with great agony but waited for their return and for their letters'. 'A simple analysis of historical records, shows that by 1872, almost half of those who went as indentured labour had returned to their homes' (ibid.: 33). He further suggests that the 'myth of non-acceptance was only a means of deterring Indians from returning: an act which meant a loss of "seasoned hands"; incurring the cost of a new labourer and the possible payment for the return fare which had been promised to workers' (ibid.: 34).

Prasad's grandfather was never able to return to India and died in Fiji in 1962, years after completing his *girmit.* The stories of India that he had narrated to his grandson filled in Prasad, a sense of nostalgia and an intense longing to go to the country and retrace his roots. He undertook the journey in 1974 and found his family in India. They were ecstatic and showed him the letters they had received from his grandfather in Fiji in 1928, 1945 and 1948 'To the family, they were a source of comfort and consolation.... They were treasured like family jewels' (Prasad 2010: 27). The matriarch of the family took charge and massaged coconut oil on the scalps, hands and legs of Prasad and his wife making a profound statement, 'Ram aur Sita banwas se padhare hain' (ibid.: 37). Prasad discovers in this voyage to his 'homeland', that he had found new joy and a new identity in his roots. 'My ancestral roots were like the umbilical cord that ties mother and child together' (ibid.: 41). He also looks at the two views he had had of India. 'One as told by *Daadaji* and the other as I read about India through the eyes of the Western media' (ibid.). After visiting his homeland, he observed that his view of India gave him 'a sense of dignity and pride and an appreciation' that he was 'the bearer of a proud heritage' (ibid.: 42). He concluded from his visit to India that the memories of *girmit* have 'been wrongly buried in shame' and since then, Prasad has become 'a crusader battling against the stigma of *girmit*' (ibid.: 43).

This chapter explores the narratives of the *girmitiyas* in Fiji, whose voices have been lost in the colonial master discourse where they are heard about but not heard from. Their narratives open up the discourse to a different set of experiences and project 'their' indenture as a counter to the official narrative. The narratives of indenture are not just memoirs of pain, anguish, trauma and betrayal, they are also accounts of courage, resourcefulness and resistance. These are some of the common themes that run across these narratives. There is a dearth of *girmitiya* voices during the period of indenture and most oral resources are undocumented. Totaram Sanadhya's is one of the rare extant texts of the period and his narrative holds the answers to some of the questions on indenture. The book carries within it the struggle of the marginalized group of the indentured Indians in Fiji and is thus open to interpretation. Only through narrating the journey of his life is Sanadhya able to present some form of resistance to the official discourse that surrounds him.

On the other hand, Prasad's narrative works on a different scale since his is an 'inherited' experience. His encounter with indenture is fragmented between his 'Indianness' and between his Indo-Fijian identity and works in a very objective way. While deconstructing the colonial discourse in his narrative, he makes an equally striking case against the postcolonial establishment. He does this from the multicultural hyphenated post-colonial position that allows him to deconstruct and reconstruct the experience of indenture through a postcolonial counter-discourse.

From a gender perspective, there is no extant female voice from the indenture period in Fiji. We do hear the narratives of Kunti and Narayani but these are not in their own words. Both these women returned to India and while Kunti played a major role in the indenture abolitionist movement, their fate is unknown and their voices are largely absent or have been omitted from public memory.

The conditions in Fiji determined the sensibility of indenture to a large extent. It is a documented fact that the tasks in Fiji were heavier than those in the Caribbean plantations. In other aspects too, indenture in Fiji was a harsher experience than the one faced by the indentured people in the Caribbean. While it was traumatic for all *girmitiyas,* nostalgia was a key determiner in the way the Fiji Indians looked back at the homeland. The Caribbean experience carried greater tones of acculturation and assimilation in their adopted land. The next chapter will look into the characteristics and features governing the indenture experience in the Caribbean.

WORKS CITED

Ali, Ahmed, *Girmit: Indian Indenture Experience in Fiji*, Suva, Fiji: Fiji Museum, 2004.

Bhabha, Homi, *The Location of Culture*, London: Routledge, 1997.

Burton, John Wear and Arthur James Small, *The Fiji of Today*, London: Kelly, 1910.

Carter, Marina and Crispin Bates, 'Empire and Locality: a Global Dimension to the 1857 Indian Uprising', *Journal of Global History* 5.1, 2010, pp. 51-73.

Foucault, Michel, *Society Must be Defended: Lectures at the College De France 1975-1976*, New York: St. Martin's Press, 1997.

———, 'Of Other Spaces, Heterotopias', *Architecture, Mouvement* 5, 1984, pp. 46-9.

Ghosh, Amitav, *Sea of Poppies*, Gurgaon: Penguin Books India Pvt. Ltd., 2015.

Gillion, Kenneth L., *Fiji's Indian Migrants: a History to the End of Indenture in 1920*, Melbourne: Oxford University Press, 1973.

Hirsch, Marianne, *Family Frames: Photography Narrative and Postmemory*, Cambridge, MA: Harvard University Press, 2016.

———, *The Generation of Postmemory Writing and Visual Culture after the Holocaust*, New York: Columbia University Press, 2012.

———, 'Past Lives: Postmemories in Exile', *Poetics Today* 17.4, 1996, pp. 659-86.

Kelly, John D., *Fiji Indians and the Law, 1912,* Suva, Fiji: Suva Museum, 1991.

Kumar, Ashutosh, *Coolies of the Empire Indentured Indians in the Sugar Colonies, 1830-1920,* Cambridge: Cambridge University Press, 2017.

Kumar, Kapil, 'Colonial Exploitation, Resistance and Forced Migrations: The Indian Scenario in the Era of Indenture Labour', *Resistance and Indian Indenture Experience: Comparative Perspectives,* ed. Maurits S. Hassankhan, Brij V. Lal and Doug Munro, New Delhi: Manohar, 2014, pp. 19-49.

Lal, Brij V., *Bittersweet: the Indo-Fijian Experience*, Canberra: Pandanus Books, 2004.

———, *Chalo Jahaji: On a Journey through Indenture in Fiji*, Canberra: ANU Press, 2012.

———, 'Veil of Dishonour: Sexual Jealousy and Suicide on Fiji Plantations', *The Journal of Pacific History* 20.3, 1985, pp. 135-55.

Lal, Brij V. and Clem Seecharan, *Girmitiyas: the Origins of the Fiji Indians*, Lautoka, Fiji: Fiji Institute of Applied Studies, 2004.

Lal, Brij V. and Doug Munro, 'Non-resistance in Fiji,' *Resistance and Indian Indenture Experience: Comparative Perspectives*, ed. Maurits S. Hassankhan, Brij V. Lal and Doug Munro, New Delhi: Manohar, 2014, pp. 121-56.

Lal, Brij V., Peter Reeves and Rajesh Rai, eds., *The Encyclopedia of the Indian Diaspora*, New Delhi: Oxford University Press, 2007.

Long, Maebh, 'Girmit, Postmemory, and Subramani', *Pacific Dynamics* 2.2, 2018, pp. 161-75.

Mclean, Sarah, 'Places Where Reality Feels Altered', theodysseyonline, 2 August 2016, Web. 22 April 2019, www.theodysseyonline.com/amp/liminal-spaces-2478165167/

Mishra, Sudesh, *Tandava*, Melbourne: Meanjin Press, 1992.

———, 'Time and *Girmit*', *Social Text* 82.2, 2005, pp. 15-36.

———, *Diaspora and the Difficult Art of Dying*, Dunedin: University of Otago Press, 2002.

———, *Diaspora Criticism*, Edinburgh: Edinburgh University Press, 2006.

Mishra, Vijay, *The Literature of the Indian Diaspora: Theorizing the Diasporic Imaginary*, London: Routledge, 2014.

———, 'Voices from the Diaspora', *The Encyclopedia of the Indian Diaspora*, ed. Brij V. Lal, Peter Reeves and Rajesh Rai, New Delhi: Oxford University Press, 2007, pp. 120-39.

Peirce, Penney, *Transparency: Seeing Through to Our Expanded Human Capacity*, Oregon: Beyond Words Publishing, Incorporated, 2017.

Pirbhai, Mariam, *Mythologies of Migration, Vocabularies of Indenture: Novels of the South Asian Diaspora in Africa, the Caribbean, and Asia-Pacific*, Toronto: University of Toronto Press, 2009.

Prasad, Rajendra, *Tears in Paradise: Suffering and Struggles of Indians in Fiji, 1879-2004*, Auckland, N.Z.: Pindar, 2010.

Rai, Satish, *In Exile at Home: A Fiji Indian Story*, Kindle edn., Amazon Asia-Pacific Holdings Private Limited, 2013, Web. 27 March 2017.

Roopnarine, Lomarsh, 'A Critique of East Indian Historiography in the Caribbean', *Labor History* 55.3, 2014, pp. 389-401.

Rushdie, Salman, *Imaginary Homelands: Essays and Criticism 1981-1991*, London: Granta, 1991, pp. 10-12.

Sanadhya, Totaram, *My Twenty-one Years in the Fiji Islands*, tr. Uttra Kumari Singh and John Dunham Kelly, Suva, Fiji: Fiji Museum, 1991.

———, *The Story of the Haunted Line*, Suva: Fiji Museum, 2003.

Tinker, Hugh, *A New System of Slavery: The Export of Indian Labour Overseas 1830-1920*, London: Hansib, 1993.

Torabully, Khal, and Marina Carter, *Coolitude: An Anthology of the Indian Labour Diaspora*, London: Anthem Press, 2002.

CHAPTER 3

The *Jahajis:* Indentured Indians in the Caribbean

'But I never left home.
I carried it away with me –
here in my darkness, in myself'
(Bhatt 2014: 105)

EACH DIASPORA HAS its own history and process and it is not altogether possible to homogenise the diasporic experiences of an entire community. In the case of the indentured diaspora too, the same equation applies since no two experiences of indenture in the colonies were the same. Indenture was a global phenomenon and while certain characteristics that applied to the agreement/contract were uniform, the experience of the indentured labourers was heterogeneous. The majority/minority axis, which is primarily based on the relation of power, played a crucial role in indenture dynamics in each plantation colony.

This heterogeneous nature of the diaspora is keenly observed by theorist Stuart Hall in 'Cultural Identity and Diaspora'. He finds that the experience of the diaspora is, 'defined, not by essence or purity, but by the recognition of a necessary heterogeneity and diversity; by a conception of 'identity' which lives with and through, not despite, difference; by hybridity' (Hall 2014: 35). Hall further believes that 'diasporic identities are those which are constantly producing and reproducing themselves anew, through transformation and difference' (ibid.: 36). This chapter illustrates that experiences of indenture cannot be homogenized and that there are several noted points of difference when they are plotted on the spatio-temporal axis.

Owing to their common point of origin, Indian indentured people have historically been spoken of in homogeneous terms. While the global indentured diaspora community does share common characteristics based on the definitions provided by postcolonial theorists William Safran, Robin Cohen and Vijay Mishra, there are several limitations to this approach of classifying their experiences as uniform. Current research demands a comparative study of the indentured experience in order to look at the convergences and divergences across the plantation colonies. The history and understanding of indenture cannot be confined to the limits of either the homeland or the host land. Each distinct group of Indian indentured immigrants comprises a whole, made up of many journeys to different parts of the world, occurring over very different periods. The experiences of each group thus, vary considerably, and some theorists even agree that the talk of shared identities and experiences of the indentured diaspora at the global level is meaningless.

When slavery was finally abolished in 1838, the freed African slaves chose to not work on the sugar plantations anymore. Those who could not look for alternative sources of employment asked the colonial planters for higher wages for their labour but were denied the same. The Caribbean, unlike Fiji, had been host to African slavery and the apprenticeship system before the arrival of Indian indentured labourers on the islands. The culture of pre-existing plantation slavery was so deeply entrenched in the colonies in the Caribbean that the plantation owners continued to treat the newly indentured Indians in a manner similar to slaves. Historian Hugh Tinker has brought out in his influential book, *A New System of Slavery* that there was only one factor in which indenture differed from slavery—that indenture was meant to be temporary while slavery had been a permanent condition. Author Basdeo Mangru (2004: 28) also agrees with Tinker and states that as a bound labourer, the indentured worker was subject to laws imposed by the planters and was denied the right to strike. The indenture system thus gave the colonial planters the control which they had sought since the abolition of slavery. Richard B. Allen (2016: 38) in his paper 'Origins of the "New System of Slavery"' contends that between 1831 and 1922, a total of 542,045 Indians were indentured and sent as plantation workers to the Caribbean. Britain sent the first Indian indentured labourers to the Caribbean from the port of Calcutta to British Guiana (now Guyana) in 1838.

Literature written by the indentured diaspora in the Caribbean offers a unique perspective of the system as it unfolded across islands. These narratives offer an enduring knowledge of the legacy of indentured labour. Gaiutra Bahadur's *Coolie Woman: The Odyssey of Indenture* (thereafter *Coolie Woman*) portrays a panoramic picture of Indian indentured labour in Guiana (Guyana) and offers a gendered perspective of women in the indenture. It narrates the story of her great grandmother Sujaria, who had come to Guiana as an indentured labourer in 1903. It also weaves together the 'entangled histories' of the many other indentured women 'from the moment they left their villages, through their middle passages, through their reinvention and struggle in a new world' (Bahadur 2013: 177). Sujaria was 'a pregnant woman travelling alone' and like 'most Indians who migrated, she did not have a last name' (ibid.: 10). Bahadur's narrative continues to raise questions as it traces the journey of Sujaria, from her home in India to the long voyage on *The Clyde*. It sketches her arrival as a 27-year-old indentured labourer to the island and, thereafter, her becoming a *coolie* on the plantation. (The term *coolie* was used by Europeans and Creoles to address Indian indentured labourers in the Caribbean in a dehumanising manner). Her immigration pass lists her as a *Brahman* named Sheojari. Also included as an aside is a scribbled note 'Pregnant 4 mos' (ibid.: 18). The book charts her life narrative through her indenture till her death aged 89 in 1962. It also draws the narratives of other Indian women indentured into the system.

Peggy Mohan's *Jahajin* is a culmination of the many voices belonging to indentured women sent to Trinidad in the Caribbean. The chief protagonist in this narrative is 110-year-old Deeda, who narrates her journey from India. Sifting through the annals of her memory, she speaks in her native Bhojpuri. Born in Basti in a *Kahaar* (palanquin bearer) family, Deeda was married at 7 and had given birth at 12 to a son named Kalloo. Her husband was a domestic migrant worker who had gone in search of work, leaving behind a 16-year-old wife and a 4-year-old son. When severe drought struck, Deeda fell prey to the machinations of an *akrati* and left her home, setting sail to Trinidad as an indentured worker.

Bahadur narrates, 'mystery darkened the lives of many women who left India as coolies' (ibid.: 26). According to a law stipulating 40 women for every 100 men in a ship bound for the colonies, the recruiters were forced to meet the quota of convincing women to indenture. This was no easy task as women rarely came into direct contact with the recruiters. Officially, women recruiters were not allowed in the system. However, male recruiters outsourced this task to women who could easily convince the other women to indenture themselves and board the ships bound for the British plantations. 'The law that aggravated the shortage of women, the 1883 Indian Emigration Act, was intended to stop wives from passing as widows or single women to escape their husbands' (ibid.: 27). According to the 1891 census of the United Provinces (the region from which the maximum number of indentured labourers were recruited), 90 per cent of girls aged between ten and fourteen were already married. This made the task of female recruitment considerably difficult for the recruiters.

Most of the indentured immigrants to the Caribbean came from North India, primarily Uttar Pradesh and Bihar, and spoke Bhojpuri. Many factors acted as catalysts in their decision to emigrate. 'The practice of imperial capitalism destroyed traditional livelihoods, plunging weavers into unemployment by flooding India with factory-made textiles from England' (ibid.: 25). Severe famines (24 in the last quarter of the nineteenth century) also resulted in large-scale displacement. Historian Romesh C. Dutt has written in his book, *The Economic History of India in the Victorian Age*, 'It is literally a fact and not a figure of speech that agricultural labourers and their families in India generally suffer from insufficient food from year's beginning to year's end' (Dutt 1969: 12). At the same time, the changes in the land revenue system further compounded the problems of the peasants by shifting the power matrix into the hands of the landowning classes who were the beneficiaries of the British practices. They imposed arbitrary taxes on a rural populace that was already reeling under the extreme deprivation caused by famines. In *Indian Diaspora in the Caribbean,* anthropologist Kumar Mahabir informs that the system of taxation was so severe that the practice of *kanya vikray* (sale of young daughters in marriage to elder men) developed to enable peasants to withstand the adverse conditions (Mahabir 2009: 3). Author and historian Lomarsh Roopnarine has conducted extensive research on the indenture system in the Caribbean. He has found that 'Besides North India, the main supplier of migrants to the Caribbean came from the sprawling Madras Presidency in South India' (Roopnarine 2003: 120). There were a lesser number of emigrants going from South India than those from the north. According to Roopnarine, 'They constituted only 8.5% of the total Indian emigrants to British Guiana'. There was lesser demand for them from the plantations owing to their bad reputation of 'being disinclined to work, difficult to manage, quarrelsome and migratory' (ibid.).

David Northrup (1995: 29) informs that Trinidad had been taken by the British from Spain in 1797 while British Guiana had been acquired from the Dutch in 1814. During the era of slavery, these two colonies had received the largest number of African-born slaves (ibid.: 18-19). On 5 May 1838, two ships, *Whitby* and *Hesperus,* holding 396 Indian labourers arrived in Guyana. Of these, only 22 were women and among them, six were just girls.

John Scoble, who was the representative of the British Anti-Slavery Society in Guyana at that time, made serious allegations against the treatment of the indentured people and called for an end to the system. He had the statistics to prove his contention. Just 18 months after their arrival in Guyana, 67 of the labourers had died owing to various reasons. A majority of them had committed suicide. The others had succumbed to various tropical diseases. This led to the suspension of indentureship for a while. However, the planters were able to sway the people in power and indentured migration was restarted to the Caribbean in 1845. Peggy Mohan (2007: 12) notes, 'The first wave of migration had not produced a viable community in Trinidad… Their death rate had been very high, both on the ships and on the plantations. And being almost all men, they had left no children in Trinidad'.

Roopnarine (2003: 123) has also highlighted the role played by the colonials in the recruitment process. In his article, he writes, 'Surreptitious recruitment processes were guided by the belief that "people of colour" were inferior whose lot could only be improved through labour and discipline, a contemptuous characteristic of imperialism and colonialism'. In a land struck by famines and repressive land regulations, the *akratis* were able to convince enough Indian men fraudulently to indenture. Only a fraction of the affected people signed up for indenture but the number of those who did was very significant at that time. Traditionally, Indian society followed rigid caste hierarchies. For a Hindu, going overseas was tantamount to losing caste, which was the single most important identifier in the Indian social milieu. Losing caste was akin to losing their identity. Children above the age of ten were particularly at risk and susceptible to indenture. Poet and critic Khal Torabully (2002: 24) narrates that since 'indenture contracts could be signed from the age of ten years and upwards, minors could find themselves engaged to an estate overseas for lengthy periods'.

It was when the 1883 Indian Emigration Act regulation of 40 women per hundred men came into force, that the *akratis* found it difficult to meet the gender quota. No ship would be allowed to sail if it did not meet this ratio. This led to several cases of kidnapping, deceit and forceful detention of the women labourers in the sub-depots. Bahadur (2013: 26) says that 'mystery darkened the lives of many women who left India as coolies'. To make the situation worse, in 1903, a law was passed which did not allow any married woman to emigrate without the permission of her husband. Recruiters thus looked for women who had no one to provide for them. The most desperate lot was the socially vulnerable women who were easy targets for the recruiters. Bahadur cites the report of Sir George Grierson, the British civil servant posted in Bihar who observed that the female emigrants consisted of four groups:

> The wives of men who had already been to the colonies and had returned to fetch them, destitute widows with no one to take pity on them, prostitutes and 'married women who have made a slip, and who have either absconded from their husband's house with or without a lover or who have been turned out of doors by their husbands' (Bahadur 2013: 33).

These statistics have given rise to one of the greatest myths of indenture regarding the type of women who became indentured. Women in indenture have been classed as 'morally degenerate' by the colonial narrative.

Widows fleeing *sati* (Hindu custom of immolating widows on the funeral pyre of their husbands) were subject to acute hunger and poverty. The only alternative available to them (before indenture) was prostitution. Bahadur notes, 'There is a reason the word *randi* or *ranri* can mean both young widow and prostitute in both the Bhojpuri and Bengali languages' (ibid.: 35). Married women whose husbands had taken on another woman and women who were ill-treated by their in-laws also had no recourse to an alternative other than suicide; neither did the women who had been seduced and then abandoned. In the Indian social order, they were already rejects, standing on the periphery. To show indenture in a positive light, the British demonstrated its civilizing influence by liberating oppressed women from what they perceived as a barbaric and heathen culture. Indenture would save their lives. It is not difficult then to understand why the women emigrated despite strong social taboos.

The testimonies of the women who indentured show 'glimpses of headstrong women, determined to go or not to' (ibid.: 31). Were they, to borrow critic Charu Gupta's (2015: 1345) phrase, 'innocent victims or guilty migrants?' By recovering their voices from official petitions, reports, songs and letters, Gaiutra Bahadur and Peggy Mohan have constructed their protagonists as gendered beings standing on the intersections of sexuality and morality. The indentured subaltern woman has many sides and layers to her persona. She was indeed a victim of deception and misinformation. It is equally true that in many instances, her choice to indenture was a deliberate choice that accorded her agency. But was this not a pseudo choice? Faced with prostitution or suicide, what alternative did she have except to get indentured?

Indenture was praised by the colonists as a liberating experience for the oppressed lower caste woman in India. Was it equally true for the women belonging to the upper echelons of Indian society? These contestations are significant in deconstructing the assumption of a single cultural identity ascribed to the *coolie* women. The fixated binary of disempowered women forced into migration versus the female voices on consensual migration needs to be carefully re-analysed. There are two main narratives of indenture for women, each centring around kidnap and escape. Until recently, everything written about the Indian women in indenture has been written by men who have presented polarized images of these women. During the years of indenture, single low caste Indian women were perceived as immoral and were looked upon with suspicion. They faced economic and sexual exploitation at the hands of the planters as well as by their Indian male protectors. Mohan's narrator, Deeda, comes to Trinidad as a 'single woman, but she was married, and she had a child with her' (Mohan 2007: 15). Deeda narrates her life story, 'I was married before I came. And my husband is still in India. I came alone and left him behind' (ibid.: 16). Belonging to the lower caste of Kahaars, Deeda informs that she was seven when she married and thirteen when she had a son, whom she brought along with her to Trinidad. Owing to the severe drought in India when her son Kalloo was four years old, Deeda's husband, a migrant worker, went to a place near Allahbad to work. Deciding to wait for her husband in her home in Basti, Deeda realised that they would have starved if she didn't find work. She decides to take her son with her to Faizabad in search of work. On her way she '. . . met the *arkatiniya,* the lady who was recruiting people to go with her as migrants… to go to a place called "Chini-dad", a land of "chini", sugar'. The female recruiter convinced Deeda to go for only one year, '. . . and then they bring you back. Plenty of money' (ibid.: 18).

Colonial records estimate that, '. . . whether willingly or unwillingly, two-thirds of indentured women left India unaccompanied by men' (Bahadur 2013: 39). Belonging to the upper class of Brahmins, Gaiutra Bahadur's great grandmother, Sheojari was 27 when she emigrated as a pregnant single woman to Guiana. No Brahmin girl in 1903 would have willingly crossed the *kalapani* (dark water) for to do so would be to lose her caste. Interestingly, 76 per cent of the indentured women travelling to the colonies in 1903 were travelling alone (ibid.). Garden Reach Depot in Calcutta was the place from where all emigrants to the Caribbean would depart. At the same depot docked those *coolies* who were returning after completing their indentures. Voices would call out, 'Look at the *jeeta janazza*, the walking dead' (Mohan 2007: 23). The Garden Depot was also the place where the metamorphoses of the new emigrants would begin. On their arrival at the depot, the emigrants were given a new set of clothes to wear. To combat the rough weather they would have to face around Africa's southern tip, the women were allotted '. . . two flannel jackets, a woollen petticoat and worsted stockings.' The men received '. . . woollen trousers, a red woollen cap and trousers. . .' (Bahadur 2013: 44).

Bahadur quotes anthropologist John D. Kelly, who remarked that indenture did not 'recruit coolies'. Rather it 'made coolies' (ibid.: 29). Many upper caste Hindus let go of their *janeu* (sacred thread worn by Brahmin boys when they turn thirteen years of age) in the waters of the Hooghly river. New identities were overlapping the older ones. Bahadur's ancestor, named 'Sheojari' in India, became 'Sujaria' in Guiana. While the men had the *janeu,* the women owned nothing that was a manifestation of their caste and class status. What they could change was their name. It may also be possible that they were changing their names to stay hidden and undocumented if they had run away from their homes. Mohan's ancestor, 'Janki' (a synonym of Sita, Lord Ram's wife, who accompanies him in exile in the Hindu epic *Ramayan*) in India is renamed 'Sunnariya' in Trinidad. It is Sunnariya who renames another woman, 'Parbati' calling her 'Deeda' (a mangling of the name 'didi' used to address an elder sister). Speaking with a sense of pride in its hybrid origins, Deeda calls it her 'creolized name'. (Mohan 2007: 24)

At the depot, men and women had to undergo a medical examination to ensure they were free from diseases. Men were subjected to a thorough examination of their genital organs and their anal region to check for any venereal diseases. It was extremely humiliating for the Indians. The journey to the Caribbean islands took at least three and a half months. The sea voyage was looked upon as an object of fear. Hinduism declared all seafarers removed from caste. On their return, the indentured would be cast adrift without the umbilical cord of religion. Bahadur (2013: 46) discovers that 'Upper-caste

Hindus wanting to study in England argued that religious tradition allowed travel for merit—for education, for progress, pilgrimage—as long as no polluting contact occurred'. The strong social order would never accept indenture as pardonable on any of the grounds used by the upper caste Hindus to travel overseas. For a majority of the single women travelling to the colonies, the voyage was a metaphor of flight to safety and freedom. In any case, whether belonging to the low or high castes in India, the women were marginalized and restricted to domestic roles. They were 'owned' by the men. Travel to a new place was looked upon with hope for a new beginning, away from the social order that marked them as 'others' in their own country. Still, the severing from the motherland tendered a deep wound, one that has still not been filled a century later.

Survivors of indenture have recounted memories of the moment of departure being one of collective weeping, wailing and breast-beating as the boat journeyed down the Hooghly. There were many instances of the indentured throwing themselves overboard and drowning to escape crossing the oceans. It is pertinent to note here that there are greater instances of men committing suicide than women, both on the ships and in the plantations. The alienation, uprootedness and emotional turmoil linked to nostalgia were more keenly wrought in the men than in the women. As pointed out earlier, women who had been brought into indenture (whether voluntarily or under duress) had become outcastes in Indian society owing to their crossing the *kalapani*. There could be no return home for them. In fact, a home would be denied to them even if they returned.

Men, on the other hand, despite the crossing of the *kalapani,* were privileged. On their return, they knew they would be welcomed home. This perpetuated a sense of nostalgia towards India, transforming the homeland as a defence against the trauma of parting. Nostalgia refers to a sense of loss, a perpetual feeling of loss and a strong yearning of returning. It created a sense of temporary optimism in the *jahajis* who were backed by a contract that promised a return. However, nostalgia offers a return only in memory and nostalgia towards India was decidedly less in the women undergoing indenture.

Bahadur's narrative also unearths the voice of one woman, fleeing with her daughter to save her from female infanticide. Generations later, her great granddaughter says they were fortunate 'that no one was able to put salt under our tongues—because of our heroic great grandparent, who preferred to cross the *kalapani*' (ibid.: 48). The indentured women were, on the whole, setting out in the hope of making a new life that would be free from caste and religious restrictions. They were looking forward to working alongside men and earning their own money.

Onboard the ship, the toilets 'served as a bizarre portal to the women aboard, where "puddings" were occasionally left as sad enticements for sexual favours' (ibid.: 51). Since women received fewer chapattis than men did, lack of food was reason enough for women to resort to desperate measures to get it, including sleeping with the white seamen and the Indian *lascars* (seamen) on these ships. The lack of a rigid rule that would enforce the 'no-sex with female immigrants' clause, as well as the absence of any penalties allowed the sexual abuse to continue unabated on board the vessels. The Surgeon Superintendent on the ship, although in charge of the emigrants, had technically no authority over the crew members. He could not discipline them into any action. The surgeon was paid a set amount of money for each emigrant he brought alive to the colony. In Guiana, the surgeons lost one shilling for each man who died on board. Thus, he was responsible for the medical condition of the indentured Indians during the voyage. Some surgeons adopted a paternalistic attitude towards the Indians while some proved to be the perpetrators of the sexual liberties taken with the women. A rare testimony cited in *Coolie Woman* informs, 'One night the surgeon came down between the decks, took me by the arm, and dragged me into his cabin, and had connexion with me.…I was not a prostitute in India' (ibid.: 58-9). When they tried to complain to the Protector of Immigrants, the women found the colonial narrative characterizing them as 'sluts'. Whether they gave in willingly in return for 'pudding' or were sexually molested and raped, the indentured women in colonial history have been marked as 'shamelessly immoral'.

Jeremy Poynting's paper 'East Indian Women in the Caribbean: Experience and Voice' draws attention to the depiction of indentured women oscillating between 'demure child-women or exotic seductresses'. He points out that 'as wage earners under the indenture, some Indian women achieved a measure of independence, and even within the family it seems likely that women achieved some status in their role as the main preservers of Indian domestic culture' (Poynting 1987: 174).

Sickness on the long voyage was one of the many horrors faced by the indentured Indians. Apart from facing the perils of seasickness, a majority of Indians on board fell prey to a number of diseases owing to the unhygienic conditions on the ships. 'In that outbreak of measles altogether fourteen people passed away, fourteen. And half of them were children' (Mohan 2007: 60). Women also suffered more on the voyage than the men. They gave birth, had miscarriages, lost children and suffered post-partum depression. The storms on the sea were among the worst faced by the immigrants. Coming from the landlocked provinces in the Indian hinterland, most of them had never even seen the sea. The *pagal samundar* (mad seas) around the Cape of Good Hope (the southernmost point of Africa) was a novel experience for the indentured Indians. Another grave cause for concern on the ships was the breakout of fires. If someone left a burning cigarette, it could prove to be a catastrophic event. 'Infants and children lost their lives to a disproportionate degree during the crossings.' They were 'overlaid, suffocated while cradled besides a sleeping mother' and a large number were lost to malnutrition (Bahadur 2013: 63).

The ship was also the site of coming together and of the beginning of a 'collective consciousness' that would prevail over their indenture and would seep into the generations that would follow. 'The moorings of caste had loosened, and people who had left behind uncles, sisters, husbands and mothers substituted shipmates, their *jahajis,* for kin. Unravelled, they began, ever so slowly, to spin the threads of a novel identity' (ibid.: 62).

Living in close quarters below the decks had engendered a closeness that would continue to remain fast for many years. Sometimes, marriages were performed on the boats by the captains. Single women were encouraged to take up partners as protectors in the life ahead. 'He told them to couple up and he made a wedding right there' (ibid.: 73). 'Depot marriages' that took place at the depots in Calcutta, even before leaving India, were not stable in nature. Indian women, on arrival at the plantations, attempted to upscale their relations and left their 'depot husbands' for other men on the plantation who could offer them a better standard of living. Mohan informs that some of these weddings were in name only, hastily put together to allow the couple to stay in the married quarters. Bahadur believes that 'power was being renegotiated between men and women in the tween decks. What had seemed unthinkable in India was becoming conceivable as the seas were crossed. In some cases, women discovered a whole new ability to set terms and conditions' (ibid.: 72). 'One husband felt the need to promise his wife jewellery if she agreed to stay with him once in Guiana' (ibid.: 73). The emerging new man-woman relationships changed the perceptions of the immigrants towards marriage and family, the two institutions considered sacrosanct in India. In *The Black Atlantic,* Paul Gilroy (2007: 4) describes the ship as a 'living, micro-cultural, micro-political system in motion'. It was the place where the older identities would be lost and newer ones would take their place.

On the ships, the longing for the receding motherland led to moments of nostalgia, of looking back and of a hope for return. At the same time, there was a longing to belong in the new place they were setting course to. It is interesting to note that while men carried religious books binding them to the culture of the homeland, women carried seeds of assimilation and acculturation. 'In a little cloth bag she was carrying some damp soil from *muluk*, and growing in that soil was a root of *hardee*, turmeric. The masala that turns food yellow, and keeps wounds from getting infected. She was keeping it alive so she could plant it when we reached' (Mohan 2007: 64).

The pregnant women hoped their wombs would yield girls. 'We already have too many boys. . . . What we need now is some girls' (ibid.: 65). This marks a stark departure from the patriarchal society in India that demanded boys from wombs. Indenture had offered these women a sense of freedom to voice their hope and wishes for a future distinct from the one they had anticipated in India. Women carried the seeds of tomorrow in their wombs. As if the name carried positive connotations, navigating the Cape of Good Hope (the southernmost tip of Africa) shook off the sense of inertia that had made the voyagers listless. Mohan's narrator, Deeda, recollects:

> After the storm, something had happened to all of us. It had all started when Sahatoo Maharaj had stood on the deck and smiled. We stopped looking back. I think we had finally crossed the *kalapani* in our minds, changed from being the people we were before. The sad notes of the *beeraha* we had sung as we crossed that ocean had brightened into a new song, a song with no dark corners and no storms. (ibid.: 82)

Deeda goes on to add that the shipmates now had a collective identity. Those on the same boat were looked on as *apan palwaar* (our family) and they started addressing each other as *jahaji bhai* and *jahaji behen*. Their new identity, the one they chose for themselves, was *jahajis* (shipmates). In a telling comment, Deeda mentions that the further they sailed, the more they changed. They started talking in a different way. 'We stopped talking about all that happened before. It was as if we had left the people we used to be behind us, around the cape' (ibid.: 83). The sense of hope was so strong that when a black cat came aboard the ship while it was docked in the Cape of Good Hope for supplies, it was welcomed by the *jahajis*. In India, a black cat would have been considered a bad omen and centuries-old superstition would have assigned it demonic status as the bringer of ill tidings.

The Nelson Island depot in Trinidad and George Town depot in Guiana were earmarked to receive the immigrants. Here, the *jahajis* would set foot on land for the first time after approximately three months. It was an alien land and would prove to be unwelcoming to the newcomers. Guiana was termed the 'white man's grave' owing to the death-inducing diseases common on the island. Malaria and yellow fever were rampant. The geographical landscape was completely different to what the Indians had been used to back home. The son of an indentured labourer in the Caribbean, V.S. Naipaul described his father, Seepersad Naipaul's, emotions on stepping foot for the first time in the depot in Trinidad. Vijay Mishra (1996: 194) quotes Naipaul, 'My father rejecting one world, came into contact with another. In him was played out the whole tragic drama of an ancient civilization coming into contact with a hideous colonial mimicry of another civilization'.

The population in the Caribbean comprised a judicious mix of 'British, black people, Chinese, Portuguese and other mixed-race descendants of plantation workers imported over several centuries'

(Bahadur 2013: 77). The earlier slaves were wary of the arrivals of the Indians and looked upon them suspiciously. Indentured Indians made up almost 40 per cent of the population in Guiana but they lived in or near the plantations. The reason for this was the Vagrancy Law which controlled the movements of indentured workers. It allowed the police to arrest Indians if they were found two miles away from the plantations without a signed pass in their possession.

The men were promised one shilling while the women were to receive two-thirds of a shilling for a day's work on the plantations. The *coolies,* after their arrival at the depot, were taken by the officials to the plantations where they would serve the next five years of their indenture. They were housed in the 'logies' in the 'nigger yard' (a ghost of the plantations' past that had housed the erstwhile slaves). The set-up did not allow any privacy and instead championed communal living. Metal roofs and mud floors were the sum total of these lodgings. There was no furniture provided to the indentured people. There were no toilets. The immigrants compared their places of residence to stables. 'In other colonies, they used the words *narak* (Hell) and *Kasbi Ghar* (brothel)' (ibid.: 84). Protesting against the indentured people slipping into the spaces vacated by the slaves, abolitionist Reverend C.F. Andrews (2007: 69) wrote in *Impressions of British Guiana*, 'It was high time that these relics of the past, with all their evil associations, were swept clean away'.

The immigrants had carried their own relics from home, which they (dis)placed in their 'new' lodgings in the plantations. V.S. Naipaul has detailed the items that the Indians had carried with them to the Caribbean:

> It was astonishing what they did bring; but they were going to the end of the world and they came prepared for the wilderness: they brought holy books and astrological almanacs, images, sandalwood, all the paraphernalia of the religious shrines, musical instruments, string beds, plates and jars, even querns, even grinding stones… as it was, they carried India with them and were able to recreate something of their world. (Naipaul 1986: 13)

Indenture was an economic enterprise started by the colonists with profit as its final end. It was not geared to promote stable families or marital relationships on the plantations. Indian women, for probably the first time in their lives, were working and earning wages outside the home. Their relatively lesser ratio to men also gave them an edge over their sisters in India. Bahadur notes six patterns of households that took shape in the Caribbean:

> (1) A woman living alone except, perhaps, for children; (2) several men succeeding each other in a woman's home; (3) a woman passing from the home of one man to another; (4) traditionally monogamous; (5) much less frequently polygamous; and (6) some combination of three or more men and women living together without marriage. (Bahadur 2013: 87)

Owing to the shortage of women on the plantation, polyandry became a common feature in the life of the indentured. Illicit intercourse between the sexes was also common. Without women, the men turned to each other for satisfaction. However, this action carried a social stigma, not to mention that it was also punishable by law. Section 377 of the Indian Penal Code (IPC) had been introduced by the British in 1861 and was a successor to the Buggery Act of 1553 that had outlawed homosexuality in England. According to scholars Enze Han and Joseph O'Mahoney, this Act was used as a model for the legal systems in all the British colonies across the world. 'Thus, through its colonial administration, the British managed to impose and institutionalise a set of laws in its colonies that criminalized homosexual conduct' (Han 2017: 273). The 'Articles' Section of the District Court in Allahabad defines Section 377 as the Act that governs unnatural offences and reads thus, 'Whoever voluntarily has carnal intercourse against the order of nature with any man, woman or animal shall be punished with imprisonment for life, or with imprisonment for a term which may extend to 10 years, and shall be liable to fine' (*Section 377 of IPC*, 12 March 2019). The predecessor to Section 377 IPC, the Buggery Act was passed in England under the reign of King Henry VIII and had made sexual relations between men a criminal offense punishable by death. In Britain and its colonies, sodomy remained a capital offence punishable by hanging until 1861. Then, in 1885, the British Parliament '. . . passed an amendment sponsored by Henry Du Pré Labouchere, which created the offence of "gross indecency" for same-sex male sexual relations, enabling any form of sexual behaviour between men to be prosecuted' (*Encyclopedia Britannica*, 12 March 2019).

The colonial government had expected the Indian indentured men to turn to local women of African descent in the Caribbean. However, in this, the colonials did not meet much success owing to the 'mutual antipathy between the races' (Bahadur 2013: 88). Caste and race prejudice did not encourage any mixing of the blood. Further, the Indian men viewed the women of African descent as untouchables. Social anthropologist, R.K. Jain (1986: 156), in his paper 'The East Indian Culture in a Caribbean Context: Crisis and Creativity' explains that 'One of the most fascinating aspects of the initial period of interculturation among the East Indians in Trinidad is their encounter with the racist ideology'. The Creole women, in turn, thought of the Indian men to be heathens and interlopers on their land. In any case, there were enough African men for them to choose from on the islands.

During their period of indenture, the Indian women enjoyed a degree of independence as they earned their own wages. The paucity of women also accelerated their emancipation. They could leave their husbands and marry another, or simply live with him without marriage. The social mores had collapsed with the breakdown of the caste barriers. Women could also marry across caste lines. 'New hierarchies emerged across the dark waters' (Bahadur 2013: 92). When colonists emphasised that women could do in the colonies what was unthinkable in India, they negated the idea about the choices of women being necessitated by pragmatism. The *sirdars* and drivers were in greater demand for their superior rank in the plantation social order. Next in importance were those men who had served their indenture and were financially secure and stable. In some cases, they even paid off their woman's indenture. In exercising the choice to select and change partners, the indentured women were choosing their own protection. A segment already marginalized and subaltern in an alien terrain, they were bold in protesting against the sexual exploitation by the planters. Overturning the tradition of giving dowry to a bride (part of the marriage ritual in India), the parents of the brides in the Caribbean were able to demand a 'bride price' for their daughters. From being seen as a financial liability in India, they had become an economic asset to their family under the indenture system. This is not to say that their lives were easy despite the rosy picture painted by the colonials. The plantocracy (according to the online *Oxford English Dictionary*, 27 March 2019: a population of planters regarded as the dominant class, especially in the West Indies) on the one hand, and their own husbands and partners on the other, conspired as a strong force to curtail the freedom of the indentured women.

The women soon realised that the plantation was no less than a jail for them and their five-year contract no less than a sentence. Other than the full-day back-breaking task that had to be completed on the plantation, the women were expected to cook and keep home for their men. Elder women filled the role of *khelaunis* (child-minders). Young children, under the age of 10, were not allowed to go to the fields during crop time. They had to be left with the *khelaunis*. It is to these remarkable women that can be attributed the survival of Bhojpuri (the language spoken in the eastern parts of Uttar Pradesh) in the Caribbean. The immigrants who first came to the Caribbean as indentured people spoke either Khari Boli or Bhojpuri, depending on their place of origin in India. When the children of the indentured people from these two regions went to the *khelauni* they started conversing in the dominant language, which was Bhojpuri. Slowly, Khari Boli made way for Bhojpuri in the plantations. Peggy Mohan (2007: 146) informs, 'Bhojpuri is a totally different language from Hindi and is grammatically closer to Eastern languages like Bengali'. It was less fragmented in the Caribbean than it became in India and served as a 'unified *lingua franca*' for the indentured community in the plantations. In India, Bhojpuri is looked upon not as a language but as 'a chain of dialects' since the dialect changes every ten kilometres. In Trinidad, one dialect of Bhojpuri (the one spoken in the Indian village of Basti) became more dominant and displaced the others. The *khelaunis* came from this region and since the children spent a long time under their supervision, Bhojpuri became the language of the plantation. Community child-rearing practised by the women in the estates was the single most important cause for the retention of Bhojpuri in the islands. Language also gave them a collective identity. Deeda felt she was 'still in India, in a way, still speaking the same language, but living in a different Indian village' (ibid.: 136).

Indentured women were vested with the role of protectors of their culture and in tandem with their defined role, they soon converted the immigrant communities into 'imagined communities'. 'Imagined

Communities' is a term coined by political theorist Benedict Anderson (2016: 6) in his book with the same title. He '. . . depicts a nation as a socially constructed community, imagined by the people who perceive themselves as part of that group'. Anderson argued that the nation is imagined '. . . because the members of even the smallest nation will never know most of their fellow-members, meet them, or even hear of them, yet in the minds of each lives the image of their communion' (ibid.). His main argument is based on anti-colonial consciousness shaping national identities in colonised societies. The identities within the imagined communities are real and are based on a shared culture, language and history.

In *Coolie Woman*, Gaiutra Bahadur postulates how the shared culture of the *Ram Leela* (dramatic performance of the *Ramcharitmanas*) brought the immigrants together, both on and off the plantations. There were 'lavish ten-day carnivals' which brought in spectators from far and even attracted vendors,

> Telling the story, in addition to its religious and allegorical significance, provided a social life for the indentured and their descendants. They sang the Ramcharitamanas in small jam sessions called *goles*.... Invitations sometimes came from boat brothers and boat sisters on other plantations. But often, Ramayan sessions were more informal, impromptu ways to pass the evening (Bahadur 2017: 108).

In terms of assimilation and acculturation into the host culture, it was once again, the women who led the way. They adapted to the culture of the adopted land. When the indentured Indians had first arrived on the plantations, the Creoles (descendants of the African slaves) were the inhabitants of the land and the *coolies* (Indian indentured labourers) were the 'outsiders'. Marina Carter and Khal Torabully (2002: 62) have argued in *Coolitude* that, 'Colonial societies hitherto composed of Creoles and Europeans, united at least superficially, by language and religion, did not readily or quickly accept the presence of "aliens" in their midst'. R.K. Jain (1986: 154) explains that creolisation was a distinctly Caribbean process of cultural identity formation. 'It was a two-way process mainly between the Europeans and the Negroes—with the mixed or coloured population playing a catalyst role'. Within a year of indenture, the costume and diet of the Indian community came under the influence of the dominant Creole practices. The changes in Indian dance and music in the Caribbean followed the form and spirit of the Creole performances. Theorist Edward Brathwaite (1974) in *Contradictory Omens: Cultural Diversity and Integration in the Caribbean* has used the concept of 'interculturation' in the context of the Creoles and indentured Indians in the Caribbean. The Indians 'borrowed' from the Creole music to produce a hybrid Chutney music. They began to dance to the beats of Afro-Caribbean Calypso music. The women stopped wearing the traditional Indian costume *saree*. Instead, they started wearing long skirts (*ghaghra*) and long blouses (*jhula*) (Mohan 2007: 146). The *orhni* worn with this ensemble was transparent. Later, even this was replaced with a belted dress of mid-calf length with the *orhni* covering the head.

Language also underwent a major change. Creole was spoken during the day to communicate with the Creoles. Bhojpuri was spoken only among the indentured people. *Dal puri* (little fried *rotis* and lentils) was an Indian dish. It was creolised into 'doubles' (little fried *rotis* made up into sandwiches with spicy *chana* as filling). The staple *rotis* became bigger in size in the plantations. Women chose convenience over elaborate cooking. Waking up at 4 am to prepare food before going to the fields to work did not augur well for ornate meals. 'Doubles' could be eaten on the go just like sandwiches while larger-sized *rotis* meant it would take lesser time to cook them. The Creoles also borrowed from the Indians. In his article, Ravindra K. Jain (1986: 158) informs that there were common celebrations of each others' festivals. 'The Indian (Muslim) religious feast of *hossey* (known in India as *tazia)* has been observed jointly by the East Indians and Negroes at least since 1850'. He adds, 'Two cultural characteristics of this celebration, the beating of drums (*tassa*) and the playing with sticks (*gadka*), form the nuclei on which the East Indian and Negro root-traditions converge'.

One of the greatest manifestations of the 'interculturation' that was unique to the Caribbean could be witnessed during the time of carnival. Literary theorist and semiotician, Mikhail Bakhtin (1984: 10) has introduced the literary concept of 'carnivalesque', which is characterised by a mocking or satirical challenge to authority and the traditional social hierarchy. He argues that a carnival is not really a performance since it does not differentiate the spectator from the performer. It offers a site of resistance to authority and a space where cultural change can take place. The carnival thus fulfilled a dual motive—of acculturation with the dominant society of the host land and of resistance against the dominating European powers in the plantocracy. Abigail Ward, in her article, writes about the depiction of the carnival in *Jahajin*, 'One of the most striking moments suggesting a transracial connection, and even harmony, is during carnival, when the float of an African-Trinidadian friend of the narrator is devised as a sailing ship, carrying *jahajis* from India'. She believes, 'This float suggests a hybridity, or coming together of African- and Indian-Caribbean peoples and traditions which extends to its musical accompaniment' (Ward 2013: 276). 'Along with the steel band that supplied the Calypso music, they had added a whole lot of *dholaks* and *tassas* for the rhythm' (Mohan 2007: 218).

The lyrics of the calypsos also marked the ongoing change in the Caribbean society. In one calypso written by The Mighty Killer and quoted by Vijay Mishra (1996: 213) in '(B)ordering Naipaul: Indenture History and Diasporic Poetics', the words are:

Long ago was Sumitra, Ramnalawia
Bulbasia and Oosankilia
But now is Emily, Jean and Dinah
And Dons and Dorothy.

Stuart Hall (1978: 155) has theorised the East Indians (Indentured Indians) of Guyana and Trinidad as 'ethnic collectives' exemplifying the characteristics of plural cultural forms. Vijay Mishra has encapsulated the six characteristics given by Stuart Hall that define the growth and persistence of such forms,

> (1) The existence of a large, ethnically identifiable community that (2) enters the socio-economic system only after its basic structures have been formed; (3) the presence of strong cultural traditions which (4) were not broken by other competing traditions as in the case of Afro-West Indians under slavery; (5) the presence of a relatively enlightened democratic apparatus that did not insist upon either forced assimilation or ethnic cleansing; and (6) a community that can live and work under conditions where inherited cultural traditions can be both preserved and transmitted (Mishra 1996: 210).

In his seminal collection of essays, *The Location of Culture*, Homi K. Bhabha (1997: 28), speaks about the concept of 'hybridity' as an in-between third space straddling different cultures. He marks hybrid identities as '. . . neither the One … nor the Other…but something else besides'. Bhabha maintains that the hybrid operates in an interstitial space which is neither fixed nor static but allows '. . . difference without an assumed or imposed hierarchy' (ibid.: 4). In his theory of the 'third space of enunciation' he suggests that the hybrid is articulated in the liminal space that emerges during a point of interaction between two or more individuals (ibid.: 54). In other words, the third space is the space of hybridity. Indenture constituted many such third spaces—the depot, the ship, the plantation, the colony, the carnival—in each of these places, hybridity was being articulated and enunciated.

Nasser Mustapha (2012: 44), in his chapter 'Muslims in the Caribbean', informs that approximately '15 per cent of the Indian indentured immigrants were Muslims'. His research shows that owing to 'their need to preserve their faith in an alien environment, they became very defensive and introverted'. However, they managed to maintain group solidarity, which in turn helped them keep their cultural traditions alive in the plantations. They had not come to the Caribbean to settle and were constantly looking back to India. This led to persistence in their beliefs and clinging to their Indo-Muslim faith. The African slaves had been living in the colonies before the arrival of the Indian immigrants under the indenture and had resisted acculturation and conversion to Christianity. However, the rigid conditions on the plantations had made it difficult for them to retain their distinct faith and tradition. With the influx of indentured Indian Muslims, Islam was re-introduced in the Caribbean. This trajectory helped in stabilising the Islamic faith in the Caribbean, and despite the inherent differences in the practising faiths of the Muslims from Africa and the Muslims from India, they were able to reach a common consensus on compatible doctrines.

Critics Raymond Chickerie and Bibi Halma Khanam (2016: 112) in their article 'Hindustani Muslims in Guyana' state that on 5 May 1838, when the first two ships carrying indentured labourers from India reached British Guyana, they were carrying 424 passengers. Of these, 90 *jahajis* (approximately 21 per cent) were Muslims. 'The male-female ratio on the first two ships was almost 28 to one' (ibid.: 116). This shortage of women initially led to serious problems that harmed the social fabric of the Muslim family but over time, the family system recovered and the faith managed to survive and thrive. They followed the teachings of the *Holy Koran* and the word of the Prophet Muhammad and '. . . by 1891, there were 29 mosques to 33 Hindu temples' in Guyana (ibid.: 117). Owing to the shortage of women, Muslim men married Hindu women who converted to Islam. One of the major changes that took place in the Caribbean, and probably part of the process of acculturation, was that women did not practice *purdah* (the custom of covering their head and face with a veil). It hindered the women working in the plantations who finally chose convenience over an outward manifestation of faith.

One of the Muslim celebrations that became a point of harmony between the people of different faiths residing in the Caribbean was the practice of *tazia* (it was observed on the tenth day of Muharram). The festivities associated with the day '. . . took on more of a "carnival-like" atmosphere and which gradually lost its religious significance over the years' (ibid.: 124). It became so secularised that Creoles, Hindus and Muslims alike joined in the revelry and made the consumption of alcohol part of the celebrations. The Christians were concerned with the involvement of the Creoles in the festival. They feared the Creoles would be converted back to their Muslim faith and tried their best to keep them away from the celebrations.

The Hindu-Muslim relationship in the Caribbean was very cordial and friendly, unlike the relationship they shared in India. The ship had forced people of all faiths to come together in the shared space and turned them all into one collective—they were no longer Hindus or Muslims or even Brahmins or Ahirs. Instead, they were all *jahajis,* sitting together, eating from the communal pots, sleeping in the same shared space, crying together for the lost homeland and even praying and celebrating with each other. Munshi Rahman Khan, an indentured Muslim who sailed to the Caribbean in 1898 has given a first-person account, published as *An Autobiography of an Indentured Labourer,* which details his years in the islands from 1874-1972. He talks about

'. . . the Brahmins suddenly becoming Shudras. . .' on the ship. 'There was no longer any interest in maintaining the sanctity of caste and creed . . .', which in turn led to closer Hindu-Muslim relationships (Khan 2005: 78). They came from the same districts in India and spoke similar languages. In the colonies, they even helped each other build temples and mosques. The shortage of women had also led to inter-religious marriages between Hindus and Muslims.

Ravindra Jain also highlights in his article that initially, neither the British government nor the plantation officials in the Caribbean were interested in converting and binding the indentured Indians to the Catholic and Anglican Church. To them, the Indians were a labour force with an attached economic value. They categorized the *coolie* as a 'bird of passage' and believed that 'any time and effort spent on converting him was a wastage since he would necessarily revert to his heathen ways once back in India' (Jain 1986: 159). To that end, their only interest in the indentured Indian was as a labour unit involved in the generation of profits for the plantocracy.

It was the Canadian Presbyterian Church that initiated the process of converting the *jahajis.* Their missionaries did so by using education and by building schools for Indian children. In *Jahajin,* Peggy Mohan (2007: 140) has delineated the entire process of assimilation and acculturation from the telescopic lens of conversions to Christianity in Trinidad. The Canadians were 'goras, yes, but they were not British, and not French Creole … Besides they could all speak Hindi'. Further, in a bid to attract the Indians to convert, the missionaries 'Indianised' the Church for the indentured people. *Bhajans* and *kirtans* (Indian devotional songs) were sung in the churches and the missionaries spoke Hindi and Bhojpuri to communicate with the Indians.

Peggy Mohan hints at underlying tones of 'mimicry' when she suggests that conversions offered 'a chance to be seen as a serious part of a big group' (ibid.: 140). Post-colonial theorist, Homi Bhabha notes that the colonised subject tries to adopt the mannerism of the coloniser. He calls this 'mimicry' which at times can produce ambivalence since the result is a subject 'almost the same, but not quite' (Bhabha 1994: 86). Mimicry is not just blindly copying something or someone. It is to do with the colonisation of the mind of the colonized. To the racially 'othered' and victimized *coolies*, mimicking the colonists became the ultimate desire. Conversion was a step towards imitating the attitude, language and culture of the coloniser. Perhaps, the indentured people believed that conversion to Christianity would allow them, who occupied the lowest rung on the social ladder whether in India or the Caribbean, to transcend their state and come out at a higher point in the karmic wheel—be on an equal footing with the coloniser. Alternatively, there could also have been an understanding that there would be no return to the homeland and they would now have to become part of the new landscape they inhabited. Assimilating the culture of the host land would allow them to 're-caste' themselves.

As part of the cycle of conversion, the immigrants were given Christian names. 'The men could keep their Indian name as a last name, and put the Christian name first' (Mohan 2007: 141). The change in name was significant in renegotiating their identity. It indicated that they were actually Indian and part of the community. Deconstruction and reconstruction are simultaneous processes. Caste had been deconstructed on leaving India but in converting to Christianity, the immigrants had found a new identifier of belonging. Conversions also mapped a struggle that could only be won by moving up the social ladder and bettering themselves. Apart from breaking the final shackle imprisoning the immigrants to an archaic caste system, religion would give them a much-needed education. Generations later, if their descendants travelled 'home' to India, they would be able to meet the Brahmins without the burden of caste.

The Indian Hindu system of defining identity, which centred around caste had broken down in the communal depots and on the voyages undertaken by indentured people. Instead, they were subjected to racial discrimination by the colonisers. The creoles too looked down upon the Indians who had arrived to work at the plantations in their place. In *Orientalism,* Edward Said has elucidated the migrant history of settler colonies as one based on hegemony and 'othering' created by the oppressors. Race and class are both euro-centric concepts. While race has its roots in creed and skin colour, class is associated with economics. When the *jahajis* lost their anchor of caste, they felt a vacuum. So acute was the helplessness caused by this loss that some of the Indians committed suicide. The others looked at the means of survival open to them. Conversion to the dominant religion contained the seeds of assimilation and acculturation. Race could compensate them for their loss of caste. With conversion, they would be able to gain a stronger identity in the host land and escape the 'othering' that had become their lot in the Caribbean. In this reference it is important to quote Frantz Fanon (1986: 18), who suggests in his seminal book, *Black Skin, White Masks,* 'The colonized is elevated above his jungle status in proportion to his adoption of the mother country's cultural standards'. Getting an entry into Christianity would give them agency, along with economic benefits, as well as help them gain the sympathy of society. It would also give them representation. Theorist Stuart Hall (1997: 15) opines representation to be '. . . an essential part of the process by which meaning is produced and exchanged between members of a culture'.

Despite the immigrants converting to Christianity, in the hope that it would give them representation in the society, the colonists were not initially in favour of educating the entire population of the *coolies*. In 1904, Governor Swettenham officially curtailed access to education for Indian girls in Guyana. In the face of protests, he inserted a 'grace period' to appease the children's rights activists who were demanding compulsory education in the plantations:

> For the first ten years in the colony, Indian immigrants who kept their boys out of school would be spared fines for breaking the law. But no Indian, immigrant or native-born, no matter what tenure in the colony, would ever incur penalties for keeping their girl children home. The edict stayed in effect for three decades. (Bahadur 2013: 204)

The Hindu revival during this period put further brakes on the emancipation of Indian women. Lacking formal education, they were instead coached in housewifely duties and taught to be loyal and devoted to their husbands.

A telling passage from V.S. Naipaul's (1992: 78) *A House for Mr Biswas* reads thus,

> "She is a good child. A little bit of reading and writing even."
>
> "A little bit of reading and writing." Mr Biswas echoed, trying to gain time.

Seth, chewing, his right hand working dexterously with roti and bans, made a dismissing gesture with his left hand.

"Just a little bit. So much. Nothing to worry about. In two of three years, she might even forget".

This dialogue between Mr Biswas and Seth (his future father-in-law) regarding the virtues of Shama (Biswas' future wife) is evocative in its silence on Shama's point of view regarding her marriage.

The archetype of 'Sita' in the *Ramayan* as the ideal woman was placed in front of the women for them to emulate. The attempt of the Canadian Mission was to emphasise the importance of housewife duties. The identity of the women was fixed in relation to societal parameters of gender and caste. If they tried to resist the oppressive patriarchal and sociocultural claim on the Indian family, the women were at once branded immoral, abused and punished. Indian indentured women in the Caribbean thus bore the brunt of the worst kind of violence perpetrated by men.

'Othering' of indentured women in the Caribbean began even before they were recruited. The term 'othering' was coined by renowned postcolonial theorist, Gayatri Chakravarti Spivak (1994: 74) in her seminal essay 'Can the Subaltern Speak?' It is defined by her as '. . . a process by which the empire can define itself against those it colonizes, excludes and marginalizes'. By creating a postcolonial subject through its hegemonic framework, the colonial discourse silences the subaltern and pushes it to the margins. Since indenture in the Caribbean followed the abolition of slavery, the planters continued with their belief in seeing women as unproductive and did not seek their presence beyond a bare minimum in the plantations. They were unwilling to pay for the cost of an immigrating Indian woman who was perceived unproductive in the labour economy. This led to a skewed gender ratio among the first wave of indentured immigrants arriving in the Caribbean. It was only later that a set ratio of one woman to four men was enforced by the Emigration Act passed in 1860.

Even later, a certain dichotomy continued to persist in the 'type of woman' required for the plantations. A better class of woman would have been unsuitable to the hard work required in the sugarcane fields. Women of 'low moral character' were not preferred and prostitutes were immediately disqualified. Nevertheless, during the entire period that the system of indenture was in force, it was marked by a distinct shortage of women. Able-bodied male workers were very obviously preferred over women who would not have been able to complete the 'heavy work' in the plantations. The shortage of women led to social problems within the migrant community. The Indian men who had to leave behind their wives wanted to return to India. The British had realized the need for a settled community of indentured labourers in the Caribbean. A self-perpetuating community would lower the costs of recruitment and shipping, as well as the cost of the return voyage. Thus, tight controls over women indentureship were loosened to aid the plantation owners whose needs dictated the official regulations. In her article 'Women and Indentureship in Trinidad and Tobago 1845-1917: Freedom Denied', critic Rhoda Reddock (2008: 44) claims that the requirement of women was linked to the requirement of a 'self-reproducing, cheap and stable work force'. Additionally, such women were expected to bring stability in the lives of the immigrants, remain docile to their men and also work in the fields at lower wages compared to the men. Statistics show that a majority of the Indian women who indentured were single women and had accepted the agreement to work in exchange for wages.

During the initial years of indenture, the women in the colonies enjoyed a certain sense of freedom away from the set social norms prevalent back home in Indian society. This freedom, however, became the source of unmitigated sexual jealousy in the Indian men. Jeremy Poynting has pointed out in his article 'East Indian Women in the Caribbean' that the indentured experience of the indentured women was one of multiple oppression. He suggests, 'The reason for both the possibilities and the miseries of the Indian woman's experiences during the indenture period was her scarcity' (Poynting 1987: 133). The agency exercised by the women added fuel to the Indian male's inability to have sole power and monopoly over his partner. He desired to establish complete control over his woman. She did not want to let go of her new-found-freedom willingly. This created an atmosphere of hostility which was ultimately responsible for the 'wife murders' in the Caribbean.

Sexual abuse of the Indian emigrants by the officials on the ship had only been a prelude to what would come their way in the colonies. Peggy Mohan focuses sharply on the sexual molestation of Indian women by overseers on the plantations. She narrates an incident in detail, and in doing so, voices, not just the act itself but also the reaction of the Indian community to the liberty taken by the overseer. 'Her *orhni* was off her head, her clothes were dirty, and her eyes had a bright crazy look ... she rushed to pick up a *lota* and started washing herself. Then she tore off her skirt and threw it aside' (Mohan 2007: 150). The narrator gives the reader a look into the mind of the young Sunnariya who has been molested by an official on the plantation. 'The look in her eyes is something I will never forget. As if she didn't care anymore. As if there was nothing worse that could happen to her now' (ibid.: 151).

When questioned about the sequence of events, Sunnariya tells the story differently each time. It is from the reaction of her father to her molestation that one can understand the place occupied by the Indian *coolie* in the plantation hierarchy. Expected by cultural and social mores to protect his woman and his family, the indentured man could only stand mutely on the side because he is not allowed to voice his grievance. On learning that his daughter had been molested but not raped, Sunnariya's father's reaction is telling. 'At first, he cried in relief, for all he might have lost, but had not.' He then '. . . cried in outrage, as a man who was now just a *coolie*, a proud man who was expected to sit by and let things like this happen to the women in the barracks, his own daughter' (ibid.: 154). Finally, in an action that is symbolic in itself, he picks up the cutlass and tests the blade to ensure that it is sharp enough. No one stops him because all the Indians on the plantation know that he will take *badla* (revenge) for his daughter's dishonour. This was the way of things in India. Since justice in any colonial court would be denied to the victims, they were left with no other choice than to take justice into their own hands. The colonial government was under a legal obligation to respect the immigrants' culture but that was only writing on a piece of paper. In reality, the courts always sided with the plantation officials.

The indentured women on the plantation were twice victimised, both by the colonials and the Indian men alike. Sexually abused by the Europeans, they could not even look to their own men for help and protection. The sexual jealousy that pervaded the minds of the Indian men made them perpetrators of extreme violence towards their women under the guise of 'honour crimes'. Gaiutra Bahadur (2013: 103) highlights the sheer scope and volume of the violence indentured women was subjected to on the plantations. 'More than thirty-five wounds covered her body. Laungee had been cut in 18 places. While being hacked to death, she had also been beaten'. The immediate cause behind this violence was the use of the word *dougla* (mixed-breed) by Laungee while cursing her man, Badal. It was a racial slur, and to a caste-conscious Indian, it was the worst insult imaginable. The defence lawyer for Badal argued that he could not be blamed as 'his reputed wife had been unfaithful and his country's traditions dictated that he punish her' (ibid.: 104). Ironically, the word used by Laungee to curse Badal can be said to hold some truth. The quiet Indian man who had undergone indenture had indeed become a sort of mixed-breed. His actions were governed by his traditions even though he was not living in his own country.

French Algerian postcolonial theorist, Frantz Fanon (2001: 152) in *Wretched of the Earth* reveals '. . . an underlying psychosis in the subject, which is a result of the colonial oppression practised by the colonizer', thereby resulting in an identity crisis for the colonised. Fanon also exposed the 'native elite' who, along with the colonial masters, became oppressors of the 'natives'. In the plantation society, the native elites were the Indian *sirdars* who mimicked the colonisers and looked down upon the indentured Indians. The *coolies* were thus made to feel like they were second-class citizens in the host land. They were now 'thrice-marginalised'; the colonial officials and plantation owners were first on the list of social order, while the second and third place belonged to the *sirdars* and the indigenous people (ex-slaves), respectively.

Some observers attribute the blame for this horrific violence against women to an alleged 'culture of violence', which allowed for violence as an accepted code for resolving disputes by linking it to a colonial legacy. The indentured men were treated barbarically and beaten violently by the colonisers. The evolution of this culture of violence in the Caribbean was historical in nature. The region had witnessed sustained violence during the era of slavery. The emancipation of slaves and the coming of the indentured Indians did not change the mindset of the European plantation owners and the culture of violence became deeply embedded in the colonial psyche. To enforce their superiority, the plantation owners left no stone unturned to punish the *coolies*.

One of the most common forms of punishment in the colonies was flogging and '. . . managers, overseers and drivers regularly punished their workers by thrashing them… The men would have internalised this culture of violence practised on the plantations. Their masculinity must have been as battered as their bodies' (Bahadur 2013: 123). Critical theorist Homi K. Bhabha in 'Of Mimicry and Man: The Ambivalence of Colonial Discourse' has suggested the term 'ambivalence' to describe the confused and chaotic mental state of the colonised subject who wants to mimic the coloniser. He defines the relationship between the coloniser and the colonised as one of extremes. The colonised subject wants to ape the master, yet feels a strong sense of repulsion and hate for the coloniser (Bhabha 1994: 88). Thus, in their ambivalent state, the Indian indentured men internalized the violence and took to victimizing their women to express it. Once the crime had been committed in a fit of anger, the men felt a sense of remorse. It was the disappointment and frustration which were a result of the indenture that had instigated them to act in a manner alien to their culture. Anticipating the loss of their wives to another suitor kept them caged in a case of constant anxiety. Indenture had managed to drive some of the men to the brink of madness.

In her book, Gaiutra Bahadur has reproduced a pamphlet written by an indentured labourer, Lal Bihari Sharma. Composed in the form of rhymed verses, it was published in 1916 as *Damra Phag Bahar* (Phagwah Songs of Demara). Holi, the Hindu festival of colours was called *Phagwah* in the Caribbean. The songs contained in this pamphlet suggest '. . . the disappointment of place—rather than race—determined the actions of Indian men' (Bahadur 2013: 124). The following verses taken from the collection bring out the angst and turmoil faced by the men very clearly.

This country, is the country of wrongdoing.
It destroys the wisdom to tell good from bad, truth from falsehood.
It leaves no sense of *dharma*.
I left my land to come to Demara,

Where they wrote my name as coolie.
I left behind my hymns and the rest of my religion.
I abandoned the paths of the Vedas
Much to my shame. I degraded my karma
Through immoral acts. (ibid.: 124-5).

The men who committed these ghastly crimes were more disoriented than others and teetered on the brink of madness. The suicide statistics of indentured men reveal the direct link between the suicide rate and the low percentage of women in the colony. Where the percentage of women was the lowest, the rate of suicide was the highest. 'In Guiana which had one of the lowest rates, the indentured still killed themselves at twice the rate that Indians in the motherland did' (ibid.: 127). In Trinidad, the indentured men fashioned a code of honour. 'If you saw your wife with another man, you killed yourself' (ibid.: 128).

The murder of women was a common feature in all the colonies that witnessed indenture. They bore multiple forms of individual and systemic violence. Uprooted and displaced from their 'home', the women inhabited liminal spaces and occupied the place reserved by colonial hegemony for the 'other'. Historian Donald Wood (1968: 152) reveals that twenty-seven murders had been committed in Trinidad between 1859 and 1863. In each of these murders, the victim was the wife or the mistress. Between 1885 and 1890, Guyana witnessed forty murders of wives or paramours by their men. The crime scenes showed ghastly images of women killed by the cutlass (the crescent-shaped tool used in the sugar cane fields). Ironically, the weapon used to sever the bodies of the women was the same that the women had used for their emancipation—the cutlass or the machete. Frantz Fanon (2001: 149), in *The Wretched of the Earth* writes, 'Colonialism is not satisfied merely with holding a people in its grip and emptying the native's brain of all form and content. By a kind of perverted logic, it turns to the past of the people, and distorts, disfigures and destroys it'.

When the number of wife murders started gaining prominence in the public sphere, the colonial powers swung into damage control mode and tried to explain away the violence. 'The European elite—planters, government, officials, journalists and missionaries—

resorted to racist stereotypes. They cast the "wife murders" as morality plays in which place was irrelevant' (Bahadur 2013: 115). The problem was centrally situated in the dynamics of the plantation but the epistemic violence was given an inherently Indian character and the murders were blamed on '. . . the constitutional jealousy of the Oriental.' It was believed that the violence was '. . . due rather to the race than to the place' (ibid.: 116). Some of the officials even believed that it was the religion (Hinduism) that was to be blamed. None of them accepted that the violence was tied to the system of indenture and its functioning. Hindu and Muslim weddings officiated by *pundits* and *maulvis* were not recognised in Guyana which had legalised only Christian marriages until 1894. In the period before 1894, Indian children born of such 'unrecognized' unions were officially termed 'bastards'. Without the sanctity of a 'recognized' marriage, men and women found it easy to stray leading to jealousy and honour crimes.

The wife murders can also be analysed on the framework of psychologist Carl Jung's concept of the archetype to understand the psyche of the Indian men behind such violent crimes. Jung opined that universal, mythic characters—archetypes—reside within the collective unconscious of people the world over. These archetypes represent fundamental human feelings of experience and thus, evoke deep emotions (*Carl Jung* 23 February 2019). In the Indian context, the greatest archetype is the one perpetuated by the Hindu epic, the *Ramayan*. This book had been revered through the ages and held sacred by the Hindus. It was also one of the few relics that most of the *jahajis* carried from India. The *Ramacharitmanas* written by Sage Tulsidas begins in Ayodhya. This was also the origin of a large number of indentured people from the northern part of India, some even called Ayodhya home. The 14-year exile of Lord Ram was equated to their own exile from their home. Having these points in common, almost all the indentured people mapped their experiences with those of Lord Ram. Ravan, the foreigner, abducted Ram's wife Sita. The Europeans, in the garb of Ravan, had also abducted their women. There were just too many parallels to be ignored.

However, there were points of departure from the epic. Real-life and mythology can only entwine themselves so far. While Lord Ram waged war against the evil Ravan, the Indians did not have the ammunition needed to fight against the colonists. The colonisers had robbed them of speech and voice and left them in an ambivalent state. In such a situation, they looked at the *Ramayan,* which provided a solution with its treatment of Surpanakha, the archetype of an immoral woman. Ravan's sister desired both Lord Ram and his brother, Laxman. When she propositioned the brothers, Laxman cut-off her nose and ears to teach her a lesson. This, it seemed, was the 'prescribed' punishment for Indian women who were sexual transgressors. The nose represents honour and the cutting off of the nose marked the woman as someone without honour. Taking their cues from the epic, Indian men cut off the nose and ears of their errant wives and women. This act of brutality was one of the most prevalent forms of violence practised by the *coolies* on the plantations.

Still, it was the women who were the frontrunners in making the host land a 'home'. In *Jahajin*, Peggy Mohan connects the role of women in forming a collective identity from the Indian immigrants in the Caribbean:

> . . . the migration came across to me as a story of women making their way alone, with men in the background, strangers, extras. In history books it had always been the other way around: it was the men who were the main actors. But there was also this unwritten history of the birth of a new community in Trinidad. And it was women who were at the centre of the story. (Mohan 2007: 204)

The role played by the *coolie* women re-positions the (his)tory of Indian indenture as (her) story. They were the pioneers in migration, in assimilation, in acculturation, in appropriation and in keeping alive the language of their 'home land' in the Caribbean. As active agents of cultural exchange, the women negotiated identities and built a strong sense of collective consciousness that allowed them to bond together across generations. The following exchange between Deeda and Sunnariya in *Jahajin* clearly marks a departure from the way marriages were conducted in India without any consultation with the bride-to-be. Here Deeda tells Sunnariya, 'This is a different country. . . . The only way for women like us to manage in this place is to hold the wheel for ourselves. Don't tell me you are not glad for a chance to make up your mind' (Mohan 2007: 172). There was also greater bonding and a shared sense of sisterhood between the mother-in-law and daughter-in-law. 'She knew that for her own peace of mind the person who mattered most was her mother-in-law. The boy was less important' (ibid.: 175).

Despite being relegated to the margins, it was the women who understood the value of standard school education for their community. When in 1912, the first school for girls was started in Trinidad, it was the women who saved to send their daughters to school. Paradoxically, while the first generation of indentured women in the Caribbean had saved Bhojpuri and turned it into the *lingua franca* on the plantations, they were also quick to realise that it was a *tooti bhasha*, a dying language. The future would belong to the speakers of English. Even Creole was 'broken English'. To that end, the succeeding generations were dissuaded from learning Bhojpuri and Creole and were instead encouraged to learn English. 'Just as Bhojpuri had come out from the thumb of Hindi in the migration, and evolved into a lingua franca in its own right, women had emerged from seclusion and silence and fixed their eyes on the big wheel that steered the boat' (ibid.: 254). There could be no looking back to a 'home'. In the new land they had adopted as their own, they would have to find their own bearings. Vijay Mishra (1996: 220) believes that the 'Loss of language, in particular, meant loss of a special way of reading "home", but it also meant that the colonial experience now entered a more hybrid state because a foreign language had to be made into one's own'.

As indenture progressed into its next phase in the Caribbean, the independence that Indian women had enjoyed began to be curtailed by the planters. This was because they now wanted a settled Indian population that would reproduce future labour, thus cutting down their costs towards recruitment and immigration of new indentured Indians. Jeremy Poynting reveals that managers in the plantations '. . . began to exercise greater control over sexual relationships by, for instance, their power to transfer to another estate a man believed to be 'enticing' another man's wife'. He informs that '. . . some male immigrants also petitioned the Government of Trinidad for the right of a husband to prosecute an unfaithful wife and her partner' (Poynting 1987: 134).

It would be faulty to assume that the Indians were a completely helpless lot and did nothing to resist the rough treatment they faced at the hands of the plantation officials. Strikes were common in the plantation colonies. The causes for the strikes ranged from wage issues to unjust punishments and penalties and the sexual molestation of Indian women. One of the strikes on 13 October 1986 soon erupted into chaos and mayhem. 'The labourers, throwing stones, rushed the constables and freed the prisoners. They blocked bridges, allegedly cut telephone lines and ran to their barracks for impromptu weapons: cutlasses, sticks, shovels, their tools from the fields' (Bahadur 2013: 137). Other forms of resistance included individual assaults on the overseers and not coming to work on the plantations.

In the light of the negative opinions and reactions on the system of indenture and angry voices reproving it as 'another form of slavery', Indian freedom fighter and Gandhiji's mentor, Gopal Krishna Gokhle, on 4 March 1912 denounced indenture as '. . . a monstrous system, iniquitous in itself, based on fraud and maintained by force. . .' (ibid.: 156). Shortly thereafter, a movement to counter indenture was initiated in India with Gandhi at the helm of political affairs. The Indentured Coolie Protection Society, also known as The Anti-Indentured Emigration League was founded in Calcutta in 1914 with the sole objective of storming depots and rescuing recruits who had been indentured and held by force. By the end of the same year, the Viceroy in India reported to London that '. . . indenture had become the central issue of Indian politics, more embittering than any other. . .' (ibid.: 158).

A major breakthrough in the resistance movement came when women joined the protests on a call given by Gandhi. 'Women labourers suffer very much in the colonies, and hence women too should join the protest' (Gandhi 2017: 304). In India, women inundated the new viceroy, Lord Chelmsford's wife with telegrams, requesting her to urge her husband to stop indenture. One of the telegram's read, 'We are confident that as a woman and a mother, Her Excellency will appreciate the deep feelings of Indian women on this subject' (Bahadur 2013: 159). A deputation led by the poet-politician, Sarojini Naidu called upon Lord Chelmsford to impress upon him the urgent need to end indenture. C.F. Andrews, a Christian missionary, saw indenture as a legalised form of prostitution and called for its immediate end. Ensuring the end of indenture was one of the critical issues facing the Indian nationalists who had started resisting the British rule in India. By extension, the call to abolish indenture was a part of the freedom struggle that was played out in India but whose reverberations were felt globally across the colonies that had Indian immigrants working on the plantations. Towards the end of 1919, heeding to all forms of request, persuasion and resistance by the Indians, the colonial powers finally abolished indenture for good. No substitute or alternative system to replace indenture was envisaged.

When their term of indenture was complete, even before indenture was officially abolished, it was the men who envisioned a return to India. The women did not choose to repatriate. The reasons for this were varied but were all tied to a common aspect—the rigid caste system that prevailed in India. At the time of leaving, the women had known they would never be welcomed back. The rules of patriarchy that governed the social order in India would open doors for the returning men but close them for the indentured women. This was especially true for those men who had left behind wives in India. Some had remarried in the plantations while some had 'kept' women without the ritual of marriage. It would not be possible for them to explain the presence of this 'other woman' to the members of his family in India. Further, Indian society, which governed caste rules in India, would never recognise an inter-caste marriage:

> And I knew then that what had grown between Mukoon Singh and me was a part of that time we had had together in the barracks, in Trinidad. India would be a different story: in India, I would be just a *kahaar*, and he would be a *thakur*. A Rajput. Would he understand and protect me in India? Would he even see the problem? And would people there let us be happy? (Mohan 2007: 180)

Deeda's questions above bring to mind Salman Rushdie's (2018: 227) essay 'Imaginary Homelands' in which he quotes the famous opening sentence of L.P. Hartley's novel *The Go-Between*, 'The past is a different country, they do things differently there'.

In *Cartographies of Diaspora* theorist Avtar Brah (2018: 236) opines, 'The question of home, therefore, is intrinsically linked with how processes of inclusion or exclusion operate and are subjectively experienced under given circumstances'. He goes on to add that 'Not all diasporas inscribe homing desire through a wish to return to a place of "origin"'. He may well have been speaking for the ex-indentured Indian women in the Caribbean. Bahadur reports that in some cases when a man married a woman in the colonies, her presence would make it difficult for him to be reclaimed himself. She narrates the story of an ex-indentured Indian who arrived in Calcutta with his wife from British Guyana but only took her as far as the Howrah railway station. 'He told her and his child to sit while he got the tickets, and heartlessly deserted her' (Bahadur 2013: 168). The man would have been considered polluted since it was an inter-caste marriage. He would only be reclaimed by his family and Indian society after he abandoned her. This fear of being abandoned was so strong that women sometimes refused to set sail to India with their husbands and in-laws to avoid being discarded on arrival.

One of the conditions of the contract/agreement was the free return passage which the *coolies* could avail after ten years of indenture and it was the hope of return that allowed many to struggle through the harsh world of the plantations. What they did not realise perhaps, was that the intervening years, from their arrival in the plantation to their return to India, would have changed them completely. In India, they would become the 'outsiders'. They would have to leave the 'familiar temporariness' (Naipaul 1992: 174). Critic Vijay Mishra (1996: 227) discusses the many stories that have been 'handed down about people who returned, some true, some apocryphal, yet they all tell the same tales of disillusionment'. He also quotes Seepersad Naipaul who recreates the stories of returning Indians 'who wanted to come back to Trinidad as soon as they reached Calcutta'. Mishra believes that this '. . . suggests the usual difficulties encountered by the returnees: loss of caste, loss of language, and the simple fact that the experience of Trinidad had changed them for good'. In Calcutta, '. . . they add to the congested colony of colonial down-and-outs, or *tapuwallahs*, as the repatriates from the colony are contemptuously called' (ibid.: 202). Peggy Mohan's (2007: 181) narrator in the novel, Deeda, also talks about the letters they received in Trinidad from the returnees. 'Their letters all asked the same question: can you arrange for us to come back'? They had realised as had Naipaul (1986: 49), 'Our own past was, like our idea of India, a dream'. The dream had existed right from the beginning. Bahadur too brings out this fact in her narrative:

> In 1838, the year the Indians first arrived in the West Indies, a third of the coolies on the Plantation Belle Vue escaped by night. Twenty-two ran. They crossed the broad, silty, shark-filled Demerara by boat and wandered in the woods on the other side, searching for a way back to India. Eventually, they were found in a solitary stretch of cane field, hungry and exhausted (Bahadur 2013: 163).

During the initial days of indenture and soon after arriving at the plantations, the dream of a return caused many Indians to get disoriented and become desperate enough to believe that they could cut a path across to India from the Caribbean. Many died in their quest to return home. The *Ramayan* guaranteed a return. Lord Ram had been able to find his way back to Ayodhya after traversing plains, cutting across jungles and crossing oceans. The promise of return was also included in the agreement to indenture that the *coolies* had signed. However, just like the other terms of the contract which stood out for their duplicity, the return was also never certain.

The single-minded devotion to return to India was always at the forefront in the minds of the indentured people. Despite the written contract, the plantation owners did not follow a single policy concerning the free return passage to India. The terms of their promise kept changing over the years depending on the cheaper course of action available at the time. They weighed the idea of whether to continue bringing more temporary immigrants from India or set up the already indentured labourers. Towards the latter half of the indenture period, their ideas became more concrete. The plantation officials wanted the labourers to make a permanent home in the Caribbean, who would in turn produce a future generation of workers for the plantations. This idea contained echoes of slavery in which the children born of slaves became the property of the plantation owners on their birth. So strong was the desire to return 'home' to India that even a minor delay from the stipulated time period of the contract felt like a betrayal to the immigrants. Bahadur describes in detail the consequences faced by the plantation officials when they affected a delay in the return of the first group of indentured people:

> Ten men marked X next to their names on the sworn statement, which read, 'We want to go back to our own country. Our *matties* all want to go. They tell us to say so. … We don't want to wait. We want to be sent immediately to our home country, according to our agreement when we left home.' As a group, they refused their rations of rice and saltfish. They stopped eating for days. Then, when they could refuse no longer, they insisted on paying for food. They feared that accepting rations would leave them in debt and further indentured to the planters. (ibid.: 165)

Sometime in 1869, the colonial governments in the Caribbean islands decided to make an offer of ten acres of land instead of a free return passage to India. Some plantations even offered money as an incentive to stay in the colony instead of the return passage to India. Still, the dream of return persisted in the hearts and minds of the indentured Indians. When offers and incentives didn't work, the planters started putting obstacles on the return. To extend their stay in the plantations, the planters required the *coolies* to work for ten years (increased by a double from the earlier contracts of five years duration) in the plantations. Yet another approach was to make the *coolies* pay a part of the cost for their return. 'By 1898, ex-indentured men in Guiana had to pay for half their tickets home, and women, one-third' (ibid.).

Those who returned discovered that the landscape of India they had left had changed beyond recognition. Despite the extravagant amount they paid to restore them to their caste, they continued to face rejection by their kin and community. Tales abound of not being allowed to share the village well, among other mundane things like sharing a *hookah.* When the time came to marry their sons and daughters, they faced rejection owing to their caste being 'polluted'. Their own people shunned them as *tapuhas* or islanders (ibid.: 169).

Bahadur also quotes Gandhi, who despaired that indenture had turned the Indians into 'social lepers, not even knowing the language of the people' (ibid.). In 1920, when indenture was abolished, many of the ex-indentured people returned 'home' to be fleeced by everyone. Those who had not been able to save for their return landed up malaria-ridden, jobless and destitute in the slums of Calcutta. She cites C.F. Andrews, who compared the returnees to 'spirits thronging at the edge of the River Styx, which divides the living from the dead, "stretching forth their hands in sick longing for the other shore"' (ibid.: 170).

The ex-indentured labourers who had returned to India found they could no longer fit into the social milieu and landscape of India. They were cast adrift and didn't know where to go. The imagined homecoming had turned into an 'impossible mourning'. Having been rebuffed by their India, the ex-indentured Indians now clamoured to leave and return to the Caribbean. They were willing to do whatever was necessary to aid their return to the islands. 'Within six months of arriving, more than eighty-four repatriates showed up at British consulates in Calcutta and Madras agitating to go' (ibid.: 171). Women, as mentioned earlier, had chosen to stay on in the colonies and not repatriate to India. This was not because they did not long for a homecoming or that their sense of nostalgia was non-existent. Instead, going by Bahadur's ancestor Sujaria's reason for not returning to India, '. . . perhaps she knew that India was best kept in the past—that it would stay sweet as long as she shed tears for it, but never held and beheld it. Perhaps she was wise enough to know the subtle tricks nostalgia plays . . .' (ibid.: 172).

For the indentured diaspora, the notion of home continually brought memories and images of the journey, the ensuing displacement in the new land, seeking both 'roots' to anchor in the new homes, as well as 'routes' to return to the original home. Manpreet Kaur and Sanjaleen Prasad (2017: 154), the authors of 'Home, Migration and New Identities: Some Reflections' suggest, 'Nostalgia or reminiscing the past is yet something that a migrant is engrossed in … being far away from the homeland, the migrant continues to romanticize the homeland.' They argue that this aspect '. . . poses a barrier between the past and the present. The past lingers in the subconscious of the migrant and frequently surfaces through memory . . .'. This pensive longing for a past that exists only in memory gave rise to melancholia in the immigrants' life. Literary critic Eli Park Sonrensen (2010: 19) has suggested that '. . . melancholia is incomplete mourning that leads to schizophrenia. . .'.

To seek a cure for their feelings of betrayal, pain and distress, the indentured men on the plantations turned to alcohol in order to numb the feelings of despair. They drank as a strategy for survival and to endure the harsh conditions they faced on the plantations. 'Alcohol consumed in the company of mates, downed with the equally downtrodden, became their escape when the promises of the recruiters proved illusory' (Bahadur 2013: 203).

Rum was a by-product of sugar and was made from the fermented molasses of sugar cane. The British had introduced rum as medicine to the emigrants in the depots in India. Even before they had left for the Caribbean, alcohol had become a weakness for the indentured men. Once they reached the plantations, it became a pastime. Bahadur quotes British civil servant D.W.D. Comins, who while travelling across Demerara witnessed, '. . . coolies from the north-west who had never tasted liquor in their own country, boozing in the verandah of a rum shop. . .' (ibid.: 202). The Indians had got *ganja* (marijuana) with them to the Caribbean and initially used the drug to help them forget their sorrows. They even planted it in the islands and made a profit growing and selling it in the islands. However, the planters plotted with the missionaries and the colonial officials to turn the indentured Indians to drink rum. The officials, in order to turn the *coolies* to drinking rum, imposed a heavy license fee on growing and selling *ganja*. Converting the *ganja* smokers into rum drinkers was a win-win situation for the planters, who controlled the rum-making process in the colonies. Apart from accruing profits from the sale of alcohol, they were assured of the Indians drowning their grievances in the liquor. Tinker (1993: 212-13) observed the Governor of Mauritius saying, 'I have seen since I came to Mauritius, more instances of drunkenness among Indians than I witnessed during the whole period of my service in India'.

Alcohol consumption may have numbed the disappointment with the institution for the *coolies* but it made them fall into debt owing to spending all their hard-earned wages at the rum stores. 'Their survival strategy proved self-destructive in the long run, trapping them in multigenerational cycles of poverty and heavy drinking from which many of their descendants are still struggling to emerge' (Bahadur 2013: 203). Needless to say, there is a direct correlation between alcohol consumption and the wife murders on the plantations which have been well documented by many researchers. Thus, alcoholism in the indentured population in the colonies was also a by-product of colonialism.

The experience of women in indenture was more intense than that of their male counterparts. Contrary to the belief that they played a passive role in the indenture, the women played a truly active role in transpositioning the community in its new location. They had come as workers and not as dependents. The move from India to the Caribbean was not just physical or geographical transportation but also paralleled an emotional shift in their sensibilities with the surfacing of an existential dilemma—that of their identity in the new land. During the early days of the indenture, women did possess agency and negotiated their own terms of survival. In doing so they built a community in the Caribbean that had features of the Indian ethos, yet was distinct from the male-dominated culture that had existed in the homeland. 'The face of the Bhojpuriya community in India seemed to be male.... The female energy released in the migration must have come as a shock' (Mohan 2007: 254).

When the indenture contracts started expiring after the requisite period had been fulfilled, ex-indentured Indians (the ones who had chosen not to return to India) moved from the plantations to nearby villages to begin a 'free' life in the adopted land. In the shift, the Indian family system which had been rendered ineffective as an institution started to get reconstructed. To reconstitute the institution of family, women had to once again retreat into the domestic sphere. They did so willingly, sacrificing their 'freedom' to salvage their family. It was done for the sake of survival, '. . . the family was a collective economic unit, based on a division of labour by sex, with women working unpaid at home.' It was '. . . rebuilt on concrete pillars of custom, religion and strictly defined gender roles' (Bahadur 2013: 206).

Sociologist Patricia Mohammad (2002: 167) has described the women's acceptance as 'the collusions of women with Indian tradition to ensure the survival of the community'. Critic Sheila Ramprasad (2012: 187) reports that the ex-indentured Indian women in the domestic sphere were '. . . imaged according to a five-point ideal of womanhood—chastity, devotion towards husband, mistress of the house, to produce children who are good citizens and useful to the society, and to bring forth peace and happiness in the family and society'. Indian women in indenture were thus, both victims and agents. They played multi-layered roles in creating an Indian society in the Caribbean and were visible as a collective noun of traumatised gendered bodies.

The *jahajis* in the Caribbean experienced the trauma of uprooting and displacement on a very large scale. They moved through liminal spaces seeking connections with the host land and reconnections with the homeland while continuing to occupy the position of the 'other' in both lands. They were always on the outside looking in. From their subaltern place in the margins, they learned new ways of coping and belonging by building structures that would prove resilient and strong in the face of the hopelessness and despair that they faced in pervasive ways. The women fostered a sense of agency and despite all odds, were successful in rebuilding the family structure in the adopted land. Through their common experience of trauma, they collectivized their struggles in the alien land and engineered spaces of belonging. Homi K. Bhabha (1997: 246) seems to concur with this view when he writes, 'It is from those who have suffered the sentence of history—subjugation, domination, diaspora, displacement—that we learn our most enduring lessons for living and thinking'.

It is imperative to rediscover the muted and silenced voices of indenture '. . . so that the *coolie* can be effectively revoiced' (Torabully 2002: 214). Writers of indenture literature have been able to successfully capture the essence of the experience of indenture through grand narratives detailing the forced migration. The following chapter will take a close look at the varied and critical narrative techniques utilized by the authors to bring out the sensibility of the indentured diaspora.

WORKS CITED

Allen, Richard B., 'New Perspectives on the Origins of the "New System of Slavery"', *The Legacy of Indian Indenture: Historical and Contemporary Aspects of Migration and Diaspora,* ed. Maurits S. Hassankhan, Lomarsh Roopnarine and Hans Ramsoedh, New Delhi: Manohar, 2016.

Anderson, Benedict, *Imagined Communities: Reflections on the Origin and Spread of Nationalism,* Mandaluyong City: Anvil Publishing, 2016.

Andrews, C.F., *Impressions of British Guiana,* Chicago: Adams Press, 2007.

'Articles', *Section 377 of Indian Penal Code*, Web. 12 March 2019, <http://districtcourtallahabad.up.nic.in/articles/IPC.pdf >

Bahadur, Gaiutra, *Coolie Woman: The Odyssey of Indenture*, London: Hatchette, 2013.

Bakhtin, Mikhail, *Rabelais and His World*, tr. Helene Iswolsky, Bloomington: Indiana University Press, 1984.

Bhabha, Homi, 'Of Mimicry and Man: The Ambivalence of Colonial Discourse', *The Location of Culture*, New York: Routledge, 1994: pp. 85-92.

———, *The Location of Culture*, New York: Routledge, 1997.

Bhatt, Sujata, *Point No Point: Selected Poems*, Manchester: Carcanet Press Ltd., 2014.

Brah, Avtar, 'Cartographies of Diaspora', *The Routledge Diaspora Studies Reader*, ed. Kalus Stierstorfer and Janet Wilson, Oxon: Routledge, 2018, pp. 235-8.

Brathwaite, Edward, *Contradictory Omens: Cultural Diversity and Integration in the Caribbean*, Jamaica: Mona, 1974.

Chickerie, Raymond and Bibi Halma Khanam, 'Hindustani Muslims in Guyana: Tradition, Conflict and Change, 1838 to the Present', *Indentured Muslims in the Diaspora*, ed. Maurits S. Hassankhan, Goolam Vahed and Lomarsh Roopnarine, New Delhi: Manohar, 2016, pp. 109-40.

Dutt, Romesh C., *The Economic History of India in the Victorian Age,* vol. II, New York: August M. Kelley Publishers, 1969.

Fanon, Frantz, *Black Skin, White Masks*, London: Pluto Press, 1986.

———, *The Wretched of the Earth*, tr. Constance Farrington, New Delhi: Penguin Group, 2001.

Gandhi, Mahatma, *The Collected Works of Mahatma Gandhi,* London: Andesite Press, 2017.

'Gay Rights Movement', *Encyclopedia Britannica,* Web. 12 March 2019, <https://www.britannica.com/topic/gay-rights-movement#ref1077994>

Gilroy, Paul, *The Black Atlantic: Modernity and Double Consciousness*, London: Verso, 2007.

Gupta, Charu, '"Innocent" Victims/"Guilty" Migrants: Hindi Public Sphere, Caste and Indentured Women in Colonial North India', *Modern Asian Studies* 49.5, 2015, pp. 1345-77, Web. 21 February 2019.

Hall, Stuart, 'Cultural Identity and Diaspora', *Diaspora and Visual Culture: Representing Africans and Jews,* ed. Nicholas Mirzoeff, NewYork: Routledge, 2014, pp. 35-47.

———, 'Pluralism, Race, and Class in Caribbean Society', *Race and Class in Post-Colonial Society: A Study of Ethnic Group Relations in the English-Speaking Caribbean, Bolivia, Chile and Mexico,* Paris: UNESCO, 1978, pp. 150-82.

———, 'The Work of Representation', *Representation: Cultural Representations and Signifying Practices*, ed. Stuart Hall, London: Sage, 1997, pp. 15-64.

Han, Enze and Joseph O'Mahoney, 'British colonialism and the Criminalization of Homosexuality', *Cambridge Review of International Affairs* 27.2, 2017, pp. 268-88.

Jain, Ravindra K., 'The East Indian Culture in a Caribbean Context: Crisis and Creativity', *India International Centre Quarterly* 13.2, 1986, pp. 153-64.

Jung, Carl, 'Concept of Archetypes at Carl Jung', *Carl Jung*, Web. 22 February 2019, <https://www.carl-jung.net/archetypes.html>

Kaur, Manpreet and Sanjaleen Prasad, 'Home, Migration and New Identities: Some Reflections', *Fijian Studies* 15.1, 2017, pp. 145-58.

Khan, Munshi Rahman, *Autobiography of an Indian Indentured Labourer: Munshi Rahman Khan 1874-1972,* tr. Kathinka Sinha-Kerkhoff, Delhi: Shipra Publications, 2005.

Mahabir, Kumar, *Indian Diaspora in the Caribbean*, New Delhi: Serials Publications, 2011.

Mangru, Basdeo, *Indians in Guyana: a Concise History from Their Arrival to the Present,* Chicago, IL: Adams Press, 2000.

Mishra, Vijay, '(B)ordering Naipaul: Indenture History and Diasporic Poetics', *Diaspora: A Journal of Transnational Studies* 5.2, 1996, pp. 189-237.

Mohammad, Patricia, *Gender Negotiations among Indians in Trinidad, 1917-1945*, London: Palgrave, 2002.

Mohan, Peggy, *Jahajin*, New Delhi: HarperCollins, 2007.

Mustapha, Nasser, 'Muslims in the Caribbean', *Indian Diaspora in the Caribbean: History, Culture and Identity,* ed. Ratan Lal Hangoo, New Delhi: Primus Books, 2012, pp. 43-54.

Naipaul, V.S., *A House for Mr Biswas*, New Delhi: Penguin, 1992.

———, 'Prologue to an Autobiography', *Finding the Center: Two Narratives*, New York: Vintage Books, 1986.

Northrup, David, *Indentured Labor in the Age of Imperialism, 1834-1922*, Cambridge: Cambridge University Press, 1995.

'Plantocracy' *Oxford English Dictionary,* Web. 27 March 19, <https://en.oxforddictionaries.com/definition/plantocracy>

Poynting, Jeremy, 'East Indian Women in the Caribbean: Experience and Voice', ed. David Dabydeen and Brinsley Samaroo, *India in the Caribbean*, London: Hansib, 1987, pp. 133-80.

Ramprasad, Sheila, 'Jahaji Behen? Feminist Literary Theory and the Indian Presence in the Caribbean', *Global Indian Diaspora: History, Culture and Identity,* ed. Ajay Kumar Sahoo and Laxmi Narayan Kadekar, Jaipur: Rawat Publishers, 2012, pp. 184-207.

Reddock, Rhoda, 'Women and Indentureship in Trinidad and Tobago 1845-1917: Freedom Denied', *Caribbean Quarterly* 54.4, 2008, pp. 41-68.

Roopnarine, Lomarsh, 'East Indian Indentured Emigration to the Caribbean: Beyond the Push and Pull model', *Caribbean Studies* 31.2, 2003, pp. 97-134.

Rushdie, Salman, 'Imaginary Homelands', *The Routledge Diaspora Studies Reader*, ed. Kalus Stierstorfer and Janet Wilson, Oxon: Routledge, 2018, pp. 227-9.

Spivak, Gayatri C., 'Can the Subaltern Speak?', *Colonial Discourse and Post-Colonial Theory: A Reader*, ed. Patrick Williams and Laura Chrisman, Hertfordshire: Harvester Wheatsheaf, 1994, pp. 66-111.

Sorensen, Eli Park, *Postcolonial Studies and the Literary: Theory, Interpretation and the Novel,* London: Palgrave Macmillan, 2010.

Tinker, Hugh, *A New System of Slavery: The Export of Indian Labour Overseas 1830-1920,* London: Hansib, 1993.

Torabully, Khal and Marina Carter, *Coolitude: An Anthology of the Indian Labour Diaspora*, London: Anthem Press, 2002.

Ward, Abigail, 'Assuming the Burden of Memory: The Translation of Indian Indenture in Peggy Mohan's *Jahajin*', *The Journal of Commonwealth Literature* 48.2, 2013, pp. 269-86.

Wood, Donald, *Trinidad in Transition: The Years after Slavery*, Oxford: Oxford University Press, 1968.

CHAPTER 4

The Aesthetics of Narrative: Poetics of Indenture

'There are two kinds of tales, one true and the other false'
(Plato 2013: 376e)

NARRATIVES OF INDIAN indenture are rooted in the specific history of physical displacement and relocation, as well as of cultural transformation. They can be placed within the broad framework of post-colonial texts, diaspora discourse and migration studies. Indenture narratives carry within their folds, within the signs and the language itself, the history of trauma that is part and parcel of postcolonial writing. Philologist Ogaga Ifowodo (2013: xiii) reinforces this aspect of writing with his '. . . view of colonialism as a shattering historical trauma'.

At the same time, Donna McCormack's *Queer Postcolonial Narratives and the Ethics of Witnessing* redefines the traditional postcolonial trauma theory which depicted the witness as a professional listener who used to play out and theorise the testimony of the victims. She suggests that in its new character, the postcolonial narrative supports '. . . the willingness of listeners to take on the responsibility for an endless narrative that they must translate from embodied exchanges into a comprehensible language that is still largely incoherent in form' (McCormack 2014: 36). Vijay Mishra (2015: 382) reinforces her point of view and opines, 'Her book draws attention to the ways in which traumatic histories are shared and internalized.... To listen is to reciprocate, to be part of the experience and as such participate precisely in those bodily effects that trauma theorists have relegated to "linguistic narrativization"'.

Writers of indenture literature use various narrative techniques and devices to highlight and bring out the themes of the experiences. Despite the expression of a shared experience, what makes their works similar to or different from each other depends on the technique of narration used in their works. Before analysing the texts, it is important to answer the questions that pertain to narrative, narration and narrative techniques. This will provide an essential framework to evaluate the texts as well as the narrative skills utilised by the authors in their works. Barbara Hardy (1987: 31) defines narrative as a 'primary act of mind' and observes that '. . . we dream in narrative, remember, anticipate, hope, despair, believe, doubt, plan, revise, criticize, construct, gossip, learn, hate and love by narrative'.

In *The Cambridge Introduction to Narrative* (hereafter referred to as *CIN*), Porter Abbott (2018: 1) traces the history of the term 'narrative' to inform that it etymologically derives from the Sanskrit word *gna*, which means 'to know'. He further informs that it comes from the Latin words *gnarus* (knowing) and *narro* (telling). This links the twin purpose of a narrative 'to know and to tell'. Abbott considers a minimalistic definition of narrative to be 'a universal tool for knowing as well as telling, for absorbing knowledge as well as expressing it' (ibid.: 10). Gerald Prince (1982: 4) defines it as 'the representation of real or fictive events and situations in a time sequence'. He expands on this definition to incorporate '. . . the representation of at least two real or fictive events or situations in a time sequence neither of which presupposes nor entails the other' (ibid.). Thus, the narrative is a set of events narrated by a narrator to a narratee.

Almost all theorists have defined narrative with an insistence upon the importance of time and sequence in the events that unfold in the narration. The presence of the temporal aspect in the definition of narrative has given rise to the interchangeable use of the terms 'story' and 'narrative'. Gerard Genette (1981: 13) distinguishes between the two with the commonly accepted distinction of a story incorporating the totality of the narrated events and a narrative comprising a discourse, whether oral or written, of the narrated events.

Narrative techniques are thus important tools for the author to present his or her view to the world. Creating a narrative involves the employment of several techniques and literary devices. It is easy for the reader to neglect the framing devices that an author uses in the narrative. The introduction and preface are often overlooked as are the epigraphs. John Mullan (2006: 10) in *How Novels Work* mentions that the author owes a contract to the reader to introduce the work through a preface or introduction before thrusting into it. He believes that apart from the introduction, the title is a common form of 'authorial guidance' (ibid.: 14). The title is expected to offer clues and inform the reader about the protagonist or the setting or the location or event or content matter or theme of the work. It should justify the subject matter of the narrative (ibid.: 15).

In *Coolie Woman: The Odyssey of Indenture*, author Gaiutra Bahadur explains in the 'Preface', her controversial use of the word 'coolie' in the title:

> Much depends on who is using the word and why. I have chosen it because it is true to my subject. My great-grandmother was a high-caste Hindu.... But she left India as a "coolie".... The power of her colonisers to name and misname her formed a key part of her story. To them, she was a coolie woman, a stock character possessing stereotyped qualities, which shaped who she was by limiting who she could ever be. The word coolie, in keeping with one of its original meanings, carries this baggage of colonialism on its back. It bears the burdens of history. (Bahadur 2013: xxi)

The preface makes it clear to the reader what to expect in the narrative. Some of the keywords used, such as 'colonialism' and 'history', highlight the scope of the text. In an interview with Annie Paul conducted by *The Margins*, Bahadur expands on her reasons:

> If we scrub our words clean, we can't scrub our history clean. We can't sanitise it that way. These workers, the indentured labourers, were coolies. . . . I'm not rebranding them with that stigma by using the word in my title; I'm acknowledging the stigma. The main reason for using it was metaphorical, figurative because a coolie carries baggage. A coolie bears a burden. To me, that perfectly sums up the position of indentured women.... They had to carry the weight of expectations: the expectation that they represent the honour of a culture, that they preserve a culture, so that's why I used it. (Paul 31 March 2014)

The 'Introduction' written by John Dunham Kelly in Sanadhya's *My Twenty-One Years in the Fiji Islands* also prepares the reader with the contents of the narrative. It is a long introduction (running into 31 pages) and comprises several navigational headings, such as 'The Book and its Authors', 'How to Read this Book' and 'Who should Read this Book', which help appraise the reader about the content of the book. The author informs the reader at the onset that in this book, '. . . themes include (1) the tricks and deceits of the recruiters, (2) the loss of caste and social and moral degeneration in the lines, (3) the harshness and brutalities of white overseers, and (4) girmit life as a time of hardships and problems in general' (Sanadhya 1991: 14).

Rajendra Prasad, in his book, *Tears in Paradise*, gives a subtitle—'A Personal and Historical Journey'. In the 'Introduction' he attributes his desire to write this book to 'the small flame of passion that my *Daadaji* (paternal grandfather) and my *Daadiji* (paternal grandmother) had lit in my heart at a tender age' (Prasad 2010: 9). Thus, the reader is made aware that the author has a personal stake in writing this book. Personal narration can hardly be objective in nature but the use of the word 'historical' in the subtitle ensures objectivity in the work. Prasad claims that his observations in the book are based on several interviews and written sources of information. Since Prasad is a third-generation descendent of an ex-indentured labourer in Fiji, he voices the '. . . strong psychological impact on the lives of succeeding generations … who have inherited the stigma of shame . . .' (ibid.: 11).

The next most important thing after the title and introduction or preface is the opening sentence of the narrative, which should be arresting enough to attract the readers. The opening statement can also offer a clue to the point of view of the narration. Once the opening has been established, the narrative moves into the main part of the story or event/s that are being narrated. At this juncture, two pertinent questions arise, but they are both answered by a further reading of the narrative—who is telling the story? Is he/she an 'overt' or 'covert narrator'; and from whose 'point of view' is the narrative being relayed? Is it a 'first', 'second' or 'third person' narrator? Before discussing the other narrative techniques utilized by the author in the work, it is essential to broaden the understanding of these terms mentioned in the previous sentence. The person who relays the story is called a narrator and the act of relaying that he/she performs is termed as narration. *The Routledge Encyclopedia of Narrative Theory* (hereafter referred to as *RENT*) suggests that '. . . the image of the author is constructed not only based on text-internal clues but also based on knowledge derived from paratexts and other sources . . .' (Herman 2008: 33). The presence or 'implied' presence of a narrator influences the narrative to a varying degree.

Any discussion on the 'point of view' remains incomplete without looking at Genette's influential concept of analysing narrative technique. He notes that the earlier studies have '. . . conflated two distinct concepts, *voice* (who speaks) and *vision* (who sees or perceives)' (ibid.: 372). He objects to the earlier way of distinguishing who is speaking by referring to the grammatical person as inadequate. According to Genette, any narrator can say 'I' and so he suggests distinguishing the narrators based on their mode of participation in the narration. In *Narrative Discourse Revisited*, he classifies the narrators who participate or did participate in the events being narrated as 'homodiegetic' and those who do not or did not participate as 'heterodiegetic' narrators (Genette 1980: 244-5). Mullan (2006: 68) argues that '. . . the more characters known, the more viewpoints represented, the more difficult it becomes to maintain narrative coherence'.

Based on point of view, there are three types of narrators or narrations—first person, second person and third person. *A Dictionary of Literary Terms* offers a preliminary frame of reference for analysing the narrations. 'In the first-person narrative, the narrator speaks as "I", and is to a greater or lesser degree, a participant in the story' (Baldick 2008: 301). In this case, the story is presented by a narrator who is also a character in the narrative. All the key texts taken in this study are written in the first-person point of view. Invariably, the story revolves around the narrator as the protagonist and allows his or her innermost thoughts to be conveyed to the reader. Peggy Mohan and Gaiutra Bahadur follow this narrative technique in their works which are being studied here. It is the narrator's point of view that dictates the actions, opinions, biases and judgements in the text. This also holds true for the narration style followed by Rajendra Prasad.

Thus, the narrator provides and withholds information based on his or her own understanding of other characters and situations. Totaram Sanadhya's text also follows this proviso.

In a 'second-person point of view', the 'story gets told as an address by the narrator to a person he calls the second-person persona "you", who is represented as experiencing that which is narrated' (ibid.: 304). The second person can either be a specific fictional character or the reader of the story. This mode of narration is agreed to be the rarest mode in literature.

In the third person narrative, the narrator is someone outside the narrative and refers to all the characters in the story by their names or as 'he', 'she' or 'they'. This mode of narration offers the greatest flexibility to the author and is thus, the most commonly used narrative mode in literature. The third-person narrator stands outside the events and is completely separate from the other characters in the story. The third person singular is the most common form of narrative used by writers. It is equally common to find the singular and plural being used together in the same narrative but at different times, depending upon the number of characters being referred to at that given moment in the story.

There is, however, one drawback to the third person point of view. Unlike the first-person narration, this mode of narration does not provide adequate knowledge of the inner landscape of the focal character. The third person narrator does, however, have access to the unvoiced thoughts and ideas of all the characters in the work. This mode of narration can also be plotted along subjective/objective lines. A third person subjective narrator describes the thoughts and feelings of the character/s, while the objective narrator does not. In this case, the narrator conveys the thoughts and feelings of one or more characters in the text. The third person objective narrator tells the story in an objective and unbiased manner which excludes any description of a character's thoughts, opinions or feelings. Third-person point of view can also be held by an 'omniscient' narrator; one who has complete knowledge of the time, place, people and events in the literary text, or by a 'limited' narrator, meaning one who has complete knowledge about a single character but is 'limited' to knowing only those things that the particular character knows. The third person omniscient point of view is the most common form of narration. In this, the narrator appears to speak in the voice of the author and assumes an omniscient perspective to the story being told. Such a view permits a large-scale analysis of the character through a mental analysis by a narrator who has access to the unspoken thoughts, words and actions of all the characters in the text. Some texts also have an 'alternating point of view' in which it is common to find a shift in the mode of narration from the first person point of view to the third person narrator's perspective.

Genette (1980: 35) also offers a technique to look at temporal relations in narratives through his advancing the concepts of 'order, duration and frequency'. He looks at 'order' which concerns the relation between the succession of events in the story (chronological sequence) and their arrangement in the narrative (discourse sequence). The two sequences may either correspond or deviate either through *analepsis* (flashback) or *prolepsis* (flash-forward). 'Duration' is the term used to establish a connection between the length of time taken by the events in the story and the length in discourse time, while "frequency" refers to the number of times the events occur and the number of times they are recounted in the narrative' (ibid.: 36).

In *analepsis*, the narrative goes back in time from where the story currently is with respect to the point of time. It is a technique used to recollect and narrate what happened in the past, leading to the chain of events that have moulded the story to its current place in time. *Analepsis* is crucial in filling the gaps and creating a back-story. It is generally presented as memories of the characters and explains their background. Genette has used this narration to refer to an event after its occurrence. Both these devices are used to re-order the chronological sequence of a story by either going back or forward in the order of events. The *prolepsis*, on the other hand, takes the story forward in time from where it has reached in the narrative. It informs about the events that will take place in the future.

Rajendra Prasad, Gaiutra Bahadur and Peggy Mohan have all used *analepsis* in their narratives. As an observer and participant in history, Totaram Sanadhya begins his narration after returning to India from Fiji. When he goes back in memory to recount his experience of the indenture, he travels a great distance (to the physical landscape of

Fiji) and goes far back in time (twenty-one years earlier) to recall the events. He follows a linear narrative and opens the text with his birth, 'I was born in 1876, in Hirangau (Firozabad), in the Sanadhya family' (Sanadhya 1991: 32). Sanadhya then accelerates to describing the death of his father eleven years later and the dwindling fortunes of his family. Genette (1980: 87) believes that a narrative of uniform speed, or what he terms an isochronous narrative, does not exist. The duration or speed in narration is calculated based on the amount of text, i.e. the number of words, sentences, paragraphs or pages that are written to describe the event in storytime. In the next three paragraphs (acceleration) Sanadhya describes leaving his town in search of work. Subsequently, he is misled by an *akrati* within two months of reaching the town of Prayag and failing to find any employment. The speed of actual time in the text remains constant but the speed of the narrative fluctuates.

Generally, the past tense is used in narration since it follows in logic that the event being narrated has already been experienced in the past and it is now over. The present tense is used to emphasize the immediacy of the narrative. Since all the key texts narrate the experience of indenture as an occurrence in the past, they make use of the past tense in their narratives. Sanadhya narrates the story of his life, starting from his birth in India and includes his travel to and return from Fiji after undergoing indenture in the plantation colony. He thus uses the past tense to retell (his) story. Prasad, Bahadur and Mohan narrate the experience of the indenture of their ancestors who had served as indentured labourers in Fiji and the Caribbean, respectively. Since they are writing about a past from the present, they use the past tense in their writings. Indenture literature writers travel both mentally and physically between India and the plantations. Sometimes the authors shuffle between the remote past and the recent past but the tension remains constant. On the surface, the narrative looks episodic or fragmented, broken in different time-space, and jumps from one event or incident to another. This shows the use of memory by the narrator.

The diasporan sensibility of the writers of indenture literature contributes significantly to the variety and scope of their writing techniques. It gives them the ability to express their thoughts clearly, concisely and meaningfully. They capture the indentured Indians' conflict and dilemma, as well as their sorrows and sufferings. Their skill of narration, characterisation and stylistic virtuosity provides a deeper understanding of the subject.

'Can the Subaltern Speak?' asks postcolonial theorist Gayatri Chakravorty Spivak (1994: 98) in her celebrated essay by the same name, and subsequently proceeds to emphasise the fact that there is no collective speech of the subaltern, including that of their lives and their stories which has been narrated in their own voices and archived. This view had been a reality for the early postcolonial period but no longer holds true with the new generation of writers of indenture literature. Only two subaltern voices detailing the experience of indenture have been recorded during the history of the period. One of these voices belongs to Munshi Rahman Khan who wrote of his experience of indenture in Surinam. He wrote it in Hindi titled *Jeevan Prakash*. It was later translated into English as *Autobiography of an Indian Indentured Labourer: Munshi Rahman Khan 1874-1972*.

The other voice belongs to Totaram Sanadhya, who recounts his experience of Indenture in *Fijidwip Mein Mere Ikkis Varsh*, which he narrated to Benarsidas Chatuvedi in 1914 after returning from Fiji to India as an ex-indentured labourer. This seminal book was instrumental in uniting the struggle against abolition of what he called the *coolie pratha* (*coolie* practice). As a decisive text on indenture, it has stood the test of time and its validity holds as good today as it did in the period it was narrated.

Vijay Mishra in *The Literature of the Indian Diaspora* has characterised Sanadhya's narrative as a testimonio. Mishra (2014: 81) cites John Beverley who defines it as 'a narrative … told in the first person by a narrator who is the real protagonist or witness of the events he or she recounts'. Sanadhya's amanuensis was Benarsidas Chaturvedi, an Indian nationalist and a follower of Gandhi. In his paper 'Of Testimonios and Feeling Communities', Frederik Schröer (2016: 151) believes that Sanadhya's testimony inhabits a thin space that shares a greater border with the 'emotional rather than historical' veracity of his account. John Beverley defines testimonio as:

> a novel or novella-length narrative, produced in the form of a printed text, told in the first person by a narrator who is also the real protagonist or

> witness of the events she or he recounts. Its unit of narration is usually a 'life' or a significant life experience. Because in many cases the direct narrator is someone who is either functionally illiterate or, if literate, not a professional writer, the production of a *testimonio* generally involves the tape-recording and then the transcription and editing of an oral account by an interlocutor who is a journalist, ethnographer, or literary author. (Beverley 2004: 571)

Beverly also attests that the testimonio is not a mere record of memory that is narrated in the first person. It is essentially a plea or a request for empathy from its readers for the specific 'ethical and epistemological demands' for which it is written (ibid.: 574). This narrative thus bestows a position of power on what would have otherwise been a subaltern voice in the diaspora discourse. Sanadhya is able to voice an appeal, on his own terms, to abolish the colonial system of indenture. He is able to use his narrative voice to offer factual insight—one gained from inside Indian indenture. His writing is very high in emotional content since it has to appeal to the position in power.

Ever since it was published, Sanadhya's narrative has remained a controversial read. Frederik Schröer analyses him as a plurivocal author:

> Though convened in his narration in the first person singular, his 'I's differ. Closest to 'the ground' is the indentured ego that is almost entirely passive, forced to experience the system in all its brutality. Post-indenture, one meets a second ego, living in Fiji but slowly improving his conditions and enquiring into the conditions around him, moving gradually from passivity to activity. Finally, a third ego is the Sanadhya who has returned to British India, active and endowing meaning to his narration, directly addressing the reader in his testimonial plea. And yet, there is a fourth ego, a hidden spectre, the ghost of the journalist writer, Benarsidas Chaturvedi. His is the voice most difficult to trace, though hardly to be underestimated. (Schröer 2016: 155)

Equally telling is Sanadhya's style of characterisation in which the characters are developed in a manner to establish the themes of the text. All the characters in Sanadhya's narrative are distinct personalities whose characterisation is encoded to their involvement in the events described in the story. Apart from the tangible attributes of a character, such as age, appearance, gender, educational level, financial status, marital status, faith and ambition, the psychological aspects are focussed upon to bring out a well developed or 'round' character. The psychological make-up of a character includes emotions, beliefs, fears, desires and intentions through his or her actions and use of language.

My Twenty-One Years in the Fiji Islands is written vividly as a first-person narrative with Sanadhya narrating the episodes in his life. Although it is an 'autodiegetic narration' (Herman 2008: 36), it is not a complete autobiography because as a testimonio, it '. . . is an affirmation of the authority of personal experience, but, unlike autobiography, it cannot affirm a self-identity that is separate from the subaltern group or class situation that it narrates' (Beverley 2004: 572). The narrator makes the observations in his own voice but the style of writing is not consistent throughout. Sometimes the sentences are blunt while at other times they are ornate. However, the text is written in a simple and engaging style with the narrator telling stories and making generalisations and analysing them alongside. This makes the text easy to comprehend.

In many instances in the text, Sanadhya refers to himself in the archetypal image of Rama, the king of Ayodhya in the epic *Ramayan*. He even sub-titles one segment of the text 'My Own Ram-Story' (Sanadhya 1991: 86). Vijay Mishra (2014: 39) is of the view that 'He is the original *girmitiya* who speaks on behalf of those who participated in the first journey. He writes through the perennial narrative of the banishment of Rama, seeing his exile in Fiji in terms of the epic hero's own quest to recover his wife Sita and return to princely Ayodhya'. The main point of the comparison is the exile and the imagery drawn of the perseverance of the *girmitiyas*. It has to be remembered that the intended audience of this book was not the readers of today. That privilege was reserved for the Indian intellectual community of the early 1900s. This can be gleaned from the fact that the narrator 'makes frequent appeal to his readers, addressing them directly in order to shame them into action' (ibid.: 8). Thus, the genre of this book is not historical but polemical, which represents a strong attack on someone or something.

In many places in the text, footnotes have been provided to aid the reader. Since Sanadhya wrote this book for an informed audience, he does not offer any definitions or provide detailed descriptions about aspects that might seem obscure to readers who are not Indians.

The customs and traditions are aspects that the audience was supposed to have known and thus, their explanation is not present in the work. In his account of the indenture, Sanadhya emphatically compares indenture to slavery to underline the pathetic conditions endured by the indentured labourers in Fiji. He recounts the moment right after his disembarkation in Fiji, 'As soon as our transport arrived there, the police came and surrounded us so that we would not get away. We were treated worse than slaves there. People say that all civilized countries of the world have ended slavery. That seems quite right from the top, but it is actually an absolute delusion' (ibid.: 39).

The book was written with the intention of abolishing indenture, so it is not surprising to read the rhetoric of slavery and its abolition. Sanadhya also uses animal imagery in his narrative. He quotes various British officials who use the same terminology to address the *girmitiyas.* 'White people call these biscuits "dog biscuits" and feed them to the dogs' (ibid.: 37). In another instance, he narrates, 'I was made to sit where pigs and other animals are kept' (ibid.: 46). He also talks about being shooed away like animals if they venture close to the residence of the colonials. 'We are not allowed to come onto the *veranda* of the company's offices … we are shoved off' (ibid.: 47).

Totaram Sanadhya's testimonio presents a world that is full of Indian, Fijian and European characters. His Indian characters are shown practising age-old Indian customs and traditions, and keeping the homeland alive in the adopted land. His chief aim is to express the trauma of the Indian indentured labourers, so he portrays them as individuals facing the stark realities of their existence, as well as the combined wrath of the colonial masters and overseers. His use of the Hindi words *dukh, kasht* and *narak,* all relate to the trauma of indenture. They help in providing a complete and realistic picture of the lives of the *girmitiyas* in Fiji. He not only expresses the brutalities of the colonial masters but also presents the pitiable conditions of the *girmitiya* men and women. He focuses on their daily life and problems. The suicides by men and the exploitation of women portray a tragic testimony to the system of indenture.

Realism is the hallmark of Sanadhya's characterisation. His characters demonstrate emotions of alienation, nostalgia, and longing for their ancestral land. Deprived of social recognition and acceptance, they derive inspiration from mythological characters like Rama and compare their lives with his:

> The *Tulsidas Ramayana*, of course, had everything in it for the *girmit* experience: fourteen years banishment for the epic hero and God incarnate Rama, trials and tribulations in the black forest of Dandak, symbolic ravishing of his wife by the demon king Ravana, Rama's victory over Ravana, and his return to the utopian metropolis of Ayodhya... in broken chords and unexpected riffs telling the story of a race. (Mishra 2014: 39)

Archetypal patterns are 'complexes of properties found across a wide range of literary works, extending back to ancient poems, stories, myths and rituals' (Herman 2008: 26). Psychologist C.G. Jung perceived it as a symbol shared by all humanity, whereas Northrop Frye looked at it as a symbol shared by those within a particular community (ibid.).

The gamut of emotions expressed by the narrator connects him, as well as the other characters, with the reader. Throughout his account, the concept of *dukkha* (suffering) is given an elevated status. Its frequent occurrence is associated with a range of situations alluding to physical and emotional pain and despair, as well as a sense of loneliness and helplessness. The description of *atyachar* (atrocities) committed by the British on the Indian women is also given a lot of space in the narrative. The illustration of physical suffering related by Sanadhya in the case of Kunti and Narayani is especially telling. Narayani was forced to return to work two days after losing her son in childbirth, and upon protesting was physically beaten up and abused mercilessly by the plantation overseers:

> This poor woman was beaten so badly that her head was damaged, and until now she has stayed crazy.... Many tortures of this kind are committed there daily. These overseers know plenty of ways to beat the Indians with the kicks of their shoes, and equally plenty ways of breaking their teeth at the root with punches. These people burn clothes, kick away food, and make us suffer arbitrarily. All this is inner suffering; going to court without evidence is useless. (Sanadhya 1991: 44-5)

Sanadhya's description of the case of Kunti, graphically portrays the suffering that Indian women had to endure at the hands of overseers while trying to protect their virtue. Kunti was sent to work alone in a banana field, 'a place apart from other men and women, where no witness could see her, and nobody could hear her crying. The *sardar* and overseer went there to rape her. Kunti freed her arm and jumped into a nearby river. She was saved but her husband was beaten up mercilessly and left almost half dead' (ibid.: 43). In various situations throughout his narration, Sanadhya also recounts shared expressions of emotions, most often in the form of crying.

In his book, Sanadhya emphasises the importance and centrality of religion or belief in the lives of the indentured people. He lists the religious texts in circulation and also gives an overview of the different religious sects that were active in the colony, in particular the Arya Samaj. 'In Fiji, there are many Kabir Panthi, Ramanandi, Satnami, Gusain and so forth, many types of sadhus.... We have also made arrangements to perform the drama of Ram Lila in a few places every year ... from this, the benefit is that in the hearts of our brothers, love is made for their own religious festivals' (ibid.: 66). This gives the reader an idea of the religious landscape in Fiji at that time. The text is also rich in its description of life in the colony.

The sea voyage is highlighted as one that is manifested in the social implications of crossing the *kalapani*. In a sense, the ship that carried the emigrants from India can be seen as a chronotope. The chronotope is a multifaceted concept by theorist Mikhail Bakhtin, who insists on the 'intrinsic connectedness of time and space' through the 'thickening or materialising of time in space' as represented in a narrative or discourse. Thus, the chronotope provides 'a space for representation' where 'temporal markers' come together with the 'spatial features' to define 'historical, biographical and social relations' (Herman 2008: 64). From this explanation, it is evident that the 'chronotope' defines the genre of the literary work. In his seminal work, *The Dialogic Imagination*, Bakhtin defines the term 'chronotope' as being:

> Points in the geography of a community where time and space intersect and fuse. Time takes on flesh and becomes visible for human contemplation; likewise, space becomes charged and responsive to the movements of time and history and the enduring character of a people. . . . Chronotopes thus stand as monuments to the community itself, as symbols of it, as forces operating to shape its members' images of themselves. (Bakhtin 2017: 7)

The ship was the space where earlier relationships were wiped out and newer relationships were forged. Men had let go of their castes, women had changed their names and renamed themselves. A collective identity was born on the ship, that of *jahaji bhais* and *jahaji behens.*

Sanadhya (1991: 37) highlights the voyage undertaken on the ship in the form of a metaphorical image, 'We saw nothing but our ship going onward, making waves in the ocean.... In just the way a bird is imprisoned in a cage, we were all locked in'. This word picture shows a vessel that is both, an enclosure as well as a vehicle, which fostered the life-long and generational relationships of *jahaji bhais and jahaji behens.* The ship was thus, a world complete in itself. Social contestations clashed and were broken down, giving rise to a new social group that would link the homeland with the host land.

In their translation of Sanadhya's text, Kelly and Singh have retained some words in their original Hindi and not translated them into English. This is because the words used by Sanadhya to express his experience of 'girmit' find no parallel in the English language. He makes use of the term *girmit* while describing situations where he criticises labour and living conditions in the plantations.

Unwittingly at times, his language produces a comic effect, which is used as an affective force in his narration. He pitches a sarcastic tone when narrating the injustice faced by the *girmitiyas.* While he narrates his story, he does not present it as a catalogue of facts but as stories of lived experience. Some stories are privileged over the others in his text. The account of Kunti in which two men, a *sirdar* and an overseer, tried to rape her in the plantation, is narrated with a strong sense of outrage at what was happening to the indentured women in the colonies. His stories are told with a skill that induces an immediate response from the readers, more than the impact an official report would have. Narayani's story is also brought out by Sanadhya to encourage performative action in the narratee. Some voices are privileged over others. His long conversations on matters of faith and theology, which he held with Rev. Burton and missionary Hannah Dudley in Fiji are quoted *ad verbatim* in the form of free speech.

The book thus follows a chronological pattern, beginning with the year Sanadhya was born, records his trials and tribulations in India before journeying to Fiji as an indentured labourer. It describes the life on the plantations for the indentured labourers and also describes the lives of the ex-indentured. The book takes into account the relations between the Indians and the Fijians. It covers almost all aspects of indenture and ends with his return to India, his visit to his home in the village and his tireless work to abolish indenture. While reporting facts, it also reflects the truth from the *girmitiya* perspective, allowing the reader a glimpse into the cultural beliefs of a particular period in history.

The descendants of the Indian indentured labourers, barring a few vernacular voices, have predominantly favoured writing in English—the *lingua franca* of the world. The reason for this could be traced back to the colonial powers making people subalterns in their own countries through linguistic displacement. Thus, by writing in English, the writers of Indian indenture can identify themselves with the literary tradition of other diasporic writers across the world. They voice their concerns as global concerns in a postcolonial world and thus gain a wider readership. Post-colonial theorist, Bill Ashcroft (2002: 218) opines, 'The diasporic production of cultural meanings occurs in many areas, such as contemporary music, film, theatre and dance, but writing is one of the most interesting and strategic ways in which diaspora might disrupt the binary of local and global and problematize national, racial and ethnic formulations of identity'.

Whereas the first-generation writers lived the indenture experience, the subsequent generations have lived indenture through an inherited memory of the experience. Researcher Amit Shankar Saha (2009: 192) observes that they are 'generations away from their original homeland but their heritage gives them a consciousness of their past'. He opines that they are not governed by actual dislocation but by an inherited memory of dislocation. Makarand Paranjpe (2002: 83) notes that the first generation looks back at the homeland with a sense of nostalgia while the subsequent generations often use an elegiac tone while looking at India.

Rajendra Prasad's *Tears in Paradise* is an account of indenture in Fiji written by a third-generation descendent of a *girmitiya*. He has undertaken several interviews and explored archived written sources for information. Prasad begins his emotional narrative by re-engaging with the homeland through a return to his ancestral home in India:

The stories of *daadaji* initially created an intense desire in me to know more about my roots, about *girmit* and India. However, the subject was taboo at social gatherings. This part of Indo-Fijian history had been buried by the passage of time, and the community seemed to make a conscious effort to obliterate it from its memory because of a stigma attached to it. (Prasad 2010: 20)

It is clear then that the oral life narratives of the *girmityas* are the only sources that provide the listeners with the complete picture of indenture. To bring out the voices of *girmit*, Prasad uses 'polyphony', a narrative technique that literally means 'many voiced'. It is derived from 'the work of Mikhail Bakhtin and describes texts or utterances in which more than one voice can be heard' (Herman 2008: 443). Bakhtin identifies 'a plurality of independent and equally valid voices which are not subordinated to any single authorial hierarchy' (ibid.). Prasad uses an unending sequence of stories in his narrative, which involves a dialectical interplay of different voices. Each voice narrates an event or incident in the *girmit* past. It highlights the culture of violence perpetrated by the British against Indian indentured labourers in the colony.

When he visits his ancestral home in India, the matriarch tells Prasad, 'Son, returning without taking food would never give peace to our hearts' (Prasad 2010: 38). In the next paragraph, while taking his leave from the family, the patriarch weeps and asks him, 'When will you meet me again, my beloved?' (ibid.: 44). In the beginning of the second chapter, Prasad changes the narrative voice and retains it till the last chapter. From an autodiegetic narrator in chapter one, he shifts and occupies the third person omniscient and narrates the story of indenture in Fiji in the rest of the chapters. After the *analepsis* of chapter one, Prasad follows a linear narrative. He searches through the archives for information and provides a plethora of stories peopled with characters, recollecting their emotions and experiences. Animal imagery, as is the norm in all indenture literature, is found in abundance in *Tears in Paradise*. Prasad (2010: 57) narrates, 'Once on the mainland, the *girmityas* were herded like animals to the plantations. They were given kennel-like living accommodation—referred to as coolie lines'.

The development of characters is well etched and the minutest of details is provided in order to build a word picture for the reader.

Prasad provides information pertaining to the person's age, social configuration and religious belief, which adds to the voices in the text. The oral narratives he had listened to during his childhood days serve as a starting point to his research. He remembers with a sense of nostalgia, the many *bidesia* (song of separation and lamentation) songs he had heard in his childhood. Memories assail him and the past is opened for his perusal. In *Tears in Paradise,* Prasad uses Hindi and Bhojpuri words to create the essence of a heteroglossic text. Herman (2008: 213) defines 'heteroglossia' as '. . . the appearance in real life of that plurality of languages of class, gender, region or ideology which enter the novel in the form of dialogism resulting in a polyphonic narrative'. Further, in a polyphonic text, '. . . the plot is subordinated to the task of coordinating and exposing languages to each other'. When he describes the feelings of sorrow faced by men and women alike in the narrative, Prasad (2010: 22) uses Bhojpuri, '*Nahin ro bahini, ka kariho upar wale par bharossa rakho.* Do not cry sister; what can we do, it is His will, have faith in God'.

Allusions to the Hindu epic, *Ramayan,* are a plenty. Prasad uses symbolism of the *Ramayan* to express the emotions related to exile, conflict, culture and traditions. '*Ram aur Sita banwas se padhare hain.* It is the return of Lord Rama and Sita from exile' (ibid.: 37). This profound statement lightens the sombre atmosphere when Prasad and his wife make the 'return pilgrimage' to India. Bhojpuri is used to convert the solemn silence into laughter and jokes. Bhojpuri words are also used by Prasad to reproduce the *bidesia* songs. The essence of sadness and anguish can only be captured in the native language:

Chhoori kudari ke sangh, ab bite din au ratiyaan,
Ganne ki harihari patiyaan, jaane hamri dil ki batiyaan (ibid.: 17).

Translated into English by Prasad, the words mean, 'The leaves of sugarcane were witnesses to the sufferings of our lives, as hoes and knives became our companions day and night. Atrocities committed against them are so blatant that even the green leaves of the sugarcane bear witness to the flames of anguish that consume their hearts' (ibid.). Prasad demonstrates how through these songs, the *girmitiyas* were able to relate the grief in their hearts to inanimate objects, like the knife and the hoe.

Each of the characters in the book speaks in his or her native language. The words spoken by the Europeans are reproduced in English, the first generation *girmitiya* dialogues are written in Bhojpuri and Hindi or in Fiji Bhat. Prasad also uses vernacular words and expressions in his narrative. There is a dialectical interplay of different voices. Hybrid texts include a mix of languages—in this case, English, Bhojpuri and Hindi—and can be seen as 'anti-language', a term coined by linguist Michael Halliday in his paper 'Anti-Languages'. Halliday (1979: 165) describes the anti-language as an outcome of an anti-society '. . . that is set up within another society as a conscious alternative'. It has a social value and '. . . bears an alternative reality' in order to maintain group solidarity:

> An anti-language serves to create and maintain social structure through conversation, just as an everyday language does; but the social structure is of a particular kind, in which certain elements are strongly foregrounded. This gives to the anti-language a special character in which metaphorical modes of expression are the norm; patterns of this kind appear at all levels, phonological, lexicogrammatical, and semantic. The study of anti-languages offers further insights into the relation between language and social structure, and into the way in which text functions in the realization of social contexts. (Halliday 1976: 570).

In *Tears in Paradise*, the anti-language works to highlight the exclusive aspects of the *girmitiya* community and serves to emphasize their cultural 'othering' in Fiji.

Prasad's writing is steeped in emotions. The trauma of indenture is embedded in his memory and his work reflects the suffering and misery that his indentured ancestors faced. When trauma is written through memory, subjectivity and prejudices seep through the narrative. The credibility of memory is questioned and there is a sense of wilful deception that is at play in the writing. In the places where he speaks about the 'inherited stigma of shame', his prose takes on a poetic quality:

> I have grieved in the stillness of the night and in the deep peal of thunder, I have heard the muffled cries of our ancestors, imploring us, the descendants. . . . Yet it is the sugarcane fields that have constantly gripped my attention. Behind the picturesque beauty lies sadness, both profound and intense. . . . Even in stillness one can feel the powerful presence of spirits of sorrow

and grief exuding from these sugarcane fields. They are the spirits of our ancestors! (Prasad 2010: 21)

These lines read like a discourse on the nostalgia of home. Writing from outside India, Prasad perceives it as both, an insider as well as an outsider.

The metaphor of the *peepal* trees in the ancestral village in India carries the significance of roots. Prasad revisits this metaphor multiple times in his narrative highlighting the existential angst faced by the descendants of the indentured diaspora. The preoccupation with searching for and finding their roots is an important part of their life journey. However, this romantic lens of looking at India from Fiji is juxtaposed with the practical difficulties the author faces on reaching India. 'Even procuring train tickets in India was no small feat. Queues and congestion at the ticket booths were common … despite the apparent urgency, the betelnut-chewing booth attendant was in no hurry' (ibid.: 27). Prasad makes it clear that he 'had earlier held two views of India—one as told by *Daadaji* and the other as I read about India through the eyes of the Western media' (ibid.: 41). At the end of his journey to India and before returning to Fiji he says, 'I have found a new joy and a new identity in my roots.… I came to accept that although I was an individual, I was also part of a larger web that I could not ignore as it gave me an identity' (ibid.).

On his return to Fiji, the author feels a renewed sense of pride in his Indian heritage. He believes that his identity had been lost in the colonial atmosphere of Fiji. 'India restored in me the inner strength to see that the *sahibs* were in no way superior to me'. He decides to become a 'crusader battling against the stigma of *girmit*, which hung ominously over my community' (ibid.: 43). Prasad's narrative begins *in media res*. This is a Latin word meaning 'into the middle of things' this narrative device is used to begin the story at a crucial point in the middle (Herman 2008: 242). He then uses the technique of *analepsis* to go back in time and narrate the story. 'My research took me into the maze of infamy of indenture' (Prasad 2010: 43).

Memory cannot be archived and yet it is very real. How then, can an author write about a past that is not documented? Prasad bridges the remembered past by researching the colonial archives and recovering the voices that have been lost in traditional history. By replacing the colonial history with individual histories of the *girmitiyas,* he liberates the subaltern voices that have been silenced in the master narrative. The writing is largely driven by emotions. 'My anger led to anguish, and anguish into passion, and the passion into an obsession to restate the history of our people in a different light' (ibid.: 130).

He ends his narrative on a positive note that is filled with hope. While seeking redemption for the violence committed against the *girmitiyas,* Prasad agrees that the wrongs committed in the past cannot be exonerated but they need to be revealed. This is because, 'A community carries the burden of earlier generations that were robbed of freedom, rights and justice' (ibid.: 133). He believes that the effect of the revelation of the past '. . . would be that the history of a race of people would be restored and rebuilt on honest foundations. This generation, and those to come, would be enabled to view their history from a true perspective' (ibid.: 134).

The third and fourth generation descendants of the indentured Indians approach the subject with the objective of rewriting history. However, rewriting history presupposes that it has been written in the first place. Apart from Totaram Sanadhya and Munshi Rahman Khan, none of the first generation indentured people have written about their experiences. The second generation was stopped from revisiting indenture as the wound was too raw to be written about. Since then, the wound has only been festering and it is now, with the third and fourth generation finally writing about the experience, that it has served as a cathartic release. This process of (re)writing takes place at the level of individual histories, at the level of the community, as well as at the global level. Authors across the erstwhile plantation colonies writing on the subject bring together multiple perspectives and expand the debate.

In *Postcolonial Literature: An Introduction,* critic Pramod Nayar (2013: 72) opines that '. . . diasporic writing fluctuates between the individual and the collective as polarities'. This holds true in the literary works of the third and fourth generation descendants of indenture that show both, temporal and spatial movements. The temporal aspect entails *analepsis* (looking back to the past) and *prolepsis* (looking towards the future). The need to look back is greater in the first generation writers but the third and fourth generation also looks back into the past to rediscover their roots and come to terms with their hyphenated identity. The spatial aspect in indenture literature is revealed through a process of 'deterritorialization' (losing their home and culture in the homeland) and 'reterritorialization' (establishing a new home and assimilating into the new culture in the hostland) (ibid.: 187). The split consciousness of being Indian while simultaneously being the 'other' or 'the outsider' is brought out very efficiently in their works.

The first generation looks at the centrifugal aspect of the journey while the third generation focuses on both, the centrifugal, as well as the centripetal aspect. This means that when indentured Indians were sent to different places across the globe, the journey, with its share of anguish and trauma, proved to be greater than what they expected of indenture. The institution managed to separate men from their wives and families, and individuals from their homes and homeland. However, it also witnessed the coming together and formation of new communities, such as the *jahaji bhai* and *jahaji behen* relationship on the ship and on the plantations. In *The Location of Culture*, Homi K. Bhabha (1997: 139) opines that the diasporic scattering becomes a gathering. Thus, it can be interpreted that indentured people have, like Bhabha, 'lived that moment of the scattering of the people that in other times and other places, in the nations of others, becomes a time of gathering'.

Colonial history of indenture remains largely contested and is a subject for interrogation by the writers of indenture literature. In this counter narrative to the colonial discourse, women have remained silent, marginalized and invisible. Their role in the history of migration has been restricted to showing them as travelling wives of indentured men. Over the past two decades, literature written on indenture has shown their experience being subsumed by the indenture experience of their male counterparts. However, this has changed in the last decade with a gradual shift towards third or fourth generation women descendants of indentured migrants in the Caribbean writing about indenture. The memory of a shared past has supplied the descendants of the indentured labourers with a collective identity and consciousness.

Peggy Mohan is a fourth generation descendant of an indentured Indian. Her book *Jahajin* is a genealogical trip into indenture in the Caribbean and presents the ethnography of a lived experience through a gendered lens. Mohan's text writes against the grain of dominant narratives of the colonists and the nationalists whose records of women's experiences had rendered them invisible. Already marginalised within the racial categorisation of the colonial officials, women were further trapped within repressive gender structures reflecting their double colonisation. However, when the storyteller is a woman, like in *Jahajin* and *Coolie Woman*, the interpretation of women in indenture undergoes a remarkable change from the earlier positing. Such narratives draw the readers' attention to the myriad ways through which women pushed against the traditional gender roles within indenture.

Jahajin begins with the unnamed narrator recording the life of an ex-indentured labourer, Deeda, who is 110 years old. The title itself (meaning 'female ship-mate') suggests that the book will put indentured women in the centre of the narrative. Right in the beginning of the book, Mohan acknowledges the *Jahajins* in her life. The *Jahajin* in the title is not limited to Deeda or the narrator but encompasses all *jahajins* who emigrated from India under the indenture system. Deeda's open 'no-holds-barred' style demonstrates the readiness of women to come out with their stories and renegotiate their marginalisation in the documentation of indenture.

Deeda speaks in Bhojpuri, the language used by the indentured people who had migrated from India. The author, being a linguist, reproduces the dialogues in Bhojpuri and translates them into English alongside. Throughout the story, she takes the help of her mother, who is an 'expert' in Bhojpuri. Through the metaphorical act of translation, Mohan validates the loss of Bhojpuri language in the Caribbean. It was used by the first generation of indentured labourers who linked the language with indenture and in the act of trying to forget the trauma of indenture, refused to pass it on to the next generation. Instead, they made an active attempt to embrace 'hybridity' in language and encouraged their children to learn Creole and Standard English.

Mohan's unnamed narrator speaks in the first person but the narrative moves to Deeda who also uses a first person narrative voice.

One thus has multiple narratives across different time zones. Mohan also uses a framed narrative through which Deeda becomes the narrator of her own story.

In framed narratives, '. . . events are narrated by a character other than the primary narrator or when a character tells a tale that, although unrelated to the main story, contains a moral message for the listener in the text' (Herman 2008: 186). It is sometimes likened to 'Chinese boxes', which means story within story within story. Framing occurs when a part of the narrative is embedded within the narrative. 'Embedding refers to the narrative situation in which part of the main narrative or a significant plot detail is displaced atemporally to another location in the narration' (ibid.). In such cases, *analepsis* and flashback are framed by the current time of the narrative. When the inset narrative is not directly related to the main narrative, intercalation comes into play. However, the intercalated narrative needs to bear some thematic relevance to the main narrative. In the case of *Jahajin,* the framed narrative occurs because Deeda's oral narrative is being transcribed by the narrator for textual transmission.

Narrative framing is related to the concept of digetic levels. Since each narrating act contains another narrating act, the 'digetic level shifts from the initial extradigetic level to an intradigetic level of narration, and further to a metadigetic level of narration' (ibid.: 188). While it essentially means the same thing, narratologist Mieke Bal coined the term 'hypodiegetic narrative', 'which is preferred by many narratologists over the Genettean "metadiegetic narrative"' (ibid.: 229). The narrator in Mohan's book is an extradigetic narrator who is listening to Deeda, the intradigetic narrator, who is narrating her life story to the 'listener'. In her retelling the story of her indenture, Deeda reveals the repressed trauma and confronts it by putting it in the past, thereby encouraging a cathartic release of her own trauma in the process.

Deeda's narrative operates on two levels. In the first, she narrates the experiences of her own indenture and in the same vein; she brings in the story of Sunnariya (the narrator's great-great grandmother) as well as of the other women whose voices have been silenced in indenture history. On the other level she narrates the Bhojpuri folk tale of *Rani Saranga ki Keesa* (the story of Queen Saranga). There are thus, four ongoing narratives in *Jahajin.* In the first, the narrator occupies the present temporal location in the book. She is at crossroads in her life in Trinidad. With a Ph.D. in Linguistics on Bhojpuri language, she wants to go to India for further research. Her parents are against the idea of a return to India and there is a significant amount of tension at home over this aspiration. Her close relationship with Fyzie, an African-Caribbean boy who the narrator fancies, is also not acceptable to her parents. They belong to a generation that is still caught in the social diktats of the Indian community in Trindad yet want their children to move ahead and forward. Fyzie is a *dougla* and any relationship between an Indian-Caribbean and an African-Caribbean faces criticism like the narrator endures from her grandmother, who discourages her 'relationship with "all kind of dog and cat"' (Mohan 2007: 112).

In the second narrative strand, Deeda, a first-generation emigrant to the Caribbean narrates why she left India and signed up for indenture. She speaks in Bhojpuri as it is the only language she knows. Thus, Mohan is able to access the historical past of indenture through Deeda's narrative. This is because the testimonies of women are absent in the history written in Standard English. Semiotician Gayatri C. Spivak (1994: 103) believes that there is 'no space from which the sexed subaltern subject can speak'. However, when Deeda speaks in Bhojpuri, she wrests back linguistic control, which in turn helps her to project her history and her language over the dominant discourse. When she asks, '*Bataayi, bahin*?', 'Should I speak, sister?' in *Jahajin*, she is addressing the narrator as a sister and taking her permission to speak (Mohan 2007: 16). These two words carry the weight of a voice that has for long remained silenced and now wants to speak out and be heard. According to Spivak (2010: 36), the '. . . tendency of the author should be to reopen what was closed by colonialism: linguistic diversity'.

The third narrative strand connects Deeda's story of Sunnariya to the lineage of the narrator. Sunnariya is the great-great grandmother of the narrator who had been on the same ship that carried Deeda from Calcutta to Trinidad. They were *jahaji behens.* Critic Nalini Mohabir (2014: 114) has pointed out in her article 'Port of Departure, Port of Return: Mapping Indentured Returns to Calcutta' that most of the research on indenture in the Caribbean begins with the researcher exploring his/her own link to the past and to India through a family member's memories. Through Deeda's recounting of the life of Sunnariya, the narrator (and the reader) is able to view different life stories of women in indenture. No two experiences were exactly the same; Sunnariya had travelled with her father and brothers while Deeda had travelled alone with her young son.

The fourth narrative strand is that of Saranga, the protagonist of the folk tale that Deeda narrates in the frame story. It is through her story that the four narrative strands are connected thematically. Scholar Nivedita Mishra (2015: 4) in her article 'The Trinidadian *deewani:* Longing and Belonging in Peggy Mohan's *Jahajin*' analyses the text and finds that '. . . a close reading of the novel reveals that Deeda and the narrator constantly weave their tales around new timelines and circumstances, drawing strength from a pattern that they individually derive from the central story of Saranga'. In *Jahajin*, Saranga is a fictional character from a folktale and is used as a counterfoil by the author '. . . to study the life-choices of the other three protagonists' (ibid.: 2).

Jahajin approaches the metaphor of migration by adopting the technique of magic realism. When Deeda narrates Saranga's folk tale, she also introduces magic realism in the text. As an important postcolonial narrative device, it brings in fantastic or seemingly impossible elements into a narrative. It mixes the real and the 'phantastic' in such a manner that the real turns magical and the unrealistic seems real, thereby blurring the distinction between the 'phantastic' and the real. One example of magic realism is when a character in a story (in this case Deeda) continues to be alive beyond the normal length of life (she is 110 years old). This fact is also underlined subtly with the character being alive across several generations. 'Often the magical events in magic realism are narrated in great realistic detail but without the narrator registering surprise or commenting on their strangeness' (Herman 2008: 281). When Deeda narrates the story of Saranga, she begins by talking about two monkeys, a male and a female, with the female monkey jumping into a river and the water transforming her into a human. Further into the story, Deeda tells the narrator that the male monkey commits suicide and the monkey-turned-girl lifts the dead monkey in her arms and jumps into the cremation pyre. 'And they are reborn. This time the monkey comes back as a boy, and is called Sada Birij. And the girl is born again in a merchant's home, and her name becomes Saranga–' (Mohan 2007: 9). All of this is narrated in a matter-of-fact voice by Deeda.

German art critic, Franz Roh first used the term 'magic realism' in 1925 to refer to a style of painting. Chris Baldick (2008: 194) defines it as,

> A kind of modern fiction in which fabulous and fantastical elements are included in the narrative that otherwise maintains the reliable tone of objective realistic report, designing a tendency of the modern novel to reach beyond the confines of realism and draw upon the energies of fable, folktale, and myth while maintaining a strong contemporary social relevance. The fantastic attributes given to characters in such novels—levitation, flight, telepathy, telekinesis—are among the means that magic realism adopts to encompass the often phantasmagorical political realities of the twentieth century.

If the purpose of employing the technique of magic realism is to showcase a different perspective and extend the scope of reality, the author succeeds in this rendition. In Mohan's text, the diasporic sensibility of the four protagonists highlights the fluidity of identity. India's Parbati becomes Deeda on the ship and Janaki becomes Sunnariya. In *Ramayan,* Sita had to undergo a trial by fire. Deeda and Sunnariya undergo the trial by water on the voyage. The female monkey jumps into the river 'water' and is transformed into a human. Her identity has changed and is reminiscent of the changed identity of a migrant in the adopted country. In these instances, there is a sense of purification involved at multiple levels. At various junctures in the novel, the narrator's consciousness merges with that of Deeda's and Saranga's. In magic realism, there is no hierarchy between the two codes of real and unreal. Both are equally valid to the text and work to integrate. In the folk tale, Saranga '. . . was always looking back, buying time to think, and looking back nostalgically. . .' (Mohan 2007: 231). This connects with the narrator buying time to think while standing at the crossroads of her life. She has to choose between Fyzie and Nishant just as Saranga had to choose between Sada Birij and the Prince. Deeda has to choose between returning to India with

Mukoon Singh or staying on in Trinidad. 'Deeda was like our Saranga. Deeda had crossed the *kalapani* and become a different person, though she had kept wondering about what she had left behind' (ibid.: 256).

Mohan disrupts the temporal sequence in *Jahajin* to make her protagonists exist simultaneously in the multiple narratives. She weaves together the narrative strands belonging to different periods and transcends the linguistic jargon of a hybrid text. The content of the book dictates its form of the frame narrative and the folk tale is used to show female empowerment in the indenture. 'In this story, it's the woman who is always ahead, and she actually leaves a mate behind in order to get ahead. That isn't typical. What you're supposed to get in a Bhojpuri folktale is undying loyalty and submissiveness' (ibid.: 256). Here the author employs the narrator as her mouthpiece to show how women in the Caribbean, despite a patriarchal set-up, were forward-looking. Deeda leaves her husband behind to travel to Trinidad and then does not leave with Mukoon Singh to return to India, instead she stays back in Trinidad; Saranga leaves the Prince to find love with Sada Birij, while the narrator leaves Fyzie behind to go to India and Nishant. Saranga is Deeda and Saranga is also the narrator, all *jahajins* are Sarangas just like all the women in Dharanagri were Sarangas. Saranga is the one who takes the initiative to throw herself into the stream (in her previous life as a female monkey) and be born again. It is the male monkey, and later Sada Biraj, who is always left behind waiting. This is the story of the *Jahajin*, the indentured Indian women in the Caribbean, as well as their female successors, who threw themselves into action, leaving their men behind. The narrator is surprised to note:

> As I listened to their conversation, the migration came across to me as a story of women making their way alone, with men in the background, strangers, extras. In history books it had always been the other way around: it was the men who were the main actors. But there was also this unwritten history of the birth of a new community in Trinidad. And it was women who were at the centre of the story. The best things never did get on tape. (Mohan 2007: 204)

Deeda's narrative is a correction to the colonial history of Indian migration to Trinidad which had silenced the subaltern woman in the voyage and the plantations. Here she speaks, but the speech is ironic because it has to be brought on paper with the help of a translator. Deeda's oral narrative is in Bhojpuri because indenture can only be accessed in that language. For it to be written in Standard English, it needs a translator playing the role of a mediator and a revisionary historian. Peggy Mohan writes in her blog:

> In *Jahajin* the bridge is the eighteenth chapter. Deeda's history tale is over. Now the young narrator assumes the role of the chronicler, seeing over a vast swath of history, and sums up in quick vignettes the time between Sunnariya's wedding and the present, tracing the descent line from Sunnariya to herself, gaining a better view of the journey that has been scripted for her from the very start. (Mohan 2010)

The narrator says, 'I was going to pilot the ship out of the storm myself and find it a safe harbour' (Mohan 2007: 200). Deeda also utters the same words to Sunnariya, 'The only way for women like us to manage in this place is to hold the wheel for ourselves' (ibid.: 172). Offering a deep insight into the psychology of indenture, Mohan has used narrative techniques of interior monologues, stream of consciousness, autobiographical tones and flashbacks to bring out the sensibility of the indentured diaspora in her work.

Marianne Hirsch's framework of postmemory can also be applied to analyse *Jahajin*. The narrator talks about the incident in a high end club where she comes under the gaze of a Scottish man. When the man attempts to talk to her, the narrator takes on the persona of her great-great grandmother who was molested by a white overseer on the plantation. She experiences, what Abigail Ward (2013: 278) has termed a 'historic flashback to Sunnariya's encounter with the Scottish overseers' in her article 'Assuming the Burden of Memory'. The narrator runs away from the club and finds herself shaken up by the encounter (Mohan 2007: 165). Postmemory had taken over and the narrator revisits the trauma. 'Blackouts always had that effect on the family. They seemed to trigger memories, and then a curtain fell. They never talked about who else had these blackouts too' (ibid.: 100).

According to Hirsch (2002: 76), in her article 'Marked by Memory: Feminist Reflections on Trauma and Transmission', postmemory is a '. . . *retrospective witnessing by adoption*. It is a question of adopting the traumatic experiences—and thus also the *memories*—of others as experiences one might have had, and thus of inscribing them into one's own life story'. Postmemory is especially useful for Mohan and other writers like her who are connected to their past through language and family history. They can '. . . explore the remembrance of Indian indenture in the absence of direct experience or associated trauma' (Ward 2013: 279). The narrator's involvement in transcribing and translating Deeda's texts pulls her into experiencing a postmemory of the indenture, where she had '. . . slipped into a time gap and become Deeda' (Mohan 2007: 125). She reveals that she appropriates Deeda's memory, 'Normally I didn't take sugar in my tea. But after the hard work of the day, this evening I put three spoons of sugar into my tea and stirred. Then I remembered that Mukoon Singh was going to come for his tea any minute now. I sat up straight and looked out the window, and waited' (ibid.). This type of unique 'time travel' happens at multiple places in the book.

Postmemory is an effective element of personal and collective consciousness that carries an emotional resonance across generations of survivors of trauma. In *The Generation of Postmemory*, Hirsch (2012: 5) explains that the listener is 'shaped, however indirectly, by traumatic fragments of events that still defy narrative reconstruction and exceed comprehension'. In such cases, 'Loss of family, home, of a sense of belonging and safety in the world "bleed" from one generation to the next' (ibid.: 34). The postmemory of indenture thus pervades *Jahajin* with the narrator revisiting and rewriting the traumas faced by the earlier generations.

Mohan's description of the carnival in the Caribbean posits the manner in which the concept of 'hybridity' is dealt within a narrative on indenture. This term was first used by Mikhail Bakhtin to characterize the novel as a hybrid genre. It was appropriated by postcolonial theorist Homi K. Bhabha who '. . . reinterpreted the concept, converting it into a positive label of multicultural racial intermixing and transnationality'. It is a 'refunctionalisation of alterities within one's own cultural horizon', which broadens to integrate aspects of the foreign culture into 'one's own moral and cultural universe'. It has '. . . frequently been equated with creolisation and diasporism'. In the recent past, '. . . celebrations of hybridity were designed to liberate the subject from cultural constraints, encouraging a free appropriation of cultural markers by a process of *bricolage*'

(Herman 2008: 228). The carnival, as depicted in *Jahajin*, builds '. . . future circuits of transracial and transcultural understanding' (Ward 2013: 276).

During the indenture period, *Muharram*, a religious occasion traditionally celebrated by Muslims (called *Hosey* in the Caribbean and *Tazia* in Fiji), used to turn into a carnival with people of all cultures participating in the revelry. 'Carnivalesque' is a term used by Mikhail Bakhtin (1968: 44) to describe the carnival as an occasion offering a second life to the people '. . . who for a time entered the utopian realm of community, freedom and abundance'. It celebrated a temporary liberation from the established order and '. . . marked the suspension of all hierarchical rank, privileges and norms of prohibitions'. *Jahajin* depicts the carnival as a festival of interracial harmony and promotion of multiculturalism in the Caribbean. A float is designed by the narrator's friend, Bobby, in the shape of a 'sailing ship named the *Godavari*', the name of the ship on which Sunnariya and Deeda had sailed from India. It was a 'hybrid ship', complete with a band playing Calypso music and 'depicting the sea journey the jahajis had made from India'. Behind the ship 'was a band full of modern-day jahajis jumping up on the road to music, and sharing the spirit' of the carnival (Mohan 2007: 218-20). The author describes 'Carnival madness' as being 'in costume playing a different role, getting to be someone freer and stronger than you think you are' (ibid.: 81).

Jahajin uses the metaphor of 'search' and ties the journeys undertaken by all the four protagonists to this action. The author draws many parallels between the narrator's, Deeda's and Saranga's search for love. At the end of the folktale, Deeda informs the narrator that Saranga sat on an *udan khatola* along with her lover, Sada Birij. She also took with her the sister of the prince who wanted to woo Saranga. It is a surprise ending as there are no answers to why Saranga would take the sister of the prince with her. It is possible that after many struggles, when Saranga gets her love, she takes on the role of helping other women choose their own destiny. The sister of the prince signifies the sisterhood of *jahaji behens,* looking out for each other during the long voyage and in the plantations.

The multiple narratives of the book come together in the end. The narrator reaches India and plays the tape with Deeda's recorded voice in front of her husband. The book had begun with the travel from India to the Caribbean and it ends with travel from the Caribbean to India. 'A story could not end with its heroine still in exile. I was bringing another long journey to an end. I was back in Ayodhya in place of my great-great-great-grandmother, Janaki-didi' (ibid.: 260).

There is a distinct poetics of community building, which women writers of indenture literature project in their narratives. Their women characters experience indenture differently from their male counterparts. When the storyteller is a woman, the vocabulary she uses is distinct and the interpretation is measured on a different scale. There is an underlying counter-discourse that questions the master narrative. These writers push the boundaries of research to understand and interpret the seemingly vulnerable links that the past holds with the present.

The Indo-Caribbean women's novel is a distinct sub-genre in the area of indenture literature. Such novels trace the trajectory of the lives of indentured women by piecing together different voices and narratives almost like a mosaic. Their research on the subject uncovers many stories behind stories that have been silenced in the traditionally male-centric discourse on indenture. Theorist Verene Shepherd (2002: 7) in *Maharani's Misery: Narratives of a Passage from India to the Caribbean* points out that 'colonist historiography has tended to mute the voices of exploited people, and the subaltern, as female, was even more invisible'.

Gaiutra Bahadur's *Coolie Woman: The Odyssey of Indenture* is an ethnographic non-fiction narrative that, on the surface seems like a genealogical search of an ancestor. It is a well-written critique of colonialism and its profit-based system of indenture. A closer look reveals the carefully mined data and analysis that Bahadur has painstakingly researched by using material from official archives. She has also conducted numerous interviews to fill the gaps left in the official records. In her extensive research-driven book, Bahadur has brought out the articulations of the gendered Indian women in the indenture. Scholars Murari Prasad and Binod K. Jha (2016: 233) in their paper, 'Indian Diasporic Formations in Guyana: Reading *Coolie Woman: The Odyssey of Indenture*' suggest that, 'The coolie tag was imposed on the migrant Indian workers during the indenture era regardless of their caste and occupational backgrounds. They were reduced to stock characters conforming to a fixed pattern and having stereotyped qualities'. They commend Bahadur's act of retrieving 'the repressed history of indentured Indians, particularly the emigrant coolie women' and highlight how Bahadur has extrapolated 'the tough odyssey of the coolie women – the silent, rarely written underside of indenture experience – from the excavated material marshalled in her narrative'.

Coolie Woman opens with an epigraph taken from Adrienne Rich's 'Cartographies of Silence' in *The Dream of a Common Language*. The epigraph is telling in nature because it talks about 'silence' and 'telling' and 'history'. The epigraph sets the tone for the rest of the book which is a rich narrative combining archival research with oral testimonies and folk songs. It begins with the metaphor of a search and uses the approach of a personal memoir with the autodiegetic narrator beginning the story *in media res*. The narrative is divided into three parts; 'Embarking', 'Exploring' and 'Returning'. The travel metaphor continues throughout the narrative with Bahadur returning to the leitmotif of travel multiple times in the book. The purpose of a leitmotif is 'to represent or symbolize a person, object, place, or idea. In literary criticism, the term is frequently reduced to denoting a recurring central motif' (Herman 2008: 276). The title itself carries the word 'Odyssey' which acknowledges the motif of travel. The cartographical aspect of the voyage undertaken by the first generation of indentured migrants to the Caribbean impacts the writing of the subsequent generations. It changes the cartography of their mind which remains caught in the recurring idea of a journey. The metaphor of the journey bridges the gap between the first generation and the fourth generation (Bahadur) opening up a 'space for entanglement'.

The first chapter begins with the author giving the reader a vignette of the Bahadur family's migration from Guyana to America in 1981. She exposes the reader to the description of a family photograph taken to mark the day of travel, '7 November 1981' (Bahadur 2013: 3). Imposing the current travel of the fourth generation over the earlier odyssey of her indentured ancestor affects the temporal space of the book and prepares the reader for the subsequent *analepsis*. 'This trip led me to ask about another, more epic journey' (ibid.: 10).

Subsequently, she wonders, 'Had leaving Guyana liberated me, because I am a woman? Was it possible that leaving India has done the same for my great grandmother a century earlier' (ibid.: 15)? Bahadur uses the narrative technique of *ekphrasis*, which means *description* in Latin and subsumes 'any verbal description of visual phenomena'. It is 'a verbal representation of visual representation' and is, 'therefore, particularly suited to reconstructing the representational climate of a historical period as well as shedding light on the historicity of its media' (Herman 2008: 133).

The first part of the book visits the theme of nostalgia for the homeland that has been kept alive by the descendants of the indentured diaspora in their 'homes' across the world. The homeland is kept alive through 'shards of Hindi' spoken by the author's mother while singing *bhajans*. 'The hymns she didn't understand, from an India she had never seen, a tangible quality' (Bahadur 2013: 5). Bahadur also talks about the power of Bollywood in keeping nostalgia alive in the diaspora. 'The Bollywood megastars were gods too. Both religion and the cinema gave me the conviction that I was Indian, although I had never stepped foot in India, nor had my parents, nor had my grandparents. Bollywood and the *bhajans* gave me language' (ibid.: 6).

Bahadur's *Coolie Woman* is a historiographic narrative, one in which:

> (1) the narrative constructs a modal system that forbids the author/narrator to present undocumented first-person characters' thoughts or third-person characters' thoughts (although it may use the must-have-thought style of inferred psychologies; (2) focuses more on mentalities than on individual minds and thereby produces both distinctive discursive conventions (such as the prevalence of summary over scene) and the need to rethink focalization; and, (3) is based on a relation of homonymy between author and narrator (a historical narrative will always assert that its narrator is identical to the author) (Herman 2008: 217).

A book review posted by Lydia Pyne (2014) on 'New Pages' commends Bahadur's use of quotes through dialogues. She also calls the book a collection of historical photos where the deconstruction of the photos gives the readers a visual narrative to follow, along with faces to relate to. In the technique of *ekphrasis*, the frames often cross each other, thus, a linear narrative is not possible. The form would not suit the content. The narrative frames that Bahadur uses, pull the reader from one narrative and simultaneously make them enter into another. Pyne suggests that in writing *Coolie Woman*, Bahadur has given '. . . the indentured Indian women a voice and a legacy where these women have typically lived in exclusion, stripped of any historical voice.' The narrative gives voices and faces to those who experienced indenture. (Pyne 2014)

Interviewer Annie Paul believes that Bahadur has succeeded '. . . in representing the submerged histories of indentureship in a form that is fluent and vivid, engaging her readers in her personal hunt for answers to the mystery of her great grandmother and her unexplained departure from India at the turn of the twentieth century, pregnant and unmarried' (Paul 2014).

When she moves from the first to the second part of the book, Bahadur changes the voice from first-person narration to a journalistic overt narration of asking rhetorical questions. The rhetorical approach emphasises the 'narrative as an interaction between an author and an audience through the medium of a text for some purpose' (Herman 2008: 500). In her web article, 'Conjure Women, Coolie Women, and Impossible Stories', Briana Wheeler informs, 'In order to capture the entire story, Bahadur had to call on two different aspects of the self: the reporter and the child immigrant. A reporter's way of seeing the world is very similar to a child immigrant's way of seeing the world. They both ask questions.'

In posing her 'impertinent questions', Bahadur is able to open a dialogue with the past and seek answers that have never been documented as the indentured women were illiterate and could not write their experience. Bahadur's dialogue with the past opens the narrative to include polyphonic voices that clamour for attention. The 'term "polyphony" is derived from Mikhail Bakhtin who described it as texts or utterances where more than one voice can be heard.' In such texts, there exists '. . . a plurality of independent and equally valid voices which are not subordinated to any single authorial hierarchy'. In such texts, '. . . the narrator is afforded no special privilege and the narrator counts as one voice in a dialogue of many' (Herman 2008: 443).

Bahadur has meticulously analysed different archives, from oral history and family records to filed reports in the National Archives of different countries, to recover and narrate the alternate history of the experience of indenture. She has also cross-referenced the sources of slavery in order to bring out the mixing of cultural nuances with the archetypes of African-American folktales. In her web article, Briana Wheeler interviews Gaiutra Bahadur to understand the use of the archetype of the 'conjure woman' in an Indian diasporic text. Bahadur explains that the 'conjure woman' originated within the African American tradition, and her archetype was controversial because 'she is wrapped in the dark arts'. In Chesnutt's story, the 'conjure woman' removes another woman's voice with magic, but does not possess the power to restore it'. Bahadur uses the story in her text since it alludes to a voice that has been irretrievably stolen, just like it has for the Indian 'coolie women'. The indentured woman's voice is not heard because there are 'no direct testimonies or memoirs written by women because they were illiterate and incapable of recording their experiences' (Wheeler 2018).

Incorporating folklore and stories from other cultures serves two purposes in the narrative. In one way it dramatises the gaps within the archives and effectively shows the manner in which history is silent in the gaps, the *aporias*. Bahadur does not accept the silence in the colonial records as far as Indian women in indenture are concerned. Instead, Lisa Outer, in her article 'Female Resilience Fortitude Gaiutra Bahadur's Coolie Woman Odyssey Indenture' suggests that 'Bahadur carefully interrogates the copious archival records she mines and highlights their assumptions, their elisions, their silences and their intentional suppression and discrediting of Indian women's voices'. While speaking of Sujaria, her great grandmother who went to the Caribbean, Bahadur argues, 'The power of her colonizers to name and misname formed a key part of her story. To them, she was a coolie woman, a stock character possessing stereotyped qualities, which shaped who she was by limiting who she could ever be' (www.stabroeknews.com).

Francoise Lionnet (2011: 2) depicts 'creolization as a way of energising the field of theory and as a hypothesis with which to map out patterns of contact, migration and linguistic differences in an uneven but interdependent world'. This is especially visible in Gaiutra Bahadur's *Coolie Woman* which recreates and narrates the lives of the indentured Indian women in Guyana. Vijay Mishra (2015: 375) points out in his article 'Postcolonialism 2010-2014' that Bahadur 'has used Creole to great effect to highlight the painful postcolonial narrative'. It works as a route and reroutes the narrative to offer a subaltern view by raising the condition of the women in the plantations.

Bahadur's tone hovers between the journalistic and the academic. When she nears the end of her book, she brings the narrative back to contemporary time and talks about the lives of the descendants of the indentured Indians living in the Caribbean. The thematic sequence of the work remains undisturbed and the author closes the narrative with a recollection of her recent conversation with an ex-indentured woman, Latchmin. 'The past was a baggage that she had to heft, somehow with disfigured arms, as generations of coolie women before her had done. To survive her history, she did as they had. She thought of her family and carried on' (Bahadur 2013: 214).

Shahid Amin (2008: 1) in his prologue to *Event, Metaphor, Memory: Chauri Chaura 1922-1992* states, 'Peasants do not write, they are written about. The speech of humble folk is not normally recorded for posterity, it is wrenched from them in courtrooms and inquisitorial trials. Historians have therefore learned to comb "confessions" and "testimonies" for their evidence, for this is where peasants cry out, dissimulate or, indeed, narrate'. *Coolie Woman* appears to substantiate Shahid Amin's observation and expands the scope to include the subaltern voices belonging to India's indenture diaspora. Authors seeking to recover these silent voices have to play the role of historians in order to view and present the complete picture to their readers.

Theorist Mariam Pirbhai (2010: 47) looks at the narrative techniques employed by women novelists from the Caribbean. She writes, 'Indo-Caribbean women novelists arguably work in tandem with historians in the memorialisation and excavation of women's narratives, for they not only strive to fill in historical gaps but also to mobilize these stories as models of cultural and feminist agency for present generations'.

Totaram Sanadhya had witnessed history and narrated his experience as a testimonio in *My Twenty-One Years in the Fiji Islands,* while Rajendra Prasad has provided an in-depth analysis of indenture in Fiji. Writing from the Caribbean and offering a gendered perspective, Peggy Mohan uses the techniques of the frame narrative and magic realism to show indenture in Trinidad. Gaiutra Bahadur's extensively researched genealogical page-turner uses the techniques of polyphony and *ekphrasis* to recover the silenced female voices during the period of indenture in Guyana.

Postcolonial theorist, Edward Said has spoken of the postcolonial narrative as one which is a counter discourse, reclaiming the lost voices that speak in direct contrast to the western hegemony. He talks about the '. . . colonised breaking free of Western narratives or theologies and representing or narrating themselves, for themselves and others' (Herman 2008: 452).

Indenture writers utilise various techniques to revise and recreate the history in order to challenge the hegemonic discourse that privileges the west and tries to dominate over and silence the 'other'. The role of the writers becomes very crucial and critical in this process since the history they excavate cannot be created. It can only be narrated through literature as the medium of expression. Writers of indenture literature debate and broaden the intellectual discourse while influencing each other. Apart from describing the social, cultural, economic, psychological and political perspectives and experiences of the subject, these writers also analyse the structures and techniques that are the framework on which the colonial discourse is built. Only after they understand the tropes on which the western theory is based can the writers of indenture literature build parallel and opposing structures to shift the narrative towards a postcolonial understanding of the experience.

The effects of labour, loss and longing that were part and parcel of indenture have found an experience-centric vocabulary in literature. In *Mythologies of Migration, Vocabularies of Indenture,* Mariam Pirbhai (2009: 120) suggests that some words are exclusive to and have become appended to the experience of indenture. No text on indenture can function without employing the words—*girmit, coolie, dougla, akrati, kalapani,* etc. These words have, in recent times, become an intrinsic part of the poetics of indenture.

WORKS CITED

Amin, Shahid, *Event, Metaphor, Memory: Chauri Chaura 1922-1992*, Berkeley: University of California Press, 2008.

Ashcroft, Bill, Gareth Griffiths and Helen Tiffin, *The Empire Writes Back*, Oxford: Routledge, 2002.

Abbott, H. Potter, *The Cambridge Introduction to Narrative*, Cambridge: Cambridge University Press, 2018.

Bahadur, Gaiutra, *Coolie Woman: The Odyssey of Indenture*, Gurgaon: Hatchette India, 2013.

Bakhtin, Mikhail, *Rabelais and His World*, Cambridge: MIT Press, 1968.

———, *The Dialogic Imagination: Four Essays*, Austin: University of Texas Press, 2017.

Baldick, Chris, *Dictionary of Literary Terms,* New York: Oxford University Press, 2008.

Beverley, John, *Testimonio: On the Politics of Truth*, Minneapolis: University of Minnesota Press, 2004.

Bhabha, Homi, *The Location of Culture,* New York: Routledge, 1997.

Felman, Shoshana and Dori Laub, *Testimony: Crises of Witnessing in Literature, Psychoanalysis and History*, New York: Routledge, 1992.

Genette, Gerard, *Narrative Discourse: An Essay in Method*, tr. Jane E. Lewin, Ithaca: Cornell University Press, 1981.

———, *Narrative Discourse Revisited*, tr. Jane E. Lewin, Ithaca: Cornell University Press, 1980.

Halliday, M.A.K., 'Antilanguages', *Language as Social Semiotic,* London: Edward Arnold, 1979: pp. 164-82.

———, 'Anti-Languages', *American Anthropologist* 78.3, 1976, pp. 570-84.

Hardy, Barbara, *The Collected Essays of Barbara Hardy: Narrators and Novelists*, Brighton, Sussex: The Harvester Press, 1987.

Herman, David, Manfred Jahn and Marie-Laure Ryan, eds., *Routledge Encyclopedia of Narrative Theory*, London: Routledge, 2008.

Hirsch, Marianne, 'Marked by Memory: Feminist Reflections on Trauma and Transmission', *Extremities: Trauma, Testimony, Community*, ed. Nancy K. Miller and Jason Tougaw, Urbana: Illinois University Press, 2002, pp. 71-91.

———, *The Generation of Postmemory: Writing and Visual Culture after the Holocaust,* New York: Columbia University Press, 2012.

Ifowodo, Ogaga, *History, Trauma and Healing in Postcolonial Narratives: Reconstructing Identities,* New York: Palgrave Macmillan, 2013.

Kaur, Manpreet and Sanjaleen Prasad, 'Home, Migration and New Identities: Some Reflections', *Fijian Studies* 15.1, 2017, pp. 145-58.

Khan, Munshi Rahman, *Autobiography of an Indian Indentured Labourer: Munshi Rahman Khan 1874-1972,* tr. Kathinka Sinha-Kerkhoff, Delhi: Shipra Publications, 2005.

Lionnet, Francoise, *The Creolization of Theory*, Durham, NC: Duke University Press, 2011.

McCormack, Donna, *Queer Postcolonial Narratives and the Ethics of Witnessing*, London: Bloomsbury Academic, 2014.

Mishra, Nivedita, 'The Trinidadian Deewani: Longing and Belonging in Peggy Mohan's Jahajin', *Postcolonial Text* 10.3 & 4, 2015, pp. 1-19.

Mishra, Vijay, 'Postcolonialism 2010-2014', *The Journal of Commonwealth Literature* 50.3, 2015, pp. 369-90.

———, *The Literature of the Indian Diaspora: Theorizing the Diasporic Imaginary*, London: Routledge, 2014.

Mohabir, Nalini, 'Port of Departure, Port of Return: Mapping Indentured Returns to Calcutta', *Small Axe* 18.2, 2014, pp. 108-22.

Mohan, Peggy, *Jahajin*, New Delhi: HarperCollins, 2007.

———, 'Writing Jahajin', *Jahajin*, 12 July 2010, Web. 12 April 2019. <http://peggymohan.blogspot.com/>

Mullan, John, *How Novels Work*, Oxford: Oxford University Press, 2006.

Nayar, Pramod K., *Postcolonial Literature: An Introduction*, New Delhi: Pearson, 2013.

Outer, Lisa, 'Female resilience and fortitude in Gaiutra Bahadur's Coolie Woman: The Odyssey of Indenture,' *Starbroek News*, 12 May 2014, Web. 11 April 2019. <https://www.stabroeknews.com/2014/features/in-the-diaspora/05/12/ female-resilience-fortitude-gaiutra-bahadurs-coolie-woman-odyssey-indenture/>

Paranjape, Makarand, 'Triple Ambivalence: Australia, Canada, and South Asia in the Diasporic Imagination', *Australian Canadian Studies* 20.2, 2002, pp. 81-113.

Paul, Annie, 'A Coolie Woman's Work is Never Done', *The Margins*, 31 March 2014, Web. 18 March 2019. <http://aaww.org/coolie-womans-work-gaiutra-bahadur/>.

Pirbhai, Mariam, *Mythologies of Migration, Vocabularies of Indenture: Novels of the South Asian Diaspora in Africa, the Caribbean and Asia-Pacific*, Toronto: University of Toronto Press, 2009.

———, 'The *Jahaji-Bhain* Principle: A Critical Survey of the Indo-Caribbean Women's Novel, 1990-2009', *The Journal of Commonwealth Literature* 45.1, 2010, pp. 37-56.

Plato, *Republic*, tr. C.J. Emyln Jones and William Preddy, Cambridge, MA: Harvard University Press, 2013.

Prasad, Murari and Binod K. Jha, 'Indian Diasporic Formations in Guyana: Reading Coolie Woman: The Odyssey of Indenture', *Asiatic* 10.2, 2016, pp. 231-44.

Prasad, Rajendra, *Tears in Paradise: Suffering and Struggles of Indians in Fiji, 1879-2004*, Auckland, N.Z.: Pindar, 2010.

Prince, Gerald, *Narratology: The Form and Functioning of Narrative*, Berlin: Mouton, 1982.

Pyne, Lydia, 'Coolie Woman', *New Pages,* 20 August 2014, Web. 22 April 2019. <https://www.newpages.com/item/26701-coolie-woman>

Reddock, R., 'Indian Women and Indentureship in Trinidad and Tobago, 1845-1917: Freedom Denied', *Caribbean Quarterly* 54.4, 2008, pp. 41-68.

Saha, Amit Shankar, 'Exile Literature and the Diasporic Indian Writer', *Rupkatha Journal on Interdisciplinary Studies in Humanities* 1.2, 2009, pp. 186-96.

Sanadhya, Totaram, *My Twenty-one Years in the Fiji Islands,* tr. John Dunham Kelly and Uttra Kumari Singh, Suva, Fiji: Fiji Museum, 1991.

Schröer, Frederik, 'Of Testimonios and Feeling Communities', *Südasien-Chronik - South Asia Chronicle* 6.1, 2016, pp. 149-74.

Shepherd, Verene, *Maharani's Misery: Narratives of a Passage from India to the Caribbean,* Trinidad: The University of West Indies Press, 2002.

Spivak, Gayatri C., 'Can the Subaltern Speak?', *Colonial Discourse and Post-Colonial Theory: A Reader,* ed. Patrick Williams and Laura Chrisman, Hertfordshire: Harvester Wheatsheaf, 1994, pp. 66-111.

———, *Nationalism and the Imagination,* Calcutta: Seagull Books, 2010.

Toolan, Michael J., *Narrative: A Critical Linguistic Introduction,* Oxon: Routledge, 2007.

Wheeler, Brianna, 'Conjure Women, Coolie Women, and Impossible Stories', *The Sewanee Purple,* 10 April 18. Web. 09 May 2019. <https://thesewaneepurple. org/2018/04/10/conjure-women-coolie-women-and-impossible-stories/>

Ward, Abigail, 'Assuming the Burden of Memory: The Translation of Indian Indenture in Peggy Mohan's *Jahajin*', *The Journal of Commonwealth Literature* 48.2, 2013, pp. 269-86.

CHAPTER 5

Emerging from Indenture/ship: Evolving Being and Belonging

'There are no headstones, epitaphs, dates.
The ancestors curl and dry to scrolls of parchment.
They lie like texts
Waiting to be written by the children'
(Dabydeen 2006: 12)

THIS BOOK AIMS to bring together the experience of Indian indenture across different geographical locations to deepen an understanding of the system and interpret the sensibility of the indentured diaspora. The story of indenture began with the abolition of slavery in the 1830s. Since then, there has been no dearth of literature comparing indenture to slavery. Initial writings on indenture followed this well defined 'neo-slavery' paradigm and the focus rarely moved beyond looking at indenture as 'a new system of slavery' (Hugh Tinker) or as 'a clever euphemism for slavery' (Kowlasar Misir). Such writings generally portrayed the indentured labourers as helpless victims bemoaning their fate. There was hardly any in-depth work done on this subject and thus, initial research in this area remained largely descriptive and very rarely analytical.

As a further limitation, indenture literature has remained focussed either on an individual (Sanadhya and Munshi Rahman Khan) or a particular colony (*Fiji's Indian Immigrants* by K.L. Gillion). In today's scenario, the focus needs to shift from such individual and place-specific experiences to enlarge and include a comparative perspective on indenture. The topic needs to be examined in all its complexity and requires a shift from its parochial outlook to one that encompasses the entire experience.

A pertinent question asked with respect to ongoing research on the topic centres around the relevance of indenture literature in today's age. Postcolonial theorist, Homi K. Bhabha (1994: 246-7), suggests in his chapter 'The Postcolonial and Postmodern' in *The Location of Culture* that 'It is from those who have suffered the sentence of history—subjugation, domination, diaspora, the displacement—that we must learn our most enduring lessons for living and thinking'. Indenture was a period in Indian history that sent around 1.3 million Indians as contract labourers to countries as far in the east as Fiji and as far in the west as the Caribbean. Looking at the wide geographical area it covered, an attempt to revisit indenture as a global system carries significant weight in the current age. The indenture diaspora today approximates 4.5 million '. . . who are the offspring of indenture coolies' (Gubili 2018: 193). According to the UN World Migration Report of 2018, '. . . the Indian diaspora is the world's largest, with slightly more than 15.6 million people from India living overseas' (*GK Today*, 18 December 2017). This means that the descendants of the indentured diaspora comprise 28.8 per cent of the total Indian diaspora. This is a fairly large percentage and can no longer be ignored in contemporary times owing to a number of factors, ranging from economic to political.

Clare Anderson (2009: 99) in her paper 'Convicts and Coolies: Rethinking Indentured Labour in the Nineteenth Century', calls for '. . . a change in the frame of analysis of Indian indentured migration'. Critic Madhavi Kale (2000: 3) in her book, *Fragments of Empire: Capital, Slavery and Indian Indentured Labour Migration in the British Caribbean*, support Anderson and suggests a '. . . broadening of research interests that allow us to move beyond the outdated debates about whether indentured labour was "free" or "unfree"'.

Acknowledging the current need for exploring all paradigms, this study engages a broad range of theoretical, conceptual and analytical tools across disciplines to demonstrate that there exists a strong potential to analyse indenture beyond the fixed categories of 'slavery' and 'neo-slavery and the established entities of 'local' and 'global'. It looks at the 'entangled histories' with the agenda of rediscovering the voices of indenture and 'hearing' from them in the postcolonial discourse. In their article, 'Indian Indenture: Speaking Across the Oceans', Goolam Vahed and Ashwin Desai (2012: 196) pose a series of interrelated questions,

> How did Indian indenture tie in with other forms of mobilisation of Asian and African labour by Westerners during this period? What are the similarities and differences between indenture and slavery? What is the relationship between Indian indenture and Britain's Asian convict labour regime during the nineteenth century? What kinds of constraints did workers under the different labour systems face? What was the form and nature of resistance among workers? What were the perceptions of the labour migrants themselves and how did these evolve? What was the particular evolution of caste, ethnic, 'race', and gender relations in the colonies? How did North and South Indians relate to each other? How did the indentured view India? Why did the aftermath of indenture have different outcomes in different colonies?

To find the answers to these questions, it is important to look at Indian indenture from a comparative perspective. The narratives studied in this book describe the experience of indenture in Fiji and the Caribbean. These narratives offer a holistic view of indenture and include the gendered perspective.

In the literary sphere, the writing slowly progressed from arguing about whether indenture was a new form of slavery to mining the colonial records and archives to recover the lost voices in Indian indenture. In these writings, history and literature came together to bring out a clear representation and record of the colonial past. To delve deeper into a subject, it becomes imperative to look at the literature that is born of the particular history. Literary writings on indenture thus offer a perspective, hitherto unnoticed or under-represented in its history. This is because colonial history itself is a manipulated record and offers a limited colonial perspective through a politics of representation.

To a large extent, the experiences of the indentured people across the colonies, on the surface at least, replicate each other and call attention to the seemingly uniform nature of indenture. However, this is only on the surface. As Vijay Mishra (2014: 55) states in *The Literature of the Indian Diaspora,* 'Implicit in our rendition of the *girmit* ideology has been a resistance to a homogenizing narrative'. There were, however, very definite convergences about the experiences across the colonies. The indentured Indians were regarded as outsiders in the colonies they were sent to. The reason for this can be traced to their own unwillingness to let go of their Indian customs and traditions, especially in Fiji. Vijay Mishra extrapolates that,

> The Indians, as an instance of a cultural minority, persist in seeing themselves as a group symbolically marginalized and excluded from the nation. Indeed the Caribbean as a collective excludes the Indian from its image of the nation which remains primarily Creole. At the same time in Fiji and Trinidad, Indians have fiercely resisted any dilution of their cultural difference and have steadfastly refused symbolic incorporation into a prior, more fluid and mobile, 'ethnic' category. (ibid.)

This work also examines the convergences and divergences in the experience of indenture faced by the *girmitiyas* in Fiji and the *coolies* in the Caribbean. Theorists favouring the idea of convergence believe that societies that are subject to similar political, economic and legal pressures ultimately end up developing on similar lines. This presupposes that all the plantation colonies that were host to indentured labour would develop similarly. However, practice is generally removed from theory and in the case of indenture at least, it has been noticed that the Indian indentured communities in the Caribbean and Fiji developed in ways distinct from each other.

Starting from the agreement (contract), which followed more or less the same stipulation, most of the aspects of indenture across the colonies were uniform. The betrayal by the *akratis,* the loss of caste and subsequently their identity, the shared camaraderie of the *jahaji bhais* and *behens* on the ships, the kind of work allotted on the plantations and the patterns of resistance—these were some of the common features of indenture across the Caribbean, as well as in Fiji. The other side of indenture, which included the sexual intimacies of Indian women with the colonial overseers and other Indian men, the dependency on alcohol, wife murders and violence, were also a global condition of the system.

However, against the backdrop of the unifying experiences, there were divergences based on how the experience was wrought, as well as the challenges that were unique to each colony. Divergences are as significant as convergences when examining the system of Indian indenture. They offer a heterogeneous look at an apparently homogeneous system. A comparative perspective enriches an understanding of the indentured experience which was not static across colonies. While the system remained fairly consistent after the initial phase was over, it was still marked by a lot of ambiguity, especially in the first two decades. The rules and regulations kept changing based on the whims and fancies of the colonial officials and nothing was fixed.

The experience of indenture varied across different parts of the world based on several factors, such as the terms of the contract entered into by the labourers with the British, the colony they were sent to, as well as the officials responsible for their voyage and subsequent housing in the plantations. The terms of the contract were also not fixed and kept varying to suit the needs of the plantation owners. They varied from two to five years in the beginning and were only later fixed for five years with the option of the indentured person continuing the indenture for a further five years if desirous of a free return passage to India. However, the central feature of the system which allowed for penal sanctions for any breach in the contract ensured that the 'fixed' term also remained open to change. Owing to considerable backlash and resistance to this 'change-at-will' feature, an ordinance was passed to ensure that some sense of consistency should prevail. Passed in 1854, this ordinance remained active till 1917.

The penal feature of the indenture system meant that the labourers could be held and prosecuted as criminals for the most trivial of offences. They were not allowed to leave their respective plantations and even then, were required to carry a pass stipulating that they had been granted permission to leave the plantation. Theorist Sherry Ann Singh (2013) in her article 'The Experience of Indian Indenture in Trinidad: Arrival and Settlement', states that the '. . . the dynamism of the experience of Indian indenture is evident in the multifarious debates that it has spawned; debates that continuously reaffirm the global presence and contribution of the Indian indenture diaspora'.

Since indenture was the immediate successor of slavery, the impact of slavery on indenture is an important factor in analysing the different experiences in Fiji and the Caribbean. The plantation colonies in the Caribbean were already employing slave labour before they received indentured labour. This was not the case in Fiji which had been annexed by the British as late as 1874 and never witnessed slavery. The Caribbean colonies lacked a native society. Slavery had changed their social landscape and made them settler colonies. The emigrant Indians in the Caribbean had to negotiate with a plural society that comprised of Europeans, native Caribbean population and emancipated Afro-Caribbean slaves. In Fiji, the Indians taken as indentured labourers had to share space with a reluctant indigenous population, i.e. the iTaukei. The Fijians were naturally suspicious of the Indians who came from British India and thus kept the newcomers on the periphery, not allowing them the physical or social space to integrate or assimilate. The end result was that the indentured Indians were cut off from mainstream society and placed into isolated communities in the plantations.

Examining the experience of indenture is thus crucial to understand the global mobility of the Indian diasporic community. Critic Nienke Boer (2019), in her article 'Indenture', believes that 'Studying and teaching texts about indentured laborers allows us to intervene in debates within both subaltern studies and "history from below", as we think about the agency of the indentured laborers' (*Global South Studies*). For literary theorists and critics, indenture literature opens up a wide canon of texts that can be used to build literary frameworks on which the system can be studied and analysed. Vijay Mishra (2014: 22), for example, argues for what he calls a '*girmit* ideology' within the literature emerging out of South Asian indenture: *girmitiya*, being one of the terms by which the indentured labourers came to be known. In her seminal work, *Mythologies of Migration, Vocabularies of Indenture,* literary theorist Mariam Pirbhai (2009) look at certain words that are exclusive to defining the experience of indenture. According to her, no text on indenture can function without employing the words—*girmit, coolie, dougla, akrati, kalapani,* etc., which have, in recent times, become an intrinsic part of the poetics of indenture. Khal Torabully and Marina Carter's (2002: 15) *Coolitude* attempts to disclose the 'Coolie's story which has been shipwrecked ('erased') in the ocean of a Western-made historical discourse as well as a world of publication and criticism'. The authors have underlined the aesthetics of the voyage as an essential component in indenture poetics.

By incorporating texts describing the experience of indenture in Trinidad and Guyana in the Caribbean, as well as texts depicting the experience in Fiji, the scope of this book has been broadened to include comparison, thereby allowing a deeper understanding of the system. Indenture in British Guyana began in 1838 and in Trinidad, it began in 1842, while Fiji was the last colony to receive indentured labourers in 1879. Thus, studying literary works originating from these colonies can help in generating an understanding of the changing phases of indenture.

In terms of numbers in the Caribbean, theorist Lomarsh Roopnarine's (2003: 106) article 'East Indian Indentured Emigration to the Caribbean: Beyond the Push and Pull Model' highlights the statistics. 'Guyana received 238,909 indentured people while Trinidad received 143,939 Indian immigrants'. Brij Lal's (2004: 13) book, *Girmitiyas,* an outcome of his extensive research on indenture in Fiji informs the readers that Fiji was home to 60,965 indentured Indians. In his article, 'The Odyssey of Indenture: Fragmentation and Reconstitution in the Indian Diaspora', Brij Lal also provides detailed statistics on the origins of the indentured people in India. 'For the most part, those who immigrated to the indenture colonies came from north India, initially from the districts of Bihar, then from the eastern regions of the United Provinces'. He also relates that in Fiji, '. . . the United Provinces provided 80 per cent of the immigrants, with Bihar and Bengal providing 13 per cent' (Lal 1996: 170). Historian K.O. Laurence, in his book *A Question of Labour: Indentured Immigration into Trinidad and British Guiana, 1875-1917* narrates,

> Between 1880 and 1889, 36,505 Indians emigrated as indentured labourers to British Guiana. Of these, the majority (17,505) was from modern-day Uttar Pradesh, with a remaining plurality from Awadh, Bengal, and Bihar. During the same period in Trinidad, 23,902 emigrated with a similar regional

breakdown: 11,385 from Uttar Pradesh, and a remaining 12,517 from Bengal and Bihar. (Laurence 1994: 106-7)

While exploring the nuances of indenture across the colonies, it has been noted that the system shared the recruitment patterns put in place under the contract regulations for indenture. The contracts provided for free passage from the colony back to India in exchange for five years of 'harsh labour with penal conditions' on the plantations. Those who wished to return to India after their five years were up could do so by utilizing their own funds. If they wanted a 'free' return passage to India, they would have to re-indenture and would be required to work for another five years on the plantations.

Almost every historian, critic and theorist writing about indenture has voiced their concern about suicide being a legacy of indenture. Across, the colonies, suicides had become a haunting spectre for the plantation officials who were constantly questioned about the work environment on the plantations and its link to the high number of suicides. Even before they left the territorial waters of India and set out on the long voyage to the colonies, many indentured men and women jumped overboard from the ships. This number was so high that in the later years when the ships used to sail from Calcutta, little boats used to follow them to save the Indians who jumped overboard. There were many possible causes for suicide on the long voyage. Chief among these was the loss of caste owing to crossing the *kalapani* (which was akin to facing existential angst for a Hindu). Others could not face the anxiety about an indeterminate future in an alien land and their inability to cope with the resultant stress made them jump. A third reason was the scarcity of food coupled with the depression that was owed to spending long hours in confinement under the deck. These people had never seen the ocean from their villages in the landlocked Indian hinterland. They were suddenly thrust into a vessel crossing an ocean and forced to spend between two to four months in a confined space on the ship. This affected their psychological health and prompted suicide.

On the plantations, the reasons for suicides were linked to nostalgia and acute depression emanating from the desire to return home. When they realized they were trapped and return seemed impossible, the men chose to end their lives. Statistics reveal that Fiji witnessed the highest number of suicides among all the plantation colonies. In his article, 'Veil of Dishonour: Sexual Jealousy and Suicide on Fiji Plantations', historian Brij Lal (1985: 215) writes, 'Between 1884 and 1925, over 300 Indian immigrants in Fiji committed suicide'. In his book *Chalo Jahaji*, he reports that in Fiji, the Indian suicide rate '. . . was the highest among all Indian labour importing colonies and much higher than India itself' (Lal 2012: 135). Lal also observes that a quarter of all suicides were committed within the first six months of arriving in Fiji. A majority of these suicides were committed by men. The alienation, uprootedness and emotional turmoil linked to nostalgia were more keenly wrought in the men than in the women, which explains the higher percentage of suicides among men. The suicide statistics of the indentured men in the Caribbean also reveal the direct link between the suicide rate and the percentage of women in the colony. Where the percentage of women was the lowest, the rate of suicide was the highest.

Fiji also witnessed a lesser number of conversions to Christianity than the Caribbean. The reason for this was the counter-movement launched by the Hindus against conversions, as well as the numerous attempts made to resuscitate the religion by the Hindu sects and *panths* that became active during the Hindu revival. Preserving their culture and religion was seen as an act of resistance against conversions being pressed on the *girmitiyas* by the colonial powers. The scope of Hindu conversions to Christianity was much more in the Caribbean. In Trinidad and Guyana, the Canadian Presbyterian Church initiated the process of converting the indentured people. The missionaries used education as a point of entry into the Indian homes. They built schools for the children of the Indian labourers and taught the lessons of the church in Hindi. This made it easier for the Indians in the Caribbean to convert. Conversion also gave them a chance to be seen as a serious part of a big group. The indentured Indians believed that by converting they would be able to come closer to the European race which subscribed to the Christian faith.

While the Hindus in the Caribbean converted to Christianity, the Muslim population continued to uphold their faith in the foreign lands. In Fiji, the Muslims were inseparable from their faith. They claimed that it was their religion that had saved them and given them the incentive to survive and sustain their identity in the colony. Naseer Mustapha (2012: 43), in his article, 'Muslims in the Caribbean' extrapolates, 'The indentured people of Muslim faith in Fiji formed an exclusive community in the plantations which was separate even from the Hindus'. While they celebrated the *Ram Lila* festival with the Hindus and their own *tazia* celebration during Muharram was attended by the Hindus in the colony, the Muslims remained largely aloof and chose not to mix and mingle with the Hindus or with the indigenous population in Fiji. The case in the Caribbean islands was very different from that of Fiji. In the colonies of Trinidad and Guyana, the Muslims intermingled with the Hindus and with the Creoles. The religious feast of *hossey* (*tazia*) was observed jointly by the Indians and the Creoles. Approximately fifteen per cent of the Indian indentured immigrants in the Caribbean were Muslims (ibid.: 44). This group was a minority within a minority in the plantations. They had a strong sense of group solidarity, which in turn helped them keep their traditions alive and intact in the colonies. The African slaves were predominantly of Muslim faith and had been living in the colonies before the arrival of the Indian immigrants. While they had resisted conversion to Christianity during the years of slavery, the rigid conditions on the plantations had made it difficult for them to retain their faith in its entirety. Indenture brought an influx of indentured Muslims from India, and Islam was re-introduced in the Caribbean.

Fiji and the Caribbean also differed with respect to the outlook of acculturation and assimilation that the indentured immigrants followed in the adopted land. The *girmitiyas* of Fiji resisted assimilation into the host culture and retained their own cultural ethos. In *Chalo Jahaji*, Brij Lal gives an evocative account of the emotions of the Indians in Fiji,

> They seemed to be shipwrecked by fate in a place they did not, perhaps could not, fully embrace, and they could not return to the place they so dearly loved. They were a people caught in between the tensions of culture and history, resisting assimilation into the ways of their adopted homeland by re-enacting archaic customs from a remembered past (Lal 2012: 26).

The Caribbean situation was very different from the circumstances in Fiji. Owing to the previous settler population of the emancipated slaves, Trinidad and Guyana had become plural societies. In such societies, assimilation was the norm, and acculturation was the keyword. The women who immigrated to the Caribbean were pioneers in assimilation and acculturation, and in keeping alive the language of their 'home land'. As active agents of cultural exchange, the women negotiated identities and built a strong sense of collective consciousness in the plantations. Within a year of their indenture, women stopped wearing the traditional Indian *saree*. Instead, they started wearing long skirts (*ghaghra*) and long blouses (*jhula*) (Mohan 2007: 146). Gradually, even this was replaced with a belted dress of mid-calf length with an *orhni* (veil) covering the head.

In terms of language, it is interesting to note that just as they had held on fast to their Indian customs and traditions, the indentured labourers in Fiji managed to keep their language sacrosanct. The growth of the Indo-Fijian community was possible owing to the emergence of the common language called Fiji *Bhat* (Fiji Hindi), which is a vernacular form of the dialects spoken in Hindi, Bhojpuri and Awadhi in the North Indian states from where the *girmityas* had come. They kept the language of their homeland alive in the plantations and strictly refused to let go of it. Over the years, it became a determinant of their distinct identity. Refusal to adapt to language change in the foreign land is a clear indication of the intentions of the indentured Indians in Fiji. It goes to show that they had no intention of settling permanently in Fiji and were always looking back at India with a longing to return. The women continued to wear *sarees* and the men stuck to their Indian *kurtas* and *dhotis*. The *girmitiyas* also continued to savour the same recipes followed in the Indian hinterland. It seems there was a tacit agreement to return to India and any effort made towards assimilation and acculturation was viewed as unnecessary.

However, in the Caribbean, language underwent a major change. Creole was spoken during the day to communicate with the Creole population in Trinidad and Guyana. Bhojpuri was spoken only among the indentured people, and even then it was restricted to the first generation of the indentured people. Speaking the coloniser's language was an act recognized by the Indians as a means of getting closer to the Western civilization which they seemed to have accepted as part of their conversion to the Christian faith. Food also underwent a phase of 'creolisation'. *Dal puri* (little fried *rotis* and lentils) was an Indian dish. It was creolised into 'doubles' (little fried *rotis* made up into sandwiches with spicy *chana*, i.e. chickpeas, as the filling). The staple *rotis* (flat round Indian bread made from wheat flour) became bigger in the plantations.

The difference in the practices of land legislation followed in the Caribbean and Fiji was a big cause for the inability of the Indian people to get assimilated in Fiji. The Land Reforms put in place by the British government in Fiji did not allow Indians to own land in the colony. They could only lease the land from the Fijians. The land had always been the basis of livelihood for most Indians. However, freehold land was denied to the Indians and the leasehold land was difficult to afford for the *girmitiyas*. Eminent historian Sarva Daman Singh in *Indians Abroad* writes,

> Throughout the history of Indian settlement in Fiji, they have been helplessly dependent on leases which have been the only means of obtaining land. Indian reliance on Fijian land became the determining factor of relations between the two races. 83 per cent of the land was inalienably Fijian. In 1917, 51.7 per cent of Indian holdings were native leases. In terms of Gordon's dispensation, Fijians would always be the masters of the land; Indians would be tenants subject to Fijian willingness, and the capital would come from the Europeans. (Singh 2003: 213)

The Caribbean followed different legislation for land ownership, which proved to be advantageous to the ex-indentured Indians. The colonial powers running the plantation colonies in the Caribbean wanted their profits to keep growing. They had witnessed the end of slavery and the subsequent troubles undertaken towards finding an alternative to the problem of finding cheap labour to work in the plantations. Once the Indians had adjusted to the Caribbean society it was hoped by the colonists that the idea of a return to India would fade away. However, the sense of nostalgia, especially for the men, was so acute that as soon as their ten years of indentureship would be drawing to a close, they would be raring to return to India. The plantation owners knew that the loss of this labour force would impact their profit-generating enterprise. To keep the ex-indentured Indians from going back to India, the colonial governments in the Caribbean islands decided to make an offer of ten acres of land instead of a free return passage to India. This legislation was passed in 1869 and some plantations even offered money as an incentive for the Indians to stay on in the colony instead of the return passage to India. It was hoped that this money would be invested by the Indians in buying land in the colony.

Women in the Caribbean took up this offer of land in lieu of return fare to India because they had chosen not to repatriate. This is because the women who had left India knew that they would have no home in India to return to. The rules of patriarchy that governed the social order in India would open doors for the returning men but close them for the indentured women. This was especially true for those men who had left their wives behind in India. Some had remarried in the plantations while some had just 'kept' women without the ritual of marriage. It would not be possible for such men to explain the presence of the 'other woman' to the members of their families in India.

During the years of indenture, one aspect remained uniform across all the colonies. The male-female sex ratio remained skewed throughout the entire period of indenture, with women numbering only 30 to 40 per cent of the total number of men. Initially, this disparity in their numbers accorded women the agency they had lacked in India. Women used this agency to better their financial condition in the plantations. They were also looking for security and chose men who could look after and protect them. Since Indian marriages were not recognised in the plantations, women used this anomaly to leave their physically, socially or financially 'weak' husbands to climb up the social ladder by finding someone more suited to their requirements. Thus, the comparatively lesser ratio of women to the men in the plantations also became a factor in degrading the social and sexual standards in the plantations.

During the initial years of indenture, the women in the colonies had enjoyed a certain sense of freedom away from the set social norms that governed their behaviour in India. This freedom, however, became the source of unmitigated sexual jealousy in the Indian men since they now faced competition if they sought a relationship with an Indian woman in the colonies. Jeremy Poynting (1987: 133) has pointed out in his article 'East Indian Women in the Caribbean' that the indenture experience of the women was one of multiple oppression. He suggests, 'The reason for both the possibilities and the miseries of the Indian woman's experiences during the indenture period was her scarcity'. The agency exercised by the women added fuel to the Indian male's inability to have sole power and monopoly over his partner. He desired to establish complete control over his woman. She did not want to let go of her new-found-freedom willingly. This created an atmosphere of hostility which was ultimately responsible for the 'wife murders' in the colonies.

The degrading social and sexual standards followed in the plantations resulted in the ultimate crumbling of the Indian family system. The culture of violence that was perpetuated by the colonists in the plantation colonies became the underlying cause for the heinous crimes and horrific levels of violence committed against Indian women. Since they had to endure physical punishments and extreme violence on the plantations, the Indian men developed a pattern of violence against their women as an outlet for their psychological trauma. The culture of violence on the fields had permeated into their family life. Violence against women was common in all the colonies but it was considerably higher in the Caribbean. Fiji also saw wife murders but their number and scope of brutality were lesser than it was in the Caribbean. The indentured women on the plantation were thus twice-victimised, first by the colonial officials on the ships and plantations, and then by their own men who, instead of helping them, used to beat them up. Sexually abused by the Europeans, they could not even look to their own men for help and protection. Writing to a newspaper about the faces of women in the indenture, missionary Hannah Dudley's letter to the *Modern Review* has been quoted verbatim by Totaram Sanadhya in his book,

> They arrive in this country timid, fearful women not knowing where they are to be sent. They are allotted to plantations like so many dumb animals … they are punished by being struck or fined and are even sent to gaol. Life on the plantations alters their demeanour and even their faces.…The look on those women's faces haunts me … only about 33 women are brought out to Fiji to every one hundred men. I cannot go into details concerning this system of legalized prostitution … every few months some Indian man

murders for unfaithfulness the woman he regards as his wife. (Sanadhya 1991: 71).

While the 'wife murders' across the plantation have been placed on record and can be accessed in the archives, what is not visible is the accounts written by the women from Fiji. This is because there are no accounts written by the indentured women in Fiji. Whether it is the story of Kunti or Narayani, it was a man writing about the experience of the woman. This has been the case in most of the colonies with only the men writing about the experience. Even where the protagonist is a woman, it is a man writing and narrating the events from a woman's perspective. Such a narrative does not answer the questions since the language of trauma can be uttered only by the victim. Women in indenture were viewed as passive participants and were kept in the margins and given a secondary place in the narrative.

The gender-representation gap in indenture is very large and is felt most strongly while looking at a list of works on the labour system from across the colonies. This gap is considerably larger in Fiji because there is no woman author who has written about the experience of indenture in that part of the world. Also the Caribbean did not produce any work by a female author during the time of indenture. However, during the last two decades, women writers from the Caribbean have been very active in writing about the gendered experience. The *Kala Pani* poetics in the Caribbean was started as a literary initiative to promote a collective female voice and offer it a space to speak from. Their writings are very important towards generating an understanding of indenture since they can apply the female sensibility and offer a holistic and balanced view of Indian indenture.

While this book seeks to offer in-depth insight on indenture and bring out the interplay of the homogeneous, as well as the heterogeneous nature of the colonial labour system, there are nevertheless, some research gaps. Firstly, there are no surviving (ex)indentured labourers who could have been interviewed face-to-face. Makarand Paranjape (2002: 9) states in the 'Introduction' to *In Diaspora*,

It is also important to remember that the old diaspora, made up largely of subaltern and underprivileged classes, hardly produced any literature at all.

Theirs was still mostly an oral culture. It consisted of stories, narratives, songs, and texts which, by and large, did not enter into the print medium. This rich archive of orature and para-literature is yet to be explored.

To excavate the original voices of the *girmitiyas,* this study was limited to mining the oral archive of documentaries and viewing them with a critical and analytical eye. While the digital interface of documentaries has managed to save some voices, it does not have the human element that is considered essential in uncovering a psychological subject. The lack of original *girmitiya* voices is thus a regrettable drawback in this work.

Secondly, the second generation born to the indentured diaspora is reluctant to talk about the indenture system and hesitant to recount its trauma. This is because the first generation wanted to keep their children away from revisiting the harrowing experience of indenture. They forbade any discussion on the subject. Some of the members of the second generation, especially the descendants of the returnees, bemoaned their lack of knowledge about the system despite being physically close to it. The subject was taboo in the households. Branded as *tapuwallahs*, the returnees who had bought themselves a place back into their caste were wary about doing or saying anything to unsettle the fine balance of social order in the Indian society. They were keen to belong to India and any discussion of the foreign lands where they had laboured and suffered was studiously wiped out from the memory of their children. Peggy Mohan's *Jahajin* has made a very telling reference in this light to explain how Bhojpuri was not allowed to be spoken in the Caribbean homes of the ex-indentured labourers. They gave this diktat because they associated the language with the trauma of indenture and refused to pass it on to their children.

In his narrative, *Tears in Paradise,* author Rajendra Prasad, the third generation descendent of Fiji's indentured diaspora writes,

Until the 1960s, the influence of the pioneer generation had somehow inhibited public discussion, research or rediscovery of this important period of Indo-Fijian history. The children of *girmitiyas*, largely illiterate, were born or grew up under the turbulence of *girmit* and, subsequently, were ambivalent towards their history. This was attributed to a lack of vision in the leadership of the community and the overpowering influence of their *girmitiya* parents' unwillingness to discuss that painful era. The code of silence remained intact until the emergence of a younger generation of educated Indo-Fijians. They gained the confidence of their illiterate parents and a part of that early history began to be shed over that dark period. (Prasad 2010: 131)

Vijay Mishra (2014: 109) writes in the *Literature of the Indian Diaspora*, 'Trauma in language always arrives late, not that it never existed, but that it occurs after the event, as a deferred experience'. This encapsulation of the trauma faced by the indentured Indians finds a place in the language that is evoked in the narratives of the indenture diaspora. 'The transmission is not via identification (the classical Freudian position) but by the witnessing of the fracture in the language and by being haunted or possessed by what it hides' (ibid.: 116). Mishra also believes that when the diaspora returns to the homeland, '. . . it has no consciousness of the earlier history; it has only an experience of an Indian diasporic life-world overlaid with idioms that glorified the homeland' (ibid.: 120).

The final gap in this work is due to the lack of women voices from Fiji. This lacuna does not allow a gendered perspective to come through and permeate the analysis to give it a balanced texture. Indenture literature originating from Fiji is written by male authors and thus lacks female sensibility. We do hear about Kunti and Narayani but their accounts were ghostwritten by male writers and are thus suspect in nature. The indenture history is full of violence perpetuated against women. Gaiutra Bahadur and Peggy Mohan have been able to bring out the experiences of indentured women in the Caribbean in their texts. They have offered a very balanced narrative by depicting women not only as stereotyped victims of the system but also as a collective that wielded tremendous agency owing to their small number. The lack of similar narratives from Fiji does not accord the platform needed in this study to draw a comparative analysis of the gendered experience in the two colonies.

Cathy Caruth (2016: 268) in *Unclaimed Experience: Trauma, Narrative, and History*, believes that '. . . language is capable of bearing witness only by a failure of witnessing or representation. . .'. This essentially means that trauma can be transferred to those who have not physically witnessed it. In this sense then, '. . . the writing by the descendants of the indentured diaspora is a literal recall and transfer of the traumatic experience'. Thus, almost all '. . . literature written by descendants of the indentured diaspora is a narrative of traumatic experience being re-collected and re-enacted on paper. Whatever canvas they are mounted on, these writings are predominantly "haunted by the spectres of trauma"' (Mishra 2014: 118).

In *The Diaspora Writes Home,* theorist Jasbir Jain (2015: 208), while writing about indenture states, 'When the past is so powerful, there is every need to negotiate it'. Despite the quantum of research available on Indian indenture, there are certain aspects of the system that need to be analysed further to reveal a holistic view of this critical paradigm. The following paragraphs look at possible routes that can be taken up for further study as an offshoot of the present work. Each of these aspects can be presented either as brief overviews in research articles or developed substantially into full research theses.

In the literature available on indenture, there is a lacuna regarding the precise role played by the Indian middlemen in recruiting the labourers for the colonies. Their position in the system needs to be actively researched and analysed. It is true that without the support of the British officials in India and the plantation officials in the colonies, the middlemen could not have pursued the imperialist need of recruitment actively. Research in the past has focussed on the internal push factors that prevailed upon the Indians to emigrate. However, what has been neglected in these studies is the active recruitment conducted by the Indian middlemen who were responsible for creating awareness about indenture in the colonies as a possible source of work. How did these middlemen convince, lure and manipulate the Indians into indenture? Domestic migration was common in India but overseas emigration had been taboo owing to the Hindu belief of losing one's caste on crossing the *kalapani.* How did the middlemen tide over this fact? Did they use political, economic or psychological manipulation to make the Indians sign the indenture contract? It would also be especially telling to discover how these middlemen filled the required quota of women. Lomarsh Roopnarine (2003: 130), in his article, suggests that a study on the '. . . active recruitment and the use of Indian middlemen have to be conducted because imperialism lacked adequate linkages necessary to make Indian emigrants aware of labor opportunities and to make their displacement a just cause. . .'.

Medical humanities is a relatively new and emerging field that connects the disciplines of medicine and humanities to investigate and understand the effects of illness and disease on patients owing to the social environment they inhabit. The system of indenture was responsible for the indentured people suffering postcolonial trauma and stress disorders. Research scholars working on the complex nature of colonialism and its impact on human health can use the current research to extend the dialogue between indenture studies and medical humanities. Thomas Lawrence Long finds that 'European colonialism has had a direct, immediate and obvious impact on human health … from the effects of environmental damage to the incalculable trauma produced by colonial violence and dispossession'. Further, '. . . colonised subjects are aware that social and cultural oppression can have somatic effects that are heritable and can potentially affect the future generations' (Long 2018). Thus, knowing the history behind the large number of cases of domestic violence against women in the Caribbean can be of help during their treatment. The high numbers of alcoholism in the indentured diaspora can also be treated better if their underlying cause is noted. Similarly, the high incidence of blackouts faced by the descendants of the indentured people can be analysed by psychologists to link to postmemory and indenture. The human approach in medical treatment is an important requirement in such cases.

Research on indenture has revealed the true history of the imperialist system that has long remained buried under the colonial master narrative. Perpetrators of the widespread physical, emotional and psychological wrongs committed against the indentured people should be held accountable for their crimes against humanity. Literature on indenture should encourage a widespread and ongoing dialogue about the labour system. Until and unless the wrongs are brought to light, there will be no cause to call for reparations that are owed to the descendants of the indenture diaspora.

The current work has taken into account the various themes related to indenture in Fiji and the Caribbean. It has taken a holistic view and used the apparatus of comparing and contrasting the experiences of the indentured people in the two colonies. Experiences on the other plantation colonies can also be analysed on the same apparatus.

This framework applied in this book can thus be used as a foundation to compare and analyse the indenture experiences in the other plantation colonies, such as Africa and Mauritius, to broaden the field for further research.

It is a fact that Indian migration to the plantation colonies took place from both, north and south India. A majority of the Indians who emigrated from north India came from the United Provinces and Bihar. Some numbers also came from Punjab. It is also known that famines, droughts, new land regulations, the First Indian War of Independence of 1857, etc., were some of the factors that led to Indians signing up for indenture. However, research is rather limited on the origins of the indentured people from south India. Which provinces did they come from? What induced them to migrate? Were the push and pull factors for emigration different for south India? The answers to these questions can be answered only after extensive research has been undertaken with respect to this aspect of Indian indenture.

Another aspect of indenture that has not received enough attention is the manner in which the system was used as a possible escape route by the people who had fought against the British in 1857. It is a recorded fact that the years between 1858 and 1860 saw remarkably greater numbers of emigrants willing to be indentured. This is an anomaly because the recruitment figures of emigrants had remained low throughout the period of indenture. The middlemen had a hard time filling the depots with the requisite number of people. Forced migrations were more the norm and voluntary emigrants were relatively fewer in number. That being the case, were the *sepoys* of the 'failed' mutiny looking for an alternative to political victimisation or possible imprisonment? Informed research is required to be conducted in this area to bring out the reasons for this anomaly in emigration numbers.

One of the areas that deserves greater attention in the literature of the twice-migrants of the indentured diaspora. Further study can take into account the experience of the twice-migrated which has been a source of unrelieved trauma and has consequently given rise to a distinct social formation in the children of the indentured diaspora. Their narratives throw light on their experience as one beset with the anxiety of displacement and finally of disillusionment. The migration process of the twice-migrants is complex. It comprises two courses of direction—the first being the migration of their ancestors from India to the colonies and the second, the migration of their parents from the plantation colonies to other countries. Their experience emphasizes the issues of migrancy and also evaluates their negotiating, interrogating and navigating the cultural constructs involved in aiding the emergence of a new hybrid identity. Brij Lal (2004: 59) finds it ironic '. . . that a century later, the tension between alienation and attachment still animates the lives of many overseas Indians . . .'

Indenture is an interdisciplinary topic and while it can be researched independently, it will be most effectively analysed when studied across the disciplines of literature, history, sociology, psychology and anthropology. The topic can also be studied pertaining to its importance in the disciplines of economics and political science.

The colonial powers that had sanctioned indenture projected it as beneficial to the Indians at a time when they were plagued by famines and droughts. Thus, indenture was shown by the British in a positive light. However, this view was far from the real truth about indenture. In Sarva Daman Singh's (2003: 11) view, 'Indian indentured labour was the human subsidy paid for the pecuniary profitability of Britain's colonies. . .'. Unfortunately, the view projected by the British continued to perpetuate since the Indians who had been indentured rarely spoke about the trauma and the associated shame they had endured on the plantations. Thus, the true story of indenture was effectively marginalised at the national and international levels. There is no single work that narrates the system of Indian indenture at a global level comprehensively.

Current literature available on indenture is limited to country-specific experiences. Even where there has been a study conducted on a global level, it has remained restricted to a few themes and has neglected to cover the entire experience of indenture. While comparisons abound between slavery and indenture, there has been relatively no comparative research done on the experience of indenture in different colonies. Narratives detailing the gendered experience of indenture are also very limited with there being no published work on the gendered experience in Fiji. The existing texts, written by colonial officials or male authors have typecast the women in indenture as victims. Their agency has remained unacknowledged in such texts. Previous literature on indenture comprises texts that were written during the indenture period by missionaries and colonial officials. Later works on indenture, written after it had ended, comprise texts both by Indian and non-Indian scholars and researchers. Some of these are fictional accounts written by British authors and carry romantic undertones of relationships between the European officials and 'exotic' Indian indentured women on the plantations. These texts do not serve the purpose of this study. Of late, the literary canon of indenture is seeing an influx of narratives written by the third and fourth generation descendants of the indentured people. They are recovering and bringing out the marginalised voices while lifting the curtain to reveal the hidden truths of indenture. These narratives project the ways through which the legacy of indentureship continues to shape the lives and identities of the Indian indenture diaspora.

The interdisciplinary and critical nature of this work is intended to streamline the topic and affect a greater understanding of the system of indenture. Straddling diverse disciplines, this study is expected to reconnect the history of people and places to the homeland. Nicholas Mirzoeff (2000: 13) suggests in *Diaspora and Visual Culture: Representing Africans and Jews,* 'A diaspora ... cannot be represented from the viewpoint of one-point perspective. The space of diaspora exists in multiple times and places, encompassing those who leave as well as those who stay and those who return. It is multiple, fluid, and at times paradoxical. It is about the future as well as the past'. Thus, diaspora sensibility can be understood in terms of 'double consciousness' or as Mirzoeff claims, '. . . as a dialectic between past and present, it may also be rethought in terms of an indeterminate future to come' (ibid.). There is thus, an urgent need to critically analyse the literature on indenture to re-engage and allow India's history to be put in the correct perspective for it to be valued by future generations.

Works Cited

Anderson, Clare, 'Convicts and Coolies: Rethinking Indentured Labour in the Nineteenth Century', *Slavery & Abolition* 30.1, 2009, pp. 93-109.

Bahadur, Gaiutra, *Coolie Woman: the Odyssey of Indenture*, Gurgaon: Hatchette India, 2013.

Bhabha, Homi, 'The Postcolonial and the Postmodern: The Question of Agency', *The Location of Culture,* London: Routledge, 1994, pp. 244-82.

Boer, Nienke, 'Indenture', *Global South Studies: A Collective Publication with The Global South,* 19 March 2019. Web. 10 May 2019, <https://globalsouthstudies. as.virginia.edu/key-concepts/indenture>

Caruth, Cathy, *Unclaimed Experience: Trauma, Narrative, and History*, Baltimore: The Johns Hopkins University Press, 2016.

Dabydeen, David, *Coolie Odyssey*, London: Hansib Publications Limited, 2006.

Gillion, Kenneth L., *Fiji's Indian Migrants: a History to the End of Indenture in 1920,* Melbourne: Oxford University Press, 1973.

Gubili, Krishna, *Viriah,* Chennai: Notion Press, 2018.

'India has largest diaspora population in world: UN Report', *GK Today,* 18 December 2017, Web. 10 May 2019, <https://currentaffairs.gktoday.in/india-largest-diaspora-population-world-report-12201750869.html>

Jain, Jasbir, *The Diaspora Writes Home: Subcontinental Narratives*, Jaipur: Rawat Publications, 2015.

Kale, Madhavi, *Fragments of Empire: Capital, Slavery and Indian Indentured Labor Migration in the British Caribbean*, Philadelphia: University of Pennsylvania Press, 2000.

Khan, Munshi Rahman, *Autobiography of an Indian Indentured Labourer: Munshi Rahman Khan 1874-1972,* tr. Kathinka Sinha-Kerkhoff, Delhi: Shipra Publications, 2005.

Lal, Brij V., *Chalo Jahaji: On a Journey through Indenture in Fiji*, Canberra: ANU Press, 2012.

———, 'The Odyssey of Indenture: Fragmentation and Reconstitution in the Indian Diaspora', *Diaspora: A Journal of Transnational Studies* 5.2, 1996, pp. 167-88.

———, 'Veil of Dishonour: Sexual Jealousy and Suicide on Fiji Plantations', *The Journal of Pacific History* 20.3, 1985, pp. 135-55.

Lal, Brij V. and Clem Seecharan. *Girmitiyas: the Origins of the Fiji Indians*, Lautoka, Fiji: Fiji Institute of Applied Studies, 2004.

Laurence, K.O., *A Question of Labour: Indentured Immigration into Trinidad and British Guiana, 1875-1917,* Kingston, Jamaica: Ian Randle Publishers, 1994.

Long, Thomas Lawrence, '(Post)Colonial Health: Global Perspectives on the Medical Humanities', *Medical Humanities.* 21 December 2018, Web. 18 April 2019, <https://medicalhumanities.mla.hcommons.org/2018/12/21/cfp-postcolonial-health-global-perspectives-on-the-medical-humanities/>

Mirzoeff, Nicholas, *Diaspora and Visual Culture: Representing Africans and Jews*, London and New York: Routledge, 2000.

Mishra, Vijay, *The Literature of the Indian Diaspora: Theorizing the Diasporic Imaginary,* London: Routledge, 2014.

Misir, Kowlasar, 'Indentureship was a Clever Euphemism for Slavery', *Kaieteur News*, n.p., 19 May 2009, Web. 21 January 2019, <https://kaieteurnewsonline.com/>

Mohan, Peggy, *Jahajin*, New Delhi: HarperCollins, 2007.

Mustapha, Nasser, *Muslims in the Caribbean, Indian Diaspora in the Caribbean: History, Culture and Identity*, ed. Ratan Lal Hangoo, New Delhi: Primus Books, 2012, pp. 43-54.

Paranjape, Makarand R., *In Diaspora: Theories, Histories, Texts*, New Delhi: Indialog Publishers, 2002.

Pirbhai, Mariam, *Mythologies of Migration, Vocabularies of Indenture: Novels of the South Asian Diaspora in Africa, the Caribbean, and Asia-Pacific*, Toronto: University of Toronto Press, 2009.

Poynting, Jeremy, 'East Indian Women in the Caribbean: Experience and Voice', ed. David Dabydeen and Brinsley Samaroo, *India in the Caribbean*, London: Hansib, 1987, pp. 133-80.

Prasad, Rajendra, *Tears in Paradise: Suffering and Struggles of Indians in Fiji, 1879-2004*, Auckland, N.Z.: Pindar, 2010.

Roopnarine, Lomarsh, 'East Indian Indentured Emigration to the Caribbean: Beyond the Push and Pull Model', *Caribbean Studies* 31.2, 2003, pp. 97-134.

Sanadhya, Totaram, *My Twenty-one Years in the Fiji Islands*, tr. John Dunham Kelly and Uttra Kumari Singh, Suva, Fiji: Fiji Museum, 1991.

Singh, Sarva Daman, *Indians Abroad*, Gurgaon, Haryana: Hope India Publishers, 2003.

Singh, Sherry Ann, 'The Experience of Indian Indenture in Trinidad: Arrival and Settlement', *Caribbean Atlas*, ed. Cruse & Rhiney, 2013, Web. 10 May 2019, <http://www.caribbean-atlas.com/en/themes/waves-of-colonization-and-control-in-the-caribbean/waves-of-colonization/the-experience-of-indian-indenture-in-trinidad-arrival-and-settlement.html.>

Tinker, Hugh, *A New System of Slavery: The Export of Indian Labour Overseas*, London: Hansib Publishing Limited, 1993.

Torabully, Khal and Marina Carter, *Coolitude: An Anthology of the Indian Labour Diaspora*, London: Anthem Press, 2002.

Vahed, Goolam and Ashwin Desai, 'Indian Indenture: Speaking Across the Oceans', *Man in India* 92.2, 2012, pp. 195-213.

Bibliography

Books

Abbott, H. Potter, *The Cambridge Introduction to Narrative*, Cambridge: Cambridge University Press, 2018.

Abrams, Meyer Howard, and Geoffrey Galt Harpham, eds., *A Glossary of Literary Terms*, Boston, MA: Wadsworth Cengage Learning, 2015.

Akram-Lodhi, A. Haroon, *Confronting Fiji Futures*, Melbourne: Australian National University Press, 2016.

Ali, Ahmed, *Girmit: Indian Indenture Experience in Fiji*, Suva, Fiji: Fiji Museum, 2004.

Amin, Shahid, *Event, Metaphor, Memory: Chauri Chaura 1922-1992*, Berkeley: University of California Press, 2008.

Anderson, Benedict, *Imagined Communities: Reflections on the Origin and Spread of Nationalism*, Mandaluyong City: Anvil Publishing, 2016.

Andrews, C.F., *Impressions of British Guiana, 1930: An Emissary's Assessment*, Chicago, IL: Adams Press, 2007.

Asaolu, Richard Oluseyi, *Slavery: Abolition*, New York: Pedia Press, 2011.

Ashcroft, Bill, Gareth Griffiths and Helen Tiffin, eds., *Key Concepts in Post-Colonial Studies*, London: Routledge, 2002.

———, *The Empire Writes Back*, Oxon: Routledge, 2002.

Bahadur, Gaiutra, *Coolie Woman: the Odyssey of Indenture*, Gurgaon: Hatchette India, 2013.

Bakhtin, Mikhail, *The Dialogic Imagination: Four Essays*, Trans. Caryl Emerson, ed. Michael Holquist, Austin: University of Texas Press, 2017.

———, *Rabelais and His World*, tr. Helene Iswolsky, Bloomington: Indiana University Press, 1984.

Baldick, Chris, *Dictionary of Literary Terms*, New York: Oxford University Press, 2008.

Barry, Peter, *Beginning Theory: an Introduction to Literary and Cultural Theory*, Manchester: Manchester University Press, 2017.

Beaumont, Joseph, *The New Slavery: An Account of the Indian and Chinese Immigrants in British Guyana,* University of Warwick, Guyana: The Caribbean Press, 2011.

Beverley, John, *Testimonio: On the Politics of Truth*, Minneapolis: University of Minnesota Press, 2004.

Bhabha, Homi, *The Location of Culture*, London: Routledge, 1997.

Bhat, Chandrashekhar, *The Indian Diaspora: Historical and Contemporary Context*, ed. Laxmi Narayan Kadekar, Ajaya Kumar Sahoo and Gauri Bhattacharya, Jaipur: Rawat Publications, 2018.

Bhatt, Sujata, *Point No Point: Selected Poems*, United States: Carcanet Press Ltd., 2014.

Birbalsingh, Frank, ed., *Jahaji Bhai: an Anthology of Indo-Caribbean Literature*, Toronto, Ont: TSAR, 1988.

Booth, Wayne, *The Rhetoric of Fiction*, Chicago: University of Chicago Press, 1961.

Brah, Avtar, *Cartographies of Diaspora: Contesting Identities*, New York: Routledge, 2003.

Brathwaite, Edward, *Contradictory Omens: Cultural Diversity and Integration in the Caribbean*, Jamaica: Mona, 1974.

Buckhory, Somduth, *The Call of the Ganges*, New Delhi: Vikas, 1979.

Burton, John Wear, and Arthur James Small, *The Fiji of Today*, London: Kelly, 1910.

Campbell, Gwyn, *The Structure of Slavery in Indian Ocean Africa and Asia*, London: Frank Cass, 2006.

Carter, Marina, *Lakshmi's Legacy: the Testimonies of Indian Women in the 19th Century Mauritius*, Mauritius: Editions de l'Océan Indien, 1994.

———, *Servants, Sirdars and Settlers: Indians in Mauritius, 1834-1874*, Delhi: Oxford University Press, 1995.

———, *Voices from Indenture: Experiences of Indian Migrants in the British Empire*, London: Leicester University Press, 1996.

Caruth, Cathy, *Unclaimed Experience: Trauma, Narrative, and History*, Baltimore: The Johns Hopkins University Press, 2016.

Chatterji, Joya and David Washbrook, eds., *Routledge Handbook of the South Asian Diaspora,* Oxon: Routledge, 2013.

Clarke, Colin G., Ceri Peach and Steven Vertovec, eds., *South Asians Overseas: Migration and Ethnicity*, Cambridge: Cambridge University Press, 2010.

Dabydeen, David, *Coolie Odyssey*, Hertford: Hansib Publications Limited, 2006.

Dabydeen, David and Brinsley Samaroo, eds., *India in the Caribbean*, London: Hansib, 1987.

Dabydeen, David, Maria del Pilar Kaladeen and Tina K. Ramnarine, eds., *We Mark Your Memory: Writings from the Descendants of Indenture*, London: School of Advanced Study, University of London, 2018.

Dutt, Romesh C., *The Economic History of India in the Victorian Age,* vol. II, New York: August M. Kelley Publishers, 1969.

Emmer, P.C. and E. Van Den Boogaart, eds., *Colonialism and Migration: Indentured Labour before and after Slavery*, Dordrecht: Martinus Nijhoff Publishers, 1986.

Fanon, Frantz, *Black Skin, White Masks*, tr. Richard Philcox, London: Pluto Press, 1986.

———, *The Wretched of the Earth*, tr. Constance Farrington, New Delhi: Penguin Group, 2001.

Felman, Shoshana and Dori Laub, *Testimony: Crises of Witnessing in Literature, Psychoanalysis and History*, New York: Routledge, 1992.

Forster, E.M., *Aspects of the Novel*, London: Hodder & Stoughton, 2016.

Foucault, Michel, *Society must be Defended: Lectures at the College De France 1975-1976*, tr. Davi D. Macey, ed. Mauro Bertani and Alessandro Fontana, New York: St. Martin's Press, 1997.

Gandhi, Mahatma, *The Collected Works of Mahatma Gandhi*, London: Andesite Press, 2017.

Genette, Gérard, *Narrative Discourse: an Essay in Method*, tr. Jane E. Lewin, ed. Jonathan Culler, Ithaca: Cornell University Press, 2006.

———, *Narrative Discourse Revisited*, tr. Jane E. Lewin, Ithaca: Cornell University Press, 1980.

———, *Paratexts: Thresholds of Interpretation*, tr. Jane E. Lewin, ed. Richard Macksey, Cambridge: Cambridge University Press, 2001.

Ghosh, Amitav, *Sea of Poppies*, Gurgaon: Penguin Books India Pvt. Ltd., 2015.

Gillion, Kenneth L., *Fiji's Indian Migrants: A History to the End of Indenture in 1920*, Melbourne: Oxford University Press, 1973.

Gilroy, Paul, *The Black Atlantic: Modernity and Double Consciousness*, London: Verso, 2007.

Gubili, Krishna, *Viriah*, Chennai: Notion Press, 2018.

Hall, Stuart, *Representation: Cultural Representations and Signifying Practices*, London: Sage, 2013.

Halliday, M.A.K., 'Antilanguages,' *Language as Social Semiotic,* London: Edward Arnold, 1979.

Hangoo, Rattan Lal, ed., *Indian Diaspora in the Caribbean: History, Culture and Identity*, Delhi: Primus Books, 2012.

Hardy, Barbara, *The Collected Essays of Barbara Hardy: Narrators and Novelists*, Brighton, Sussex: The Harvester Press, 1987.

Hassankhan, M.S., Brij V. Lal and Doug Munro, eds., *Resistance and Indian Indenture Experience: Comparative Perspectives*, New Delhi: Manohar Publishers & Distributors, 2014.

Hassankhan, Maurits S., Goolam Vahed and Lomarsh Roopnarine, eds., *Indentured Muslims in the Diaspora: Identity and Belonging of Minority Groups in Plural Societies*, New Delhi: Manohar Publishers & Distributors, 2016.

Hassankhan, Maurits S., Lomarsh Roopnarine and Hans Ramsoedh, eds., *Legacy of Indian Indenture: Historical and Contemporary Aspects of Migration and Diaspora*, New Delhi: Manohar Publishers & Distributors, 2016.

Hassankhan, Maurits S., Lomarsh Roopnarine and Radica Mahase, eds. *Social and Cultural Dimensions of Indian Indentured Labour and Its Diaspora: Past Present and Future*, New Delhi: Manohar Publishers & Distributors, 2016.

Hegde, Radha Sarma and Ajaya Kumar Sahoo, eds., *Routledge Handbook of the Indian Diaspora*, Abingdon, Oxon: Routledge, 2018.

Herman, David, Manfred Jahn and Marie-Laure Ryan, eds., *Routledge Encyclopedia of Narrative Theory*, London: Routledge, 2008.

Hirsch, Marianne, *Family Frames: Photography Narrative and Postmemory*, Cambridge, MA: Harvard University Press, 2016.

———, *The Generation of Postmemory Writing and Visual Culture after the Holocaust*, New York: Columbia University Press, 2012.

Ifowodo, Ogaga, *History, Trauma, and Healing in Postcolonial Narratives: Reconstructing Identities,* New York: Palgrave Macmillan, 2013.

Jain, Jasbir, *The Diaspora Writes Home: Subcontinental Narratives*, Jaipur: Rawat Publications, 2015.

———, ed., *Writers of Indian Diaspora: Theory and Practice*, Jaipur: Rawat Publications, 2011.

Jayaram, N., *The Indian Diaspora: Dynamics of Migration*, New Delhi: Sage Publications, 2004.

Jayawardena, Chandra, *The Disintegration of Caste in Fiji Indian Rural Society*, Sydney: Angus and Robertson, 1971.

Kale, Madhavi, *Fragments of Empire: Capital, Slavery, and Indian Indentured Labor Migration in the British Caribbean*, Philadelphia: University of Pennsylvania Press, 2010.

Kamboureli, Smaro and Roy Miki, eds., *Resituating the Study of Canadian Literature*, ON: Wilfred Laurier University Press, 2007, pp. 93-109.

Khan, Munshi Rahman, *Autobiography of An Indian Indentured Labourer: Munshi Rahman Khan 1874-1972,* tr. Kathinka Sinha-Kerkhoff, Delhi: Shipra Publications, 2005.

Klass, Morton, *East Indians in Trinidad: A Study of Cultural Persistence*, Prospect Heights, IL: Waveland Press, 1988.

Kelly, John, *A Politics of Virtue: Hinduism, Sexuality and Countercolonial Discourse in Fiji*, Chicago: University of Chicago Press, 1991.

———, *Fiji Indians and the Law, 1912,* Suva, Fiji: Suva Museum, 1991.

Klein, Alison, *Anglophone Literature of Caribbean Indenture: The Seductive Hierarchies of Empire*, London: Palgrave Macmillan, 2019.

Kumar, Ashutosh, *Coolies of the Empire Indentured Indians in the Sugar Colonies, 1830-1920*, Cambridge: Cambridge University Press, 2017.

Kumar, Kapil, *Peasants in Revolt: Tenants, Landlords, Congress and the Raj in Oudh, 1861-1922*, New-Delhi: Manohar, 1994.

Lal, Brij V., *Bittersweet: the Indo-Fijian Experience*, Canberra: Pandanus Books, 2004.

———, *Chalo Jahaji: On a Journey through Indenture in Fiji*, Canberra: ANU Press, 2012.

———, *Mr Tulsi's Store: a Fijian Journey*, Canberra: ANU Press, 2013.

Lal, Brij V. and Clem Seecharan, *Girmitiyas: The Origins of the Fiji Indians*, Lautoka, Fiji: Fiji Institute of Applied Studies, 2004.

Lal, Brij V., Peter Reeves and Rajesh Rai, eds., *The Encyclopedia of the Indian Diaspora*, New Delhi: Oxford University Press, 2007.

Laurence, K.O., *A Question of Labour: Indentured Immigration into Trinidad and British Guiana, 1875-1917*, Kingston, Jamaica: Ian Randle Publishers, 1994.

Lionnet, Francoise, *The Creolization of Theory*, Durham, NC: Duke University Press, 2011.

Mahabir, Kumar, *Indian Diaspora in the Caribbean*, New Delhi: Serials Publications, 2011.

Mangru, Basdeo, *Indians in Guyana: A Concise History from Their Arrival to the Present*, Chicago, IL: Adams Press, 2000.

McCormack, Donna, *Queer Postcolonial Narratives and the Ethics of Witnessing*, London: Bloomsbury Academic, 2014.

McKay, Steven C., Aims McGuinness and Sukanya Banerjee, eds., *New Routes for Diaspora Studies*, Bloomington: Indiana University Press, 2012.

Mehta, Brinda J., *Diasporic (Dis)Locations: Indo-Caribbean Women Writers Negotiate the Kala Pani*, Jamaica: University of the West Indies Press, 2004.

———, *Notions of Identity, Diaspora and Gender in Caribbean Women's Writing*, New York: Palgrave Macmillan, 2009.

Mesthrie, Rajend, *Language in Indenture: A Sociolinguistic History of Bhojpuri-Hindi in South Africa*, S.l.: Routledge, 2018.

Miller, Nancy K. and Jason Tougaw, eds., *Extremities: Trauma, Testimony, Community*, Urbana: Illinois University Press, 2002.

Mirzoeff, Nicholas, *Diaspora and Visual Culture: Representing Africans and Jews*, London and New York: Routledge, 2000.

Mishra, Sudesh, *Diaspora and the Difficult Art of Dying*, Dunedin: University of Otago Press, 2002.

———, *Diaspora Criticism*, Edinburgh: Edinburgh University Press, 2006.

———, *Subaltern Studies*, Delhi: Oxford University Press, 1999.

———, *Tandava*, Melbourne: Meanjin Press, 1992.

Mishra, Vijay, *The Literature of the Indian Diaspora: Theorizing the Diasporic Imaginary,* London: Routledge, 2014.

Misir, Prem, *The Subaltern Indian Woman: Domination and Social Degradation*, Singapore: Springer Singapore, 2018.

MLA Handbook for Writers of Research Papers, 7th edn., New Delhi: First East-West Press, 2009.

Mohammad, Patricia. *Gender Negotiations among Indians in Trinidad, 1917-1945*, London: Palgrave, 2002.

Mohan, Peggy, *Jahajin*, New Delhi: HarperCollins, 2007.

Mullan, John, *How Novels Work,* Oxford: Oxford University Press, 2006.

Nail, Thomas, *The Figure of the Migrant*, Stanford, CA: Stanford University Press, 2015.

Naipaul, V. S., *A House for Mr Biswas*, New Delhi: Penguin, 1992.

———, *Finding the Center: Two Narratives*, New York: Vintage Books, 1986.

———, *Mauritius: The Overcrowded Barracoon*, London: Allied Newspapers, 1972.

Naipaul, V. S. and Pankaj Mishra, *Literary Occasions: Essays*, New York: Vintage Books, 2004.

Nayar, Pramod K., *Postcolonial Literature: An Introduction*, New Delhi: Pearson, 2013.

Northrup, David, *Indentured Labor in the Age of Imperialism, 1834-1922*, Cambridge: Cambridge University Press, 1995.

Pal, Adesh, Tapas Chakraborty and Kavita A. Sharma, *Interpreting Indian Diasporic Experience*, New Delhi: Creative Books, 2004.

———, *Theorizing and Critiquing Indian Diaspora*, New Delhi: Creative Books, 2004.

Paranjape, Makarand R., *In Diaspora: Theories, Histories, Texts*, New Delhi: Indialog Publications, 2002.

Peirce, Penney, *Transparency: Seeing Through to Our Expanded Human Capacity*, Oregon: Beyond Words Publishing Incorporated, 2017.

Persaud, Lakshmi, *Daughters of Empire*, Leeds: Peepal Tree, 2012.

Phelan, James, *Narrative as Rhetoric: Technique, Audiences, Ethics, Ideology*, Columbus, Ohio: Ohio State University Press, 1996.

Pirbhai, Mariam, *Mythologies of Migration, Vocabularies of Indenture: Novels of the South Asian Diaspora in Africa, the Caribbean and Asia-Pacific*, Toronto: University of Toronto Press, 2009.

Plato, *The Republic*, tr. C. J. Emlyn-Jones and William Preddy, Cambridge, MA: Harvard University Press, 2013.

Prasad, Rajendra, *Tears in Paradise: Suffering and Struggles of Indians in Fiji, 1879-2004*, Auckland, N.Z.: Pindar, 2010.

Prince, Gerald, *Narratology: The Form and Functioning of Narrative*, Berlin: Mouton, 1982.

Rex, John, *Race and Class in Post-Colonial Society: A Study of Ethnic Group Relations in the English-Speaking Caribbean, Bolivia, Chile and Mexico*, Paris: UNESCO, 1977.

Rushdie, Salman, *Imaginary Homelands: Essays and Criticism 1981-1991*, London: Granta, 1991, pp. 10-12.

Sahoo, Ajaya Kumar, *Mapping Indian Diaspora: Contestations and Representations*, Jaipur: Rawat Publications, 2017.

Sahoo, Ajaya Kumar and Laxmi Narayan Kadekar, eds., *Global Indian Diaspora: History, Culture, and Identity*, Jaipur: Rawat Publications, 2012.

Sahoo, Ajaya Kumar, Michiel Baas and Thomas Faist, eds., *Indian Diaspora and Transnationalism*, Jaipur: Rawat Publications, 2012.

Said, Edward W., *Orientalism*, New Delhi: Penguin, 2001.

Sanadhya, Totaram, *My Twenty-one Years in the Fiji Islands*, Trans. John Dunham Kelly and Uttra Kumari Singh, Suva, Fiji: Fiji Museum, 1991.

———, *The Story of the Haunted Line*, Suva: Fiji Museum, 2003.

Shepherd, Verene, *Maharani's Misery: Narratives of a Passage from India to the Caribbean,* Trinidad: The University of West Indies Press, 2002.

Singh, Sarva Daman, *Indians Abroad*, Gurgaon, Haryana: Hope India Publishers, 2003.

Smith, Abbot Emerson, *Colonists in Bondage: White Servitude and Convict Labor in America 1607-1776*, United States: The University of North Carolina Press, 2014.

Sorensen, Eli Park, *Postcolonial Studies and the Literary: Theory, Interpretation and the Novel,* London: Palgrave Macmillan, 2010.

Spivak, Gayatri Chakravarty, *Nationalism and the Imagination,* Calcutta: Seagull Books, 2010.

Stierstorfer, Klaus, and Janet Wilson, *The Routledge Diaspora Studies Reader*, Abingdon, Oxon: Routledge, 2018.

Tinker, Hugh, *A New System of Slavery: the Export of Indian Labour Overseas 1830-1920*, London: Hansib, 1993.

Toolan, Michael J., *Narrative: A Critical Linguistic Introduction,* Oxon: Routledge, 2007.

Torabully, Khal and Marina Carter, *Coolitude: An Anthology of the Indian Labour Diaspora*, London: Anthem Press, 2002.

Williams, Patrick and Laura Chrisman, eds., *Colonial Discourse and Post-Colonial Theory: A Reader*, Hertfordshire: Harvester Wheatsheaf, 1994.

Wood, Donald, *Trinidad in Transition: The Years after Slavery*, Oxford: Oxford University Press, 1968.

Articles

Anderson, Clare, 'Convicts and Coolies: Rethinking Indentured Labour in the Nineteenth Century', *Slavery & Abolition* 30 (1), 2009, pp. 93-109.

Basu, Shrabani, 'The Women Who Came from the Sea', *Telegraph*, 1 December 2013, p. 9.
Baumann, Martin, 'Diaspora: Genealogies of Semantics and Transcultural Comparison', *Numen* 47.3, 2000, pp. 313-37.
Carter, Marina and Crispin Bates, 'Empire and Locality: a Global Dimension to the 1857 Indian Uprising', *Journal of Global History* 5.1, 2010, pp. 51-73.
Chakraborti, Siddhartha, 'Travelling through Time and Space in Peggy Mohan's *Jahajin*: An Archive of Displaced People Reengaging with Language, Gender, Religious and Caste Identities', *Lapis Lazuli* 5.1, 2015, pp. 371-97.
Foucault, Michel, 'Of Other Spaces, Heterotopias', *Architecture, Mouvement* 5, 1984, pp. 46-9.
Gupta, Charu, '"Innocent" Victims/"Guilty" Migrants: Hindi Public Sphere, Caste and Indentured Women in Colonial North India', *Modern Asian Studies* 49.5, 2015, pp. 1345-77.
Halliday, M.A.K., 'Anti-Languages', *American Anthropologist* 78.3, 1976, pp. 570-84.
Han, Enze, and Joseph O'Mahoney, 'British colonialism and the Criminalization of Homosexuality', *Cambridge Review of International Affairs* 27.2, 2017, pp. 268-88.
Hirsch, Marianne, 'Past Lives: Postmemories in Exile', *Poetics Today* 17.4, 1996, pp. 659-86.
Jain, Ravindra K., 'The East Indian Culture in a Caribbean Context: Crisis and Creativity', *India International Centre Quarterly* 13.2, 1986, pp. 153-64.
Kanjilal, Pratik, 'The Books of Exodus', *Indian Express,* 2 March 2014, p. 9.
Kaur, Manpreet, and Sanjaleen Prasad, 'Home, Migration and New Identities: Some Reflections', *Fijian Studies* 15.1, 2017, pp. 145-58.
Lal, Brij V., 'The Odyssey of Indenture: Fragmentation and Reconstitution in the Indian Diaspora', *Diaspora: A Journal of Transnational Studies* 5.2, 1996, pp. 167-88.
———, 'Veil of Dishonour: Sexual Jealousy and Suicide on Fiji Plantations', *The Journal of Pacific History* 20.3, 1985, pp. 135-55.
Long, Maebh, 'Girmit, Postmemory and Subramani', *Pacific Dynamics* 2.2, 2018, pp. 161-75.
Mishra, Nivedita, 'The Trinidadian *Deewani:* Longing and Belonging in Peggy Mohan's *Jahajin*', *Postcolonial Text* 10. 3 & 4, 2015, pp. 1-19.
Mishra, Sudesh, 'Time and *Girmit*', *Social Text* 82.2, 2005, pp. 15-36.
Mishra, Vijay, '(B) ordering Naipaul: Indenture History and Diasporic Poetics', *Diaspora: A Journal of Transnational Studies* 5.2, 1996, pp. 189-237.
———, 'Introduction', *SPAN Journal of South Pacific Association for Commonwealth Literature and Language Studies,* 34.35, 1993, pp. 1-17.

———, 'Postcolonialism 2010-2014', *The Journal of Commonwealth Literature,* 50.3, 2015, pp. 369-90.

Mohabir, Nalini, 'Port of Departure, Port of Return: Mapping Indentured Returns to Calcutta', *Small Axe,* 18.2, 2014, pp. 108-22.

Paranjape, Makarand, 'Triple Ambivalence: Australia, Canada, and South Asia in the Diasporic Imagination', *Australian Canadian Studies,* 20.2, 2002, pp. 81-113.

Pirbhai, Mariam, 'The *Jahaji-Bhain* Principle: A Critical Survey of the Indo-Caribbean Women's Novel, 1990-2009', *The Journal of Commonwealth Literature,* 45.1, 2010, pp. 37-56.

Poynting, Jeremy, 'East Indian Women in the Caribbean: Experience and Voice', *India in the Caribbean,* ed. David Dabydeen and Brinsley Samaroo, London: Hansib, 1987, pp. 133-80.

Prasad, Murari, and Binod K. Jha, 'Indian Diasporic Formations in Guyana: Reading Coolie Woman: The Odyssey of Indenture', *Asiatic,* 10.2, 2016, pp. 231-44.

Reddock, R., 'Indian Women and Indentureship in Trinidad and Tobago, 1845-1917: Freedom Denied', *Caribbean Quarterly,* 54.4, 2008, pp. 41-68.

Roopnarine, Lomarsh, 'A Critique of East Indian Historiography in the Caribbean', *Labor History,* 55.3, 2014, pp. 389-401.

———, 'East Indian Indentured Emigration to the Caribbean: Beyond the Push and Pull model', *Caribbean Studies,* 31.2, 2003, pp. 97-134.

Saha, Amit Shankar, 'Exile Literature and the Diasporic Indian Writer', *Rupkatha Journal on Interdisciplinary Studies in Humanities,* 1.2, 2009, pp. 186-96.

Schröer, Frederik, 'Of Testimonios and Feeling Communities', *Südasien-Chronik-South Asia Chronicle,* 6.1, 2016, pp. 149-74.

Vahed, Goolam and Ashwin Desai, 'Indian Indenture: Speaking Across the Oceans', *Man in India,* 92.2, 2012, pp. 195-213.

Ward, Abigail, 'Assuming the Burden of Memory: The Translation of Indian Indenture in Peggy Mohan's *Jahajin*', *The Journal of Commonwealth Literature,* 48.2, 2013, pp. 269-86.

Yang, Anand, 'Peasant on the Move: A Study of Internal Migration in India', *Journal of Interdisciplinary History,* 10.1, 1979, pp. 37-58.

Web Sources

'Articles', *Section 377 of Indian Penal Code,* Web. 12 March 2019, <http://districtcourtallahabad.up.nic.in/articles/IPC.pdf >

Banerjee, Raka, 'Jahajin – Fable and Facts', *Wordpress,* 17 October 2013. Web. 22 April 2017, <www.southasainwomenwriters.wordpress.com/reviews-home/ 2013-reviews/>

Boer, Nienke, 'Indenture', *Global South Studies: A Collective Publication with the Global South,* 19 March 2019, Web. 10 May 2019, <https://globalsouthstudies. as.virginia.edu/key-concepts/indenture>

'Discovery', *The National Archives,* Web. 30 May 2018, <https://discovery.nationalarchives.gov.uk/discovery/>

Ferrari, Guillermina De, 'The Ship, the Plantation and the *Polis*: Reading Gilroy and Glissant', *Comparative Literature Studies* 49.2, 2012, p. 186, Web. 28 March 2018.

'Gay Rights Movement', *Encyclopedia Britannica,* Web. 12 March 2019, <https://www.britannica.com/topic/gay-rights-movement#ref1077994>

Galenson, David W., 'British Servants and the Colonial Indenture System in the Eighteenth Century', *The Journal of Southern History,* 44.1, 1978, p. 41, Web. 12 February 2016.

Hosein, Gabrielle Jamela, 'Dougla Poetics and Politics in Indo-Caribbean Feminist Thought: Reflection and Reconceptualization', *Indo-Caribbean Feminist Thought,* 2016, 205-23, Web. 24 January 2017.

'India has largest diaspora population in world: UN Report', *GK Today.* 18 December 2017, Web. 10 May 2019, <https://currentaffairs.gktoday.in/india-largest-diaspora-population-world-report-12201750869.html>

Jung, Carl, 'Concept of Archetypes at Carl Jung', *Carl Jung,* Web. 22 February 2019, <https://www.carl-jung.net/archetypes.html>

Klein, Alison, 'Family Ties: Embodiment of Female Laborers in the Poetry of Indenture,' *Anglophone Literature of Caribbean Indenture,* 2018, pp. 145–79, Web. 03 August 2018.

———, 'Tangled Up: Gendered Nationhood in Indo-Caribbean Indenture Narratives', *Anthurium A Caribbean Studies Journal,* 12.2, 2015, p. 4, Web. 23 January 2019.

———, 'To Have and To Hold: The Role of Marriage in Nonfiction Indenture Narratives', *Anglophone Literature of Caribbean Indenture,* 2018, 25-58, Web. 18 January 2019.

———, 'Tying the Knot: Early Depictions of Indenture', *Anglophone Literature of Caribbean Indenture,* 2018, pp. 59-101, Web. 13 June 2018.

———, ' "Seeing Greater Distances" : An Interview with Peggy Mohan on the Voyages of Indo-Caribbean Women', *Indo-Caribbean Feminist Thought,* 2016, pp. 63-72, Web. 1 April 2017.

Long, Thomas Lawrence, '(Post)Colonial Health: Global Perspectives on the Medical Humanities', *Medical Humanities,* 21 December 2018, Web. 18 April 2019, <https://medicalhumanities.mla.hcommons.org/2018/12/21/cfp-postcolonial-health-global-perspectives-on-the-medical-humanities/>

McLean, Sarah, 'Places Where Reality Feel Altered', theodysseyonline, 2 August 2016, Web. 22 April 2019, www.theodysseyonline.com/amp/liminal-spaces-2478165167/

Misir, Kowlasar, 'Indentureship was a Clever Euphemism for Slavery', *Kaieteur News*, N. P., 19 May 2009, Web. 21 Jan 2019, <https://kaieteurnewsonline.com/>

Mohan, Peggy, 'Writing Jahajin', *Jahajin,* 12 July 2010, Web. 12 April 2019, <http://peggymohan.blogspot.com/>

Nadkarni, Dev, 'Tears In Paradise, Suffering and Struggle of Indians in Fiji 1879-2004', *Blogspot,* 27 August 2011, Web. 09 August 2017, www.rajendraprasad site.blogspot.in.

Nair, Rukmini Bhaya, 'Ladies Coop', *Outlook,* Outlook Publishing (India) Private Limited, 31 March 2008, Web. 31 May 2018, <https://www.outlookindia.com/ magazine/story/ladies-coop/237061>

O'Carroll, John, 'Totaram's Ghost', *Australian Humanities Review,* 52.6, 2012, Np. Web. 22 May 2017, < http://australianhumanitiesreview.org/2012/05/01 /totarams-ghost/ >

Outer, Lisa, 'Female resilience and fortitude in Gaiutra Bahadur's Coolie Woman: The Odyssey of Indenture', *Starbroek News,* 12 May 2014, Web. 11 April 2019, < https://www.stabroeknews.com/2014/features/in-the-diaspora/05/12/ female-resilience-fortitude-gaiutra-bahadurs-coolie-woman-odyssey-indenture/ >

Paul, Annie, 'A Coolie Woman's Work is Never Done', *The Margins,* 31 March 2014, Web. 18 March 2019, <http://aaww.org/coolie-womans-work-gaiutra-bahadur/>

'Plantocracy' *Oxford English Dictionary,* Web. 27 March 19, <https://en.oxford dictionaries.com/definition/plantocracy>

Polya, Gideon, '"Tears In Paradise. Suffering and Struggle of Indians in Fiji 1879-2004' by Rajendra Prasad – Britain's Indentured Indian "5 Year Slaves"', *Countercurrents,* 04 March 2015, Web. 09 August 2017, < www.counter currents.org/polya040315.html>

Prakash, Gyan, 'Postcolonial Criticism and History: Subaltern Studies', *Oxford Scholarship Online,* 2018, Web. 19 May 2018.

Pyne, Lydia, 'Coolie Woman', *New Pages,* 20 August 2014, Web. 22 April 2019, <https://www.newpages.com/item/26701-coolie-woman>

Rai, Satish, *In Exile at Home—A Fiji Indian Story,* Kindle edn., Amazon Asia-Pacific Holdings Private Limited, 2013, Web. 27 March 2017.

Ramesar, Marianne D., 'The Impact of the Indian Immigrants on Colonial Trinidad Society', *Caribbean Quarterly,* 22.1, 1976, pp. 5-18, Web. 07 January 2016.

Reddock, Rhoda, 'Indo-Caribbean Masculinities and Indo-Caribbean Feminisms: Where Are We Now?', *Indo-Caribbean Feminist Thought,* 2016, pp. 263-82, Web. 24 October 2017.

Sawe, Elisha Benjamin, 'Aapravasi Ghat of Port Louis, Mauritius', *World Atlas.* n.p., n.d. Web. 30 May 2019, <https://www.worldatlas.com/articles/aapravasi-ghat-of-port-louis-mauritius.html>

'Slavery' *The National Archives*, n.p., n.d. Web. 27 May 2018, <http://www.nationalarchives.gov.uk/slavery/about/>

Simha, Rakesh Krishnan, 'Fiji Indians: Trapped in the Gulag of the Pacific', *eSamskriti*. 13 August 2011, Web. 12 January 2019, https://www.esamskriti.com/e/National-Affairs/For-The-Followers-Of-Dharma/Fiji-Indians--Trapped-in-the-Gulag-of-the-Pacific-1.aspx.

Singh, SherryAnn, 'The Experience of Indian Indenture in Trinidad: Arrival and Settlement', *Caribbean Atlas*, ed. Cruse & Rhiney, 2013, Web. 10 May 2019, <http://www.caribbean-atlas.com/en/themes/waves-of-colonization-and-control-in-the-caribbean/waves-of-colonization/the-experience-of-indian-indenture-in-trinidad-arrival-and-settlement.html.>

Surajbali, Preeia D., 'Indo-Caribbean Feminist Epistemology: A Personal and Scholarly Journey', *Indo-Caribbean Feminist Thought*, 2016, pp. 37-48. Web. 08 December 2017.

Trotman, David V., 'Acts of Possession and Symbolic Decolonisation in Trinidad and Tobago', *Caribbean Quarterly*, 58.1, 2012, pp. 21-43, Web. 10 December 2018.

Wajid, Sara, 'Journey of the Coolie Woman in the History of the British Empire', *The Guardian*, 19 November 2013, Web. 1 May 2015, < https://www.theguardian.com/lifeandstyle/womens-blog/2013/nov/19/journey-coolie-women-history-british-empire-indentured-labourers>

Wheeler, Brianna, 'Conjure Women, Coolie Women, and Impossible Stories', *The Sewanee Purple*, 10 April 2018, Web. 09 May 2019, <https://thesewaneepurple. org/2018/04/10/conjure-women-coolie-women-and-impossible-stories/>

Index

For Product Safety Concerns and Information please contact our EU
representative GPSR@taylorandfrancis.com
Taylor & Francis Verlag GmbH, Kaufingerstraße 24, 80331 München, Germany

www.ingramcontent.com/pod-product-compliance
Ingram Content Group UK Ltd.
Pitfield, Milton Keynes, MK11 3LW, UK
UKHW020130200926
475702UK00005B/683
* 9 7 8 1 0 3 2 3 7 7 0 4 9 *